D1191382

KING OF THE COURTROOM: Percy Foreman for the Defense

OTHER BOOKS BY MICHAEL DORMAN

WE SHALL OVERCOME

THE SECRET SERVICE STORY

THE SECOND MAN:
The Changing Role of the Vice-Presidency

KING OF THE COURTROOM: Percy Foreman for the Defense

BY MICHAEL DORMAN

Library of Congress Catalog Card Number: 68-19468
Manufactured in the United States of America
First printing

FOR MY WIFE,

Jeanne,

AND MY FIRST NEWSPAPER EDITOR,

George Carmack,

BOTH OF WHOM LOVE TEXAS AS MUCH

AS DO PERCY FOREMAN AND I.

Guilty or innocent,
Makes no difference to this gent.
He's got warehouses full of jewels.
He's got mansions and swimming pools. . . .
If hubby you should shoot,
And your mother-in-law to boot,
You'd better check out your bank account.
Be sure it's a big amount. . . .
Percy Boy is King of the Court.

Parody on "King of the Road"
sung in honor of Percy Foreman at a
Houston Press Club Gridiron Show.

INTRODUCTION

THE MOST SUCCESSFUL defense attorney in the world is a six-foot-four-inch, 250-pound Texan named Percy Eugene Foreman.

In a field as complex as criminal law, only the most foolhardy would try to classify one attorney as "the best." It would be impossible, for example, to say whether Foreman possesses greater skill than such trial lawyers of the past as Clarence Darrow, Sam Leibowitz and Max Steuer or such current-day luminaries as Edward Bennett Williams, F. Lee Bailey and Jake Ehrlich.

But, from the standpoint of results alone, none of these talented practitioners even approaches the record of Foreman. By sheer weight of statistics, Foreman's record before the bar of justice has been nothing short of phenomenal.

He has represented more accused killers than any man in history—upwards of 1000. In fact, he frequently tries more murder cases in a year than Darrow handled in his entire career. Yet, of the more than 1000 slayers he has represented, he has lost only *one* to the executioner. Perhaps even more startling is this statistic: of the 1000, only 55 have served even so much as one day of prison time!

However, to summarize Foreman's career merely in terms of statistics is to sell him short. For Percy Foreman, sad to say, is one of the last of a dying breed. He is an authentic folk hero of the criminal courts. He is the personification of the old-fashioned mouthpiece with a trick or two up his sleeve. Moreover, he has amassed an impressive record of achievements having nothing to do with trial statistics. He was, for example, president of the National Association of Defense Lawyers in Criminal Cases. He was the second attorney in history to win the American Academy of Achievement's Golden Plaque award for excellence. Today, he is perhaps the leading spokesman for the legal profession on questions involving the criminal courts. And, not least, he is one of the few attorneys in history to become a multimillionaire through the practice of criminal law.

The public generally knows Foreman only in terms of his press image—as the canny defender of such assorted "villains" as James Earl Ray, Candy Mossler and Mel Powers, General Edwin Walker, Jack Ruby and various Mafia kingpins. His public image, thus, is one-dimensional.

But Percy Foreman is a three-dimensional character if ever there was one. He is as complicated a human being as ever walked the earth. Anyone who claims to understand him completely ranks as either a liar or a fool.

Consider the fact that, while masterfully defending accused criminals against the most heinous of charges, Foreman himself has somehow managed: to get arrested on an adultery charge; to get indicted on a charge of subornation of perjury; to stand trial on charges of operating a policy (numbers racket) game; and to stand trial on charges of using abusive language to a young woman.

It goes without saying that Foreman beat the rap in each of these cases. But the wonder is that he allowed himself to get involved in such jams in the first place.

For a dozen years, Foreman has assured me that he plans someday to write an autobiography. At various times in those dozen years, he has promised to permit me to collaborate with him on such a book. But he has insisted, year after year, that the time is not yet ripe—that he must wait until he retires from the practice of law.

A Biblical scholar and ordained Baptist deacon (he describes himself as "ordained but unchurched" because of numerous rows with his Baptist brethren), he is fond of quoting from the Book of Job: "My desire is that the Almighty would answer me, and that mine adversary had written a book." He adds: "I will write a book only when I cease being an adversary."

That day, alas, may never come. The chances are that Percy Foreman will never retire from his law practice. He usually has several years' worth of cases stacked up before him. One day, his desk still cluttered with the briefs and transcripts of his trade, he may pass into that special realm of heaven reserved for defenders of the damned. His autobiography may have gone unwritten.

"That will be the world's loss," he once told me sarcastically. I agree with the statement, if not with the sarcasm.

The story of Percy Foreman—in all its complexity, the good and the evil—should be told in his lifetime. That is why I have chosen to write this book.

If it helps somewhat to unravel the enigma of our most successful criminal lawyer, it will have been worth the effort. It is hoped that the defense attorneys of the present and future will draw inspiration from Foreman's example and wisdom from his few mistakes.

It is also hoped that at least some members of the new generation of law students will see in this story evidence that there is majesty—not to mention money—in practicing before the criminal bar. No American has done more than Percy Foreman to prove that a criminal lawyer need be neither a shyster nor a beggar.

MICHAEL DORMAN

Deer Park, New York

KING OF THE COURTROOM: Percy Foreman for the Defense

1

You should never allow the defendant to be tried. Try someone else—the husband, the lover, the police or, if the case has social implications, society generally. But never the defendant.

PERCY FOREMAN

THIS SUCCINCT PARAGRAPH summarizes the Percy Foreman defense credo. For forty years, he has followed it faithfully in courtrooms from coast to coast—to the satisfaction of his clients and the horror of prosecutors and lawmen. He is the supreme advocate of the thesis that a good offense is the best defense. He has portrayed police officers as brutes and Ku-Kluxers, prosecutors as villains, and judges as incompetents. He has woven spells that have pictured sluts as maidens, killers as innocent babes, and victims as violators. For his efforts, he has suffered insults, curses, and even a vicious beating at the hands of peace officers.

Of all the cases he has tried, none so well demonstrates the Foreman defense strategy as the murder case of Jack Whitfield Bonds. In this case, Foreman truly put society on trial. It takes a defense lawyer of consummate skill and colossal gall to undertake such a monumental task. Foreman possesses both qualities in abundance.

The Bonds case was noteworthy for several other reasons. For one, it was the longest murder trial in Texas history—putting Foreman's unique talents on display for more than five weeks. For another, it represented a milestone in the use of psychiatric testimony. It is hardly unusual for a murder jury to hear complex psychiatric testimony about an accused slayer. However, in the Bonds case it was not the slayer, but the dead victim, who was psychoanalyzed during the trial. Since the victim was a fifteen-year-old boy, and since he had never even been interviewed by the psychoanalyst who testified, the testimony *was* unusual. What was even more significant was that this *ex post facto* psychoanalysis helped provide Foreman with the ammunition necessary to put society on trial.

The basic facts in the Bonds case were uncontested. That is, it was agreed by both prosecution and defense that Bonds, a forty-two-year-old Houston elevator mechanic, had shot to death William John Walden III, fifteen-year-old son of a wealthy Houston couple, on January 18, 1963. It was further agreed that the slaying had been carried out with a .38-caliber pistol and had occurred in the driveway of a drive-in grocery store.

Beyond that, however, there was agreement on little—particularly on motive, justification or precise circumstances. Foreman, who neither asks nor gives any quarter in the courtroom, was confronted by two equally hard-nosed adversaries when the case came to trial before Criminal District Judge Sam Davis in Houston's Criminal Courts Building in January of 1964. The prosecutors were Harris County (Houston) Assistant District Attorneys Erwin Ernst and Robert Musslewhite—both considerably younger than Foreman, but both solid, experienced trial lawyers. Before the Bonds trial was over, each would challenge Foreman to fisticuffs. For this was a case loaded with emotion. And, with Foreman rising to new heights of courtroom drama, it was only natural that this emotion should occasionally run rampant.

Testimony had scarcely begun before the fireworks started. It had taken a week to select a jury pledged to sentence Bonds to death in the electric chair if the evidence proved appropriate. (Juries in Texas are empowered to fix a defendant's punishment, in addition to determining guilt or innocence.) Now, on January 15, 1964, testimony got under way. Within hours, prosecutor Ernst formally accused Foreman of trying to get a state witness to lie on the stand.

The witness involved was Mrs. Beverly Chambers White, the sixteen-year-old stepdaughter of Foreman's client. The state contended that Bonds had admitted slaying young Walden and had given as his reason that the youth had molested Mrs. White, who was fifteen and unmarried at the time of the shooting.

Ernst announced in open court that he had asked a grand jury to investigate Foreman's purported tampering with Mrs. White's testimony. Specifically, Ernst claimed, Mrs. White (then Beverly Chambers) had reported to police immediately after the slaying that her stepfather had told her: "I shot Bill." But later she had written a letter to the district attorney's office, repudiating her previous statement to the police. In the letter, she said: "I don't remember anything I said in statements at the police station." Ernst claimed Foreman had persuaded Mrs. White to change her story.

Foreman hotly denied the accusation. In turn, he accused Ernst and Musslewhite of trying to pervert justice by issuing a grand-jury subpoena for Mrs. White. He argued that Texas law gave Mrs. White the right to refuse to talk to the prosecutors, except on the witness stand. By issuing a grand-jury subpoena, Foreman said, the prosecutors were seeking to get around that law and compel Mrs. White to answer their questions in the grand-jury room before she testified in the murder trial. He demanded that Judge Davis quash the subpoena.

"If you don't, you will permit the state to do with its left hand what the law won't permit it to do with its right," Foreman argued. But Davis was unmoved. He refused to quash the subpoena. In the end, the grand-jury investigation came to naught. The prosecutors were unable to sustain their charge of witness tampering. But more was to be heard from Mrs. White.

A short time later, the teenaged housewife—who had given

birth to a son only three weeks earlier—was wheeled into the courtroom on a stretcher. Her baby was in her arms, and he needed burping. The trial ground to a halt. Percy Foreman, a man of many talents (not the least of them a fine sense of news judgment), gently lifted the infant to his shoulder. Then, while spectators gaped and news photographers' shutters clicked, he proceeded to burp the baby in full view of a jammed courtroom. The resulting pictures hit front pages all over the country. And the paternal courtroom scene surely did not hurt Foreman's standing with the jurors.

But Foreman had little time to enjoy it all. By now, the trial was in full swing. Ernst called to the stand a seventeen-year-old Air Force enlisted man, William Lamonte Cross, who had been with young Walden on the night of the slaying. Cross related how Bonds had gunned Walden down in the driveway of a grocery at 14106 South Post Oak Road, in Houston's fashionable southwest section.

Foreman's defense strategy called initially for establishing that young Walden—despite coming from a respectable, well-to-do family—had been a teenage hoodlum who had molested girls, robbed and brawled constantly. If he could succeed in showing that, Foreman could then put society on trial for permitting a privileged youngster to descend to such depths.

In his cross-examination of Airman Cross, Foreman immediately launched his offensive. He claimed, in his questions, that Walden had been a member of a teenage gang called the King Cutters—a gang organized to fight, steal and to molest defenseless girls.

"Is there such an organization as the King Cutters?" he asked.

"I really don't know," Cross replied. "I've heard the name, but I don't know if it was King or Keen. All I know is that, if you wanted to be cool, you said you were a King Cutter."

Erwin Ernst objected strenuously to this line of questioning. He tried to put Foreman on the stand to question him about the supposed existence of the King Cutters. A heated exchange ensued.

Referring to Foreman's attempts to cloud Walden's name, Ernst snapped: "You've got as much compassion as an ant."

Foreman retorted: "How do you spell that—A-U-N-T or A-N-T?"

In the end, Judge Davis refused to order Foreman to the witness stand. And, throughout the trial, Foreman continued to hammer at the theme that Walden had been a teenage hoodlum.

Foreman implied in questioning Cross that the airman—as well as Walden and other purported members of the King Cutters—had been involved in numerous acts of violence and immorality. Cross adamantly denied that he personally had committed any such acts.

He was followed to the witness stand by another Air Force enlisted man who had been a friend of the slain youth. The witness, James R. Allen, an eighteen-year-old airman stationed at Amarillo Air Force Base, testified that both Walden and Beverly Chambers had attended an all-night party in a vacant house shortly before the slaying. Although many of the participants in the party had been well below the legal drinking age (Walden and Beverly had been only fifteen at the time), Allen testified that there had been considerable drinking.

Here, again, Foreman was building toward his general indictment of society. If such parties had taken place and been either condoned or overlooked by supposedly respectable parents, Foreman felt, something was radically wrong with society. And, if that were true, he could put society on trial—rather than his client.

Allen testified that, at the time of the shooting, he was considered Beverly's boy friend. Despite the allegations that Walden had molested Beverly, Allen said he did not think the slain youth had ever dated Bonds' stepdaughter.

"To my knowledge, Bill never took Beverly out once," he said. "Bill took Dwayne [Dwayne Hinson, another friend] and me to Beverly's house [a short time before the slaying] because we didn't have a car." He said he considered Beverly "a good girl." He did not define "good girl."

When Allen, Hinson and Walden went to the Bonds home on the evening of the slaying, Allen said, they asked Beverly to go with them to a drive-in restaurant. "She said her parents had taken her clothes away from her and that she was going to Mississippi the next day," he testified. "She didn't want to go. . . ."

Although no detailed explanation was given at this point in the trial, the implication left was that Bonds and his wife were sending Beverly to Mississippi to get her away from the King Cutter crowd. Numerous debates erupted between Foreman and Ernst over attempts to explore this incident, and others, during Allen's testimony. But they were mere trifles, compared with the near brawl that came about the following day.

On Saturday, January 18, Allen was still on the stand. And Foreman, still plugging away at his case against society, was trying to prove that the slain youth had been a narcotics addict. Ernst asked that the jury be sent out of the courtroom. When Judge Davis complied, Ernst called Foreman to the witness stand. This exchange followed:

Q. Are you aware this is a murder trial and not a walrus act?

A. It would be if anyone besides yourself was prosecuting this case.

Foreman, after completing his brief testimony, was not to be outdone. He promptly called Ernst to the witness stand. Picking up a thick file folder from the prosecution table where Ernst previously had been sitting, Foreman asked: "Is this your file on this case?"

Ernst, bristling at Foreman's audacity in picking up the prosecution file, replied: "Yes, and keep your stinking hands off of it."

Ernst's fellow prosecutor, Robert Musslewhite, snapped: "Give me that file and don't pick it up again!"

Still grasping the file, Foreman smiled and asked Musslewhite: "What will you do if I pick it up again?"

"Punch you in your fat mouth!" Musslewhite rasped. He then reached up and angrily ripped the file from Foreman's hands.

Foreman, still smiling as his adversaries glared at him, said softly: "I don't think you will hit me in my mouth, Bob."

It was a seemingly inconsequential incident. It had added nothing to either the prosecution or the defense case. It had all occurred out of the hearing of the jury. But, from Foreman's standpoint, it had undoubtedly helped. He had succeeded in riling the prosecutors—getting them to lose their concentration on the evidence—while all the time he had kept his cool. This is a typical Foreman tactic. He never gives the opposition the chance to coast. (As Erwin Ernst once put it: "Percy never lets up. That's one reason it's personally distasteful to try a case against him. He's always cuttin' you. He's like a football coach who rolls up the score. He's a helluva trial lawyer, but I haven't found in him any sense of gallantry.")

Whether Foreman's gallantry—or lack of it—is a pertinent subject for discussion at this point seems moot. More pertinent is his acknowledged skill in the courtroom. And, whether Ernst liked it or not, he was willing to concede grudgingly that Foreman's tactic had bothered him, thus hurting the prosecution case.

The remainder of the state's case was perfunctory. Ernst and Musslewhite called to the stand the Harris County medical examiner, Dr. Joseph Jachimczyk. He testified that young Walden was killed by a .38-caliber bullet fired into his left ear from a distance of about nine inches. A Houston homicide detective, T. D. Muckleroy, described the slaying scene and the roundup of witnesses following the shooting. Airmen Allen and Cross and other witnesses provided additional details on the shooting itself.

Before Saturday's court session ended, Ernst and Musslewhite rested their case. But any hope that the trial would soon be over was short-lived. It was now Percy Foreman's turn. And he had no intention of presenting a perfunctory defense. After all, he was about to launch in earnest his trial of society.

On Monday, January 20, Foreman called to the stand a fifteen-year-old boy billed by the newspapers as a surprise witness. The witness, Don Bennett, Jr., considerably bolstered Foreman's case by testifying to numerous nefarious acts involving the slain youth. Among other things, Bennett said that he and young Walden had operated a protection racket at their school, Albert Sidney Johnston Junior High.

"We charged about eight or ten kids two dollars a week each to guarantee them that they wouldn't get beaten up," Bennett said.

"We did this for about two weeks, but then we were caught and suspended from school."

Before Bennett's testimony was completed, however, Erwin Ernst sprang a surprise witness of his own. He asked that Bennett's testimony be interrupted to permit the surprise witness to take the stand. The new witness was another youth, Gregory Anderson, seventeen. And his testimony created an even greater uproar than that which had preceded his appearance.

In short, Anderson accused Percy Foreman of "buying" Bennett's testimony. Anderson said Bennett had boasted to him that Foreman had: rented a room for him (Bennett) for at least two weeks at Houston's Sam Houston Hotel; opened a charge account for him at a department store; paid him fifteen dollars a day for at least three days; bought him a seafood dinner and some beer; and implied he would provide Bennett with call girls.

Under Foreman's withering cross-examination, Anderson stuck to his story. He said Bennett had made the boasts both in a telephone conversation the previous evening and in a face-to-face talk in the courthouse Monday morning.

"Did Bennett tell you that I could get some girls for him?" Foreman asked.

"Yes, sir, he said you were a soft touch," Anderson replied. "He didn't say that you had offered women to him—but that he felt you would."

Anderson testified that Bennett claimed Foreman had instructed him to "keep pretty much to the truth, but just leave out certain things." Thus, for the second time in the trial, Foreman stood accused of trying to influence a witness to give warped testimony. It began to appear that he—as well as Jack Bonds and society—might be on trial.

Bennett soon returned to the stand to face a stern cross-examination by Erwin Ernst.

Q. Are you staying at the Sam Houston Hotel?

A. Yes.

Q. May I see your key?

A. Here. [Bennett handed the prosecutor a key marked "Room 518, Sam Houston Hotel."]

Q. Have you ever gone under any other name?

A. No, sir.

Q. Do you know that Room 518 at the Sam Houston Hotel is registered to a Don Havlick?

A. No, sir.

Q. Is it true that Foreman promised to furnish you, and your friends who might come to the hotel, with call girls?

At this point, Foreman hauled his huge frame out of the counsel chair and demanded that the jury be sent from the courtroom. After the jurors had filed out, he unleashed a verbal barrage at both Ernst and Judge Davis—demanding a mistrial because of the last question. In support of this demand, he then called Ernst to the witness stand once more.

Q. Mr. Ernst, you know this is hearsay testimony, don't you?

A. Yes, sir, Mr. Foreman. But there are many exceptions to the hearsay rule, and I believe this testimony is admissible to show bias on the part of your witness.

Judge Davis denied Foreman's motion for a mistrial, recalled the jury and permitted Bennett to answer the question. The youth denied that Foreman had promised to furnish him with call girls. He also denied that Foreman had paid him any money or that he planned to stay at the Sam Houston Hotel for as long as two weeks.

However, another surprise witness called by Foreman was to contradict part of this testimony. The witness: Percy Foreman himself.

Settling into the witness chair once again, while courthouse wags joked that the lawyers had spent more time on the stand than some of their other witnesses, Foreman conceded giving Bennett some cash. But he denied it was as much as fifteen dollars a day. "It was closer to ten dollars," he said. He also conceded he had bought the youth a seafood dinner, but denied buying any beer.

He said he had rented the hotel room for Bennett in the name of one of his associates and had given one room key to Bennett. "I wanted him readily accessible to the court," Foreman said. "I also wanted to protect him from harassment by the district attorney's office. And the boy had some threatening telephone calls last week, and I felt he would be safer at the hotel."

Bennett later returned to the witness stand. He testified that the junior-high-school protection racket was originally his idea. Over Foreman's strenuous objections, the youth was permitted to testify about what various witnesses to the slaying had told him.

"The way it was told to me, Bonds intended to kill," Bennett testified. "They told me Bonds stepped out with a gun in his hand and said, 'You no-good blank-blank.' Then he fired."

This version contrasted with the story of the slaying Foreman would later present to the jurors. Thus, his own witness—while helping him build his case against society—had also helped build the specific case against Jack Bonds. It should be pointed out that, although he was the man on trial, Bonds seemed at this point to be the forgotten man in the case. Foreman did nothing to call attention to his client. This was a typical Foreman maneuver. The less attention focused on the defendant, he usually feels, the better. That way, it becomes easier for him to put someone other than the defendant on trial.

Prosecutor Erwin Ernst questioned young Bennett at length about switchblade knives, weapons supposedly favored by members of the King Cutters. At one point, Ernst pulled a knife from his pocket and asked Bennett whether it was a switchblade. Foreman instantly leaped to his feet.

"Judge, I ask that you disarm Mr. Ernst," he demanded. Although Foreman kept a straight face, a roar of laughter filled the courtroom. When it subsided, Judge Davis denied the motion to disarm the prosecutor. A lengthy discussion ensued between Ernst and Bennett over whether the knife resembled a switchblade weapon that young Walden was reported to have carried constantly. The point was never firmly resolved.

Under renewed questioning by Foreman, Bennett testified that he, Walden and other teenagers—male and female—committed a number of burglaries. "They made me feel big," he said. "And I wanted my friends to think of me as big."

Foreman returned to the allegations that he had "bought" Bennett's testimony.

Q. I did give you ten dollars and no more—is that right?

A. Yes, sir.

Q. Have I ever asked you to testify to anything that is not the whole truth and nothing but the truth?

A. No, sir.

The next day, Foreman further bolstered his case against society by calling as a witness a pretty, slender fourteen-year-old girl. Though she appeared as prim as prim could be, the story Melinda Hatcher told was not prim at all. It was a story of privileged youth run wild—of drinking parties, of burglaries and of generally loose morals among the teenagers in a "respectable" section of Houston.

Melinda, chic in a blue jumper and a white blouse, with every hair brushed neatly in place, calmly testified that she had taken her first drink of hard liquor at the age of twelve, that she had participated in beer-drinking contests and that she had frequently slipped out her bedroom window at night with Don Bennett's help. She described Bennett as her sweetheart.

"Once, Don got me drunk at my house on vodka when my parents were gone," she said in response to a question from Foreman. "At other parties, I got drunk on beer and whiskey." She told how she, Bennett and Bill Walden had met at a drive-in movie one night in November of 1962. "We went to a vacant house and stayed until after daylight," she said.

Another time, she said, she and Walden engaged in a beer-drinking contest. "I said I would kiss a boy if I lost," Melinda testified. "I won. Before long, everybody at the party was drunk."

On still another occasion, Melinda said, she and Bonds' stepdaughter, Beverly Chambers, sneaked out a window at the Bonds home and went to a motel party attended by Bill Walden, Don Bennett and James Allen. "Bill Walden brought about fifteen pints of whiskey to the motel and we all got drunk," she said.

She said she, Beverly and the three boys stole some bedding from four model homes in the fashionable Westbury section of southwest Houston—where most of the youths lived—and then broke into a fifth model home and spread the bedding on the garage floor. "We couldn't keep warm," she testified. "So we left about 5 A.M." Then, at her suggestion, the party moved to the bank of a nearby bayou.

"I told Beverly to test Jim Allen—tell him that, if he loved her, he would jump into the bayou," Melinda said. Beverly put her boy friend to the test. He thereupon jumped into the water, head first. This was in November—a cold month even in Houston's southern climate.

"Was it cold?" Foreman asked.

"Yes," Melinda replied. "I believe there was ice on the bayou."

Frequently, she said, Bennett helped her sneak out her bedroom window late at night. They then took long walks to a vacant house and just talked, she testified.

The obvious question seemed to be what had happened to parental supervision and discipline in the community. Foreman promptly addressed the question by calling Melinda's parents as witnesses.

Mrs. Ruth Hatcher testified that she moved with Melinda to Miami, Florida, three days after the Walden slaying. She said she wanted to get her daughter away from other teenagers in the neighborhood. Mrs. Hatcher testified that she did not learn of Melinda's misadventures until returning from a hospital stay in December, 1962. At that time, she said, she learned that her daughter was running around with a group of teenagers who called themselves "The Hoods and Hoodesses." About a month earlier, Mrs. Hatcher testified, both Melinda and Beverly Chambers had complained that "they never had any fun at our house." As a result, she said, "I consented to give them a party." The party eventually took place at the Hatcher home on January 11, 1963—a week before Bill Walden was shot.

Erwin Ernst, in his cross-examination of Mrs. Hatcher, seemed to play directly into Foreman's hands. That is, he appeared to aid and abet Foreman in the trial of society.

Q. Mrs. Hatcher, why were "The Hoods and Hoodesses" your daughter told you about invited to a party in your home?

A. I really didn't know who was invited.

Q. Did you drink anything at the party?

A. Mr. Ernst, I'm not on trial here! [Judge Davis instructed, just the same, that she answer the question.]

A. Yes, I was drinking.

She testified that Don Bennett's father, Don, Sr., was the only other adult at the party. She said he was also drinking, but she denied knowledge of any drinking by the teenagers.

Q. Do you remember sitting on a couch with Don's father having his arm around you and drinking with you?

A. No, I do not!

Q. Where was your husband?

A. We were separated, and still are.

On the afternoon of January 18—the day Walden was slain—Mrs. Hatcher said she picked up Melinda at school just before several teenage boys, including Walden, could drive off with her. "We went to a drive-in movie," Mrs. Hatcher said. "Bill Walden and a number of the boys kept circling our car while we watched the movie."

After the movie, she said, she and Melinda just happened to drive past the drive-in grocery where the slaying occurred. She saw a crowd, stopped and then spied Walden's body.

"I saw Mr. Walden in a car and told him it didn't seem real—that I had seen his son fifteen minutes earlier," she testified. "Mr. Walden told me, 'It was bound to happen.' "

Mrs. Hatcher's estranged husband, David E. Hatcher, a forty-year-old hospital-supply salesman, got his turn next. He readily conceded that he had failed as a father, and admitted that his frustration had become so great that he had once had an "urge to kill" young Don Bennett. Hatcher said he had resigned his job as regional manager with his company in order to spend more time with Melinda. He said the manager's job had kept him out of town ninety percent of the time, so he had returned to his former job as a salesman in January of 1962.

Once again, it was Ernst who helped establish the facts that Foreman wanted entered into the record. The prosecutor drew from Hatcher, during cross-examination, testimony that the events leading up to the slaying were a "nightmare" for the divided Hatcher family.

"My daughter was becoming a terrific problem at this time," he said. He told of becoming enraged when he learned that Don Bennett had been helping Melinda slip out of the house late at night. He said he developed his "urge to kill" young Bennett at that time.

Ernst, in an apparent attempt to show that Jack Bonds' actions far outstripped this other father's, asked Hatcher: "But you didn't [kill Bennett], did you?"

"No," Hatcher said. "I couldn't find him."

Q. Did you have a real urge to get a pistol and blow his head off?

A. Yes, I did.

Q. You didn't have a pistol, did you?

A. No. I've never owned one.

Ernst then asked Hatcher whom he blamed for Melinda's escapades. Hatcher shook his head sadly. "Only myself," he muttered.

Through the testimony of Hatcher, his estranged wife and their daughter, Foreman had put into the record still more evidence aimed at advancing his case against society. If these youngsters and parents were guilty of misdeeds, he implied, then so was society. And, if society's ills had contributed to the death of Bill Walden, then society belonged on trial—along with Jack Bonds or in his place. To some, it seemed a farfetched theory. But Foreman was pressing it for all he was worth.

He called to the stand Jim Ashmore, athletic coach at the junior high attended by the teenagers involved in the case. Ashmore testified that a member of the King Cutters—or the Hoods and Hoodesses—had once thrown a bottle through a front window of his home. He conceded that teams in his gym classes were called by the names "The Switchblades" and "The Zip Guns." But it was all in fun, he implied. Foreman, for his part, implied that it might not be so funny, in the light of what had come out at the trial.

The following day, Thursday, January 23, Foreman summoned to the stand a Houston policeman, Patrolman J. W. Butzke. The officer testified that, two months before the slaying, he and his partner had stopped Bill Walden for driving with a burned-out headlight.

"What, if anything, did you find when you stopped him?" Foreman asked.

Butzke answered: "When my partner and I got to the car, we found two six-packs of beer on the floor and two open beers and beers spilled on the front seat. We ordered Walden out of the car and found a knife in Walden's right front pocket."

The officer produced the knife. It was a switchblade. Foreman demonstrated to the jury—not once, but twice—just how the blade swung out when a button was pushed. (Foreman is a leading advocate of the "live demonstration" in the courtroom. No matter how simple the demonstration is, he will invariably insist on going through with it. Some of the most newsworthy photographs ever taken of Foreman—particularly in Texas, where cameras are permitted in the courtroom—have involved such demonstrations.)

Thursday's testimony was perhaps the most meaningful in the trial, at least to that point. For the first time, attention centered on the forgotten man in the case—Jack Bonds himself. After fencing for weeks with the prosecution over whether Bonds would take the stand, Foreman announced that the defendant would testify in his own behalf. The announcement came as something of a surprise, for several reasons. First, Foreman does not make a habit of putting his clients on the stand in murder cases. Second, the decision seemed to fly in the face of Foreman's overall strategy—which was to keep as little attention as possible from falling on Bonds.

Even before Bonds was called as a witness, he suddenly became the focus of the testimony. A next-door neighbor of Bonds, Kenenth Eoff, thirty-two, gave a graphic description of events immediately following the slaying.

Eoff testified that he received a telephone call from Bonds' wife moments after the shooting. This was about 9 P.M.

"Kenneth, come quick!" Eoff quoted Mrs. Bonds as telling him. "Jack just shot and killed a boy!"

Eoff said he immediately ran next door and saw Bonds with the pistol used in the shooting. "I didn't say anything to him—I just didn't know what to say in a case like this," he testified. "I just listened. Jack told me, 'I'd give anything in the world if it hadn't happened. I hit him with . . . the gun and it went off.' "

This testimony bolstered Foreman's case considerably. For, in addition to contending that the slaying of young Walden was justifiable on the ground that Bonds had been goaded into it by the failings of society, Foreman also claimed that the shooting was both accidental and a case of self-defense. His version was that Bonds had not intended to kill Walden—merely to defend himself against a presumed concealed weapon in the youth's pocket. Bonds had meant only to scare or slug Walden with the gun, Foreman insisted, but the gun had accidentally discharged and fired the fatal bullet into the youth's head.

The evidence did not seem to support Foreman on every basic point, as we shall see. But, as we shall also see, he did a persuasive job of presenting the evidence in the light most favorable to his client.

Kenneth Eoff quoted Mrs. Bonds as saying immediately after the shooting: "I wish it hadn't happened." Eoff said that, during this period, someone in the Bonds home questioned whether it was certain Walden was dead. He said Bonds remarked: "Yes, I know he's dead."

The pastor of the church attended by the Bonds family, the Reverend Leroy S. Smith of South Post Oak Baptist Church, testified that he was summoned to the Bonds home shortly before the slaying because Mrs. Bonds was threatening to commit suicide. The Reverend Mr. Smith said that Mrs. Bonds was in a hysterical state because of her problems with her daughter, Beverly. Bonds felt compelled to slap his wife in the face several times to calm her, the minister testified. He quoted Mrs. Bonds as saying: "If this is life, I would rather go ahead and get out of it."

Further testimony about the distraught state of Bonds and his wife, Ola Mae, and about the cause of their dismay was offered by a police officer, Patrolman R. A. Drude. He said he and his partner answered a police radio call at the Bonds home on December 16, 1962, about a month before the slaying. The officers found Bonds standing guard with a pistol.

Foreman asked: "What, if anything, did Mr. and Mrs. Bonds tell you?"

Drude replied: "Mr. and Mrs. Bonds said they had been harassed during the night by a car driving by and gunning the motor, and by its occupants stopping and scratching on their windows. Mr. and Mrs. Bonds appeared worried and distraught. They pointed out a vehicle, parked down the street. I went down to investigate. I found James Allen [the friend of Walden who had testified earlier in the trial] asleep in the back seat. He said Bill Walden and another youth had been with him in the car."

Drude said he talked at length with Bonds and his wife about their problems with the teenage boys. He quoted Mrs. Bonds as telling him: "Someone is going to get killed if the situation is not cleared up!"

Foreman asked whether Bonds had mentioned receiving any threats.

"Yes, he mentioned several threats," the officer replied. "He said he got some over the telephone. There was also a message scratched on Bonds' front door, which said: 'Bonds, you are going to get yours.' "

Asked whether he had given Bonds and his wife any advice, the officer testified: "I told them they had a right to protect their property if someone tried to break in."

Thus, Foreman had scored several major points through Drude's testimony. He had shown that there was apparently genuine fear of the teenagers on Bonds' part. He had also shown that a member of the Houston Police Department had, in effect, sanctioned use of a weapon, if necessary, to protect the Bonds home. Moreover, Foreman had made another, more subtle point in his case against society. Here was a situation where tensions were obviously building. Trouble appeared certain. And yet society seemed incapable—or unwilling—to take the steps necessary to head off the trouble.

Of course, society is a vague, amorphous term. Did the police department, at this point, represent society as a whole? Did the school system, which had apparently failed to cope with the problems of the teenagers involved in the case? Did Walden's parents? And what about Bonds and his wife? They had obviously failed to solve their problems with Beverly.

The answer seemed to be that the blame lay partially at all these doors—and many others—if you accepted Foreman's general thesis. Foreman, perhaps alone in grasping the full significance of the testimony at this point, continued to pound at the "society is guilty" theme.

Another officer, Patrolman O. A. Williams, testified that he spent much of his time during late 1962 investigating incidents in which Bill Walden and other members of his gang were involved. He said the gang caused most of the juvenile-delinquency problems in the neighborhood.

Williams said he usually saw Walden about four to six times a week—either during the course of an investigation or just to chat. He testified Walden always behaved in a friendly manner toward him personally, even though he represented the law against which the youth apparently was in rebellion. Questioned about Walden's relationship with Beverly Chambers, Williams said: "He [Walden] always promised me he would leave Beverly alone."

A neighbor of Jack and Ola Mae Bonds, Mrs. Jack Duncan, testified that a long-bladed knife was stolen from her home during a burglary in September of 1962. "It has been proved that William Walden burglarized my house and kept the knife," she said. Mrs. Duncan said she knew this because all the items stolen, except the knife, had been returned to her. (Foreman was apparently trying to show through this and other testimony regarding knives that Bonds had ample reason to believe Walden represented a physical threat to the Bonds family.)

Except for another threat by Erwin Ernst to punch Foreman, the trial dragged for several days. But, finally, Jack Bonds was called to the stand. Attention was centered at last on the forgotten man. He was hardly an imposing figure. At five feet seven and 140 pounds, he was smaller than many of the teenagers who had appeared previously. Since the substance of the Bonds testimony had been tipped off by Foreman's questioning of earlier witnesses, the testimony itself proved anticlimactic.

Bonds claimed, in short, that the shooting had been both accidental and a case of self-defense. He said he had encountered Walden and Gregory Anderson the night of January 18, 1963, outside the drive-in grocery. He said the two youths got out of their car, that Anderson cursed him and that Walden put his hand in his pocket—as if to reach for a weapon. Bonds testified he struck Walden "two or three times" with his pistol and that the gun then accidentally discharged, killing Walden. Ernst subjected Bonds to a grueling cross-examination.

Q. Where was Greg Anderson when you pulled the trigger?

A. Coming around the car. . . . He was in front of the car. . . . Coming around the car.

Q. How far were you from Walden when he fell?

A. I just don't know.

Q. Why didn't you shoot Greg Anderson?

A. I didn't want to hurt anybody.

Q. Did you think he would hurt you?

A. Yes, I thought any of them would hurt me.

Q. What did you do?

A. I ran.

Q. You mean you turned your back on this gang you have described as vicious—that you say kept knives and rods and guns and pipes in their cars?

A. Yes, I did.

When the cross-examination was completed, Foreman asked his client only one question on redirect.

Q. When you say you pulled the trigger, you don't mean you pulled it intentionally, do you?

A. No, sir. I did not mean to pull the trigger.

Foreman technically rested the defense case a short time later—technically because he could be certain of prosecution rebuttal witnesses and an opportunity for the defense to try, in turn, to rebut them. The next high point in the trial came on Friday, January 31, with the lengthy testimony of the slain youth's mother, Mrs. William John Walden, Jr. An attractive, articulate woman—chic in a black velvet suit and pillbox hat—Mrs. Walden was called as a prosecution witness.

She reviewed the long history of her dead son's troubles. He was "very difficult to control, but not violent," Mrs. Walden said. She testified that she and her husband had "tried everything" to straighten him out.

"We tried private schools, public schools, taking privileges away, military academies and examinations—but nothing worked," Mrs. Walden said. "But he wasn't a violent boy."

On cross-examination, Foreman immediately attacked that last sentence.

Q. Isn't it true that your son knocked you down at least once?

A. No.

Q. Is it or is it not a fact that he threatened to kill you and your husband if you sent him to a military academy in Florida?

A. He threatened to kill himself, but not his parents.

Asked about her son's relationship with Beverly Chambers, Mrs. Walden testified: "Bill was not going with this girl."

Foreman introduced into evidence an essay written by the slain youth when he was twelve years old. The essay was to become a major piece of evidence in the case. Dated February 17, 1960, it had been written for a seventh-grade English course. Foreman handed the essay to Mrs. Walden.

Q. Do you recognize the handwriting as your son's?

A. My, my, Mr. Foreman, you are going back to when he was three years old. [She was referring to the first line of the essay, which referred to young Walden's boyhood.] I have never seen this—but it's my son's.

Foreman then read the entire rambling theme. Excerpts of interest included:

> I hate every teacher. . . . I like art and music. . . . I hate arithmetic and spelling. . . . I didn't like church, but at least I thanked God for everything He did. [A later paragraph contradicted this one, saying: "I like church."] . . .
>
> Three things I wonder about most are if I am going to heaven, who will I marry and what will I be. I would wish to go to heaven, to be filthy rich and to have fifty other wishes.

Walden mentioned again and again his desire for money and

his dislike for hard work. He wrote that he liked persons who "aren't rats, tattletails [sic], yellow or ones who think they are tough."

During Mrs. Walden's direct testimony, a large oil painting of her son had been introduced into evidence. After having Mrs. Walden identify the portrait, Ernst had placed it—facing the jury—on the judge's bench. Thus, the victim's handsome young face—seeming positively benign—had been staring at the jurors during his mother's testimony. This point was hardly lost on Foreman, who sees no detail as too insignificant to be worthy of his attention. As soon as he got the opportunity during the cross-examination, he turned the portrait face down on the judge's bench.

Then, reading from a county probation report on young Walden, Foreman asked the boy's mother numerous questions about her son. She denied various allegations Foreman had read from the probation report. His questions visibly irritated her.

"May I ask you a question?" Mrs. Walden finally asked.

Foreman replied softly: "I don't mind, but it's not proper and I prefer not to get into an argument with you."

Mrs. Walden retorted brusquely: "I'm sure you wouldn't!"

"I'm sure, too," Ernst chimed in.

Foreman, perfectly composed, addressed the bench. "Judge, will you tell the little lady [a pet Foreman expression] that this is not proper," he said. Davis agreed, and instructed Mrs. Walden that it was the lawyers—not the witnesses—who were to ask the questions. During a recess, Mrs. Walden was questioned by newsmen.

"What did you want to ask Foreman?" a reporter asked.

"I wanted to ask him what all of those records he has against Bill, and the theme he read, and all of the other testimony has to do with the murder of my son?"

Two days later, Mrs. Walden got her answer, if she was listening. In a precedent-shattering display of courtroom technique, Foreman put on the stand a psychologist who conducted an after-the-fact analysis of Bill Walden—using the very documents Mrs. Walden had mentioned as his tools for entering the slain youth's mind. Dr. Sanford Goldstone, a faculty member of the Baylor University College of Medicine, placed special emphasis on Walden's essay. After analyzing the essay, he testified, he would diagnose the youth as an "aggressive, troublesome and troubled boy who yearned for a 'magical' Utopia—but who would have settled for discipline and a father-image."

Foreman kept Goldstone on the stand for two and a half hours, providing still more evidence that society had failed both Bill Walden and Jack Bonds. The psychologist's testimony—whether truly valid or not—was critical of Walden's upbringing.

Under Foreman's questioning, the psychologist provided a paragraph-by-paragraph analysis of Walden's essay. It went this way.

Essay: "My first memory is the time I drilled a hole in the wall of my father's friend's house. I was three. . . . I called a woman who patted me on the head an ugly woman. . . . I liked to ruin things best as a little child."

Goldstone's analysis: "He was angry at the world."

Essay: "I wish my home cost $40 million and had electric tooth brush bristles, heat in the rug and floors, a swimming pool, a lake . . . an airstrip . . . a cowboy town."

Goldstone's analysis: "This is a magical world he'd like to live in and make his own. He wants nothing but pleasures. What he's actually saying is: 'I have no father and mother to discipline me.' This is an aggressive, troublesome and troubled twelve-year-old."

Essay: "The experiences I have had at church . . . I don't like going much."

Goldstone's analysis: "There is no discipline here. He's saying his parents gave him nothing in the way of comfort, discipline and guidance. He's begging for discipline."

Essay: "I like people that aren't rats, tattletails [sic], yellow or ones who think they are tough."

Goldstone's analysis: "He's telling the world that he doesn't like people who are like himself."

Essay: "I have a hobby of stamp collecting, rock collecting and building models. . . ."

Goldstone's analysis: "This is typical of this type of person. He forces himself to a certain amount of discipline by sitting down to a docile task."

Essay: "I would like to be a real astate [sic] broker, like my father. . . ."

Goldstone's analysis: "What he's asking here is: 'Where is my father? I have no father!' Again, he is begging for discipline."

Having completed his after-the-fact analysis of Walden, Goldstone turned—under Foreman's questioning—to a more orthodox analysis of Gregory Anderson, the youth who had testified about Foreman's purported "buying" of Don Bennett's testimony. Goldstone had conducted a psychological examination of Anderson at Foreman's request.

"Anderson is a youth of superior intelligence, in the upper five percent of the intelligence bracket," Goldstone testified. "He is not aggressive, and it is highly unlikely he would hurt anyone. But he indulges in gross untruths."

Goldstone did not claim that any specific statements made by Anderson during the trial were untrue. But the psychologist's testimony unquestionably hurt the state's case. For, in addition to making the charges against Foreman, Anderson had provided the prosecution with key eyewitness testimony on the slaying itself. He had contradicted Jack Bonds' story—denying, for example, that the shooting was accidental. Anderson's version was that Bonds simply walked up to Walden, leveled his pistol and fired once with the muzzle only nine inches from the youth's ear.

Foreman struck hard at Anderson's credibility as a witness. He asked Goldstone: "When did you examine this boy?"

"On August sixteenth and seventeenth," the psychologist testified.

Foreman asked: "Could he still be indulging in these 'gross untruths'?"

"Yes," Goldstone replied. "He has a weak character structure. He will follow easily and is most vulnerable to youths of his own age. Anything the crowd wanted him to do was fine with him. He wanted to be helped, and he cried for discipline."

When Goldstone stepped from the witness stand, Erwin Ernst

once again rested the state's case. Foreman then announced: "The defense rests."

Thus, at 10:41 A.M. on February 3, testimony in the longest murder trial in Texas history finally came to a halt. The case would be argued by opposing attorneys—and, indeed, by countless others—in court and out. But now the evidence was all in. What remained was in the realm of debate, then decision. What lay behind was perhaps more significant. Percy Foreman had made some law in this courtroom—merely by trying the case in the manner he had chosen. Not only had society been put on trial, but new ground had been broken in the use of psychiatric testimony.

The jury had heard fifty-nine witnesses and millions of words of testimony. Now, the time of decision neared.

It was decided to proceed with summations and Judge Davis' formal charge to the jury without recessing overnight. Erwin Ernst summed up the prosecution case in a punchy argument that lasted only twenty-two minutes. Ernst, a squatty, moon-faced man with red hair and cold slate eyes, had spent eight of his thirty-nine years as a prosecutor. Though admitting privately that he was not in Percy Foreman's class as a trial lawyer, he had never failed to give Foreman a battle royal in court. The Bonds case was no exception.

"I think we might have lost track of trying Jack Bonds for murder, and tried the juveniles of this county," Ernst told the jurors. "This was a cold-blooded, premeditated murder. It was a cruel killing of a fifteen-year-old boy by a former Marine scout, who has tried to lead us to believe that the boy needed killing. Bill Walden and his crowd needed help—but shooting one of them was not the answer."

Ernst recalled the testimony accusing Foreman of "buying" the testimony of young Don Bennett. "There is no doubt in my mind that Don Bennett shaded his testimony to fit the defense," he argued.

In his final words to the jurors, Ernst quoted a piece of philosophy. " 'Because he has the fountain of reason in him not yet regulated, a fifteen-year-old boy is the most unmanageable, insidious, sharp-witted, insubordinate, foolish, unregulated and childish of all animals,' " Ernst said. "Plato wrote this four hundred years before the birth of Christ. And times haven't changed a bit. We still have the fifteen-year-olds—and killing them isn't solving the problem!"

A hush settled over the courtroom as Ernst took his seat. The moment everyone had been awaiting was now at hand. Percy Foreman was about to begin his summation. The spectators' section was jammed. This is common. Foreman's jury speeches are legendary not only in Texas, but across the land. Lawyers and judges—as well as ordinary citizens—travel many miles to watch him in action. Foreman starts slowly and softly, holding a yellow legal pad in his hand as a sort of stage prop (more often than not, it is blank or bears only a few words). By the end of his summation, he builds to a crescendo that leaves his listeners physically, mentally and emotionally drained.

In the Bonds case, Foreman's speech was even more sensational than usual. For this case was rare—in its emotional wallop, in its legal significance and in its aspects that questioned Foreman's ethics. An indication of the importance Foreman accorded the case was provided by the fact that his eighteen-year-old son, William, an infrequent courtroom visitor, was seated in the front row of the spectators' section. Foreman would later make use of his son's presence.

He began his argument at 6:38 P.M. and did not sit down until 8:49, thus addressing the jury about six times as long as Ernst. Pulling out all the stops in his case against society, he moved a three-sided, old-fashioned church pulpit into the courtroom—saying he planned to "preach" on the subject of society's ills. The prosecution once forced removal of the pulpit, but Foreman persuaded Judge Davis to have it brought back. He "preached" behind it for the remainder of his argument.

Much of the argument was filled with a recitation of the facts already in evidence—slanted to fit Foreman's version, of course. He recalled various witnesses' testimony, recounting all the sordid details once again. His emphasis, however, was on the failure of society to cope with the problem of its wayward youth—rather than on the specific failure of any particular youngsters or parents.

He laid his case on the line in a few succinct sentences:

"We have millions to pay for a cover over a stadium [Houston's famed Astrodome] and millions to air-condition an outfield—but not enough to build a county school for delinquent boys and girls," he said.

Then, with tears streaming down his face, the supposedly hard-boiled defense lawyer denied furnishing young Don Bennett with call girls. He turned to his own teenage son.

"Stand up, Son," Foreman said. As his son rose, Foreman cried: "And they say I would furnish fifteen-year-olds with women!"

His huge frame shuddered convulsively as he sobbed again and again. Several minutes passed—laden with drama—before he resumed speaking. Not an eye in the courtroom was anywhere but on Percy Foreman. A Shakespearean actor could not have done it better.

Now, his voice still quavering, Foreman spoke of Jack Bonds.

He painted a vivid picture of a tormented man—tormented by the fear that his stepdaughter, not even his own flesh and blood but loved all the more, was being led astray. Foreman spoke of the common virtues—of home, of family, of hard work, of service to one's country as a Marine scout. But, most of all, he spoke of Jack Bonds' paternal love for his stepdaughter.

Now, the spectators strained forward to hear every syllable. Foreman, who often ends his jury speeches in a booming voice, this time used the soft sell. His voice was a bare whisper. But the jurors could hear him, and that was all that mattered. Not to be outdone by Ernst's quoting of Plato, Foreman closed his case with a quotation from Sir Walter Scott's *Lady of the Lake*.

> ". . . A tear so limpid and so meek
> It would not stain an angel's cheek
> 'Tis that which pious fathers shed
> Upon a dutious daughter's head."

Who, but Percy Foreman, would have closed on such a note? Perhaps not another attorney now practicing in our criminal courts. But, for Percy Foreman, it was a natural ending—lyrical but effective, cornpone but beautiful.

At 9:10 P.M Judge Davis, after delivering his formal charge, turned the case over to the jury. The foreman, C. Y. Yancy, a shop supervisor for a diesel-engine plant, immediately got the jurors down to work. A ballot was taken at the outset on the possible death-penalty verdict of murder with malice. It was unanimous—against conviction.

But that did not mean Bonds was off the hook. The jury still had the power to find him guilty of a lesser offense.

A second ballot was taken, on a possible verdict of murder without malice. This time two jurors voted for a guilty verdict. The other ten, however, insisted on a verdict of not guilty. A third ballot was taken. The verdict: unanimous for acquittal.

It was 10:45 P.M. The jury had considered the case for only about an hour and a half. The written verdict was handed to court clerk Ray Butts. When he read it aloud, pandemonium reigned in the crowded courtroom. Applause erupted. Mrs. Bonds rushed toward her husband and Percy Foreman. All three went into a joint, tearful embrace.

"It's wonderful!" Bonds said with a smile. "We didn't have any doubts." He kissed his wife—at the same time brushing the tears from her cheek.

"It's all over, darling," Mrs. Bonds whispered.

A shoving match—not unlike those around the goalposts at the end of a football game—ensued. Almost everyone seemingly wanted to congratulate Foreman, Bonds and other members of the defense team simultaneously. Jurors dashed from the box to embrace their wives.

"I had no doubt about it whatsoever," Foreman said. "That's why I insisted on a not-guilty verdict [rather than pleading Bonds guilty to a lesser crime]."

It is often difficult to tell whether Percy Foreman is truly moved emotionally or merely playacting. This time, with the tears still on his cheeks, his emotion seemed genuine. But we may never know for certain. He does not often discuss his inner thoughts or feelings. Although he adores a crowd of hero-worshipers around him, he appears to be the loneliest of men. Few admirers are equipped by intellect or experience to commune with him.

At any rate, he had won his case. Not only had Jack Bonds been found innocent. Society, in effect, had been found guilty.

Whether that meant anything would be done to reform society was another question. Percy Foreman once said it all, in describing jury verdicts.

"My clients don't want justice," he said. "They want their freedom."

This is no less true for society. It apparently does not want true justice. It wants its freedom to do as it pleases. And that is what keeps Percy Foreman in such great demand.

2

It's not that I'm vain, proud or egotistical.
I just don't have anything to be modest about.
PERCY FOREMAN

THE EVENING of Wednesday, May 18, 1966, was cool and clear in New York City. New Yorkers, bundled up in topcoats and fur wraps, made their way along the windy streets to the Hotel Pierre. The occasion was the annual dinner of New York's Association of Lawyers of Criminal Courts.

It was a gathering of the elite or the semi-elite (since criminal lawyers, particularly in New York, rank well below Wall Street lawyers on the social scale). Yet, if one judges attorneys by their importance to society, this was a star-studded gathering of lawyers, judges and politicians. Familiar front-page names—from New York's best-known criminal lawyer, Maurice Edelbaum, to United States Attorney (and former gubernatorial candidate) Bob Morgenthau and from rackets-buster Al Scotti to such prominent judges as Hyman Barshay, George Beldock and Irving Saypol—graced the guest list.

The guest speaker was to be Percy Foreman, fresh from new triumphs in the criminal courts of Florida and other states north and south. Foreman was no stranger to New York. He had practiced frequently in New York courts and had once held a part-ownership in a costly cooperative apartment on Park Avenue, given him as a partial fee in a divorce case.

Soon it was time for Foreman's speech. He had apologized in advance to several friends for what he felt would be a poor showing. "I'm in trial in Hartford, Connecticut, in a federal narcotics case," he said. "I haven't had time to prepare this speech, so I'll have to give them something off the cuff."

Off the cuff or not, Foreman wowed 'em. He started with a few jokes—like the old one about a lawyer's speech being like a dog's tail. "It's bound to a cur." A cur—occur. Get it? (Foreman's pet "jokes" are rarely as amusing as his spontaneous jests. He has an extremely agile mind, and his impromptu barbs are far sharper than what he considers his "jokes.")

The speech, like Foreman himself, was bombastic, iconoclastic and, in the view of some attorneys, just plain drastic. At the same time, it was highly significant in revealing Foreman's personal and legal philosophy. As he frequently does, Foreman lashed out at the American Bar Association and the legal "establishment" in general.

"The American Bar Association is an honorable organization," he said. "But the representatives of the association who are now engaged in trying to develop a code on news coverage of criminal cases are the last ones in the profession who should be doing the job. These people just don't try criminal cases."

Now he was off on one of his pet subjects—the low esteem in which criminal lawyers are held.

"The difference between a civil lawyer and a criminal lawyer is a difference in values," he said. "The civil lawyer defends money. He represents money. The criminal lawyer is primarily concerned with life and liberty. When I talk to young law students I tell them that, if they love money more than life and liberty, they should stay in their sequestered cells. But, if they value life and liberty, they should join us.

"As for press coverage of criminal cases, I think it's a mistake to assume that the bar and the press are on opposite sides. I find, in meeting with news people, that we're all on the same side—we're all trying to do the same thing. We're all trying to get the rights of the people preserved and at the same time preserve the guarantee of a public trial.

"I say it's just as foolish to try to ignore the terrific communications impact of television and radio as it is to put a buggy whip in an automobile. There are times when knowing that the press, TV and radio people are in the courtroom helps keep the court honest. I think television and newspaper cameras and radio equipment should be permitted in the courtroom. But I believe all news media in the courtroom should be hidden. In every major city, there ought to be a courtroom designed for the trial of sensational cases. That's all the press wants to cover. So a courtroom should be engineered for the convenience of the news media."

Now he turned to another pet topic—capital punishment. "The Holy Writ does not say that 'thou shalt not kill, except in groups.' The state has no more right than anyone else to take a life. People who advocate the death penalty as a deterrent to crime attempt to justify their stand by saying it should be used only in cases where there is premeditation. But, back in Texas, our legal terminology for premeditation is 'malice aforethought.' The law, as interpreted by the courts, is that 'malice aforethought' may be presumed from acts done or words spoken. No lapse of time other than an instant is required by law for a jury to convict a man of murder 'with malice aforethought.' Premeditation means nothing under such a law. Any homicide can be construed as being with malice aforethought. This gives rise to the maladministration of justice by any of various elements involved in a murder trial."

Foreman witnessed his first and only hanging at the age of eight. He not only recalls it vividly; he dwells on it frequently. It would hardly be stretching a point to speculate that the hanging, plus his boyhood environment and some urging from his mother (all of which will be discussed later in this chapter), helped lead him into the career of defending the seemingly doomed.

"If the purpose of executions is to deter crime, they should have the widest possible audience," Foreman told the New York lawyers. "It is much more sensible to hold them in public than in the wee hours of the morning in total confinement. I advocate putting executions on television. Not only that. They should all be commercially sponsored—by the light and power companies that provide the juice."

Now Foreman turned to the debate over whether recent rulings by appellate courts, some of them in cases in which he had taken part, worked to the detriment of society and to the advantage of the criminal. He particularly defended the United States Supreme Court decision in the controversial Escobedo case, which held that the police must permit a suspect to consult an attorney promptly after his arrest.

"The people who are against this ruling are those people who would like this country to be a police state," he said. "They believe that evidence should be taken from the suspect, instead of against the suspect. All of that is changed now, to the greater good of this America. And when people say to you: 'What about all the decent people; don't we have rights, too?' . . . then you must remind them that, if the blackest criminal does not have constitutional rights, neither do any of us!"

For an off-the-cuff talk, Foreman's speech received a rousing ovation. He was among his peers—or at least his would-be peers. And, though all might not agree with him, all reveled at the spectacle of seeing this living legend in action. Pete Hamill summed it up the next day in an eloquent column in the New York *Post:*

> One of the few remaining glories of this Republic was among us last night, reminding us again of the elegance and passion of the old style, and how much our poor America has lost. Percy Foreman, tall and powerful-looking at sixty-four, wearing a shirt that seemed to choke him, his pants baggy, the steel-gray hair starting its fall forward, a drink in his hand, walked among a group of his fellow criminal lawyers and by his presence alone underlined how honorable a profession the law can be when it is practiced by a man who understands the engines of the human

> heart. . . . He stood among his fellows at a pre-dinner cocktail party like a man from the King Ranch dropped suddenly into Red Hook. People came to him and congratulated him. . . . He was funny with the men and gracious with the women and, when the conversation lagged, he would look out through those crinkled Western eyes like the professional he is, counting the house. . . . Welcome to New York, Mr. Foreman: We'll never see enough of the old style.

After Foreman had finished his speech, it took him almost an hour to extricate himself from a swarm of well-wishers. It was now after 10 P.M. But he was still working. When he hires someone, he hires the best. So it seemed natural that Vincent Gillen, the high-priced private detective who was even then under fire for his role in the Ralph Nader–General Motors investigation, was on hand to report to Foreman on an assignment. At long last, Gillen completed his business with Foreman and went on his way. Now, except for one longtime friend, Foreman was alone. He invited the friend to his hotel room.

"I may be going back up to Hartford tonight," Foreman said. "But we can talk for a while."

The friend had seen Foreman hundreds of times over the years—in court and out, with a brief or a drink in his hand, in fair weather and in foul, in good health and in poor. But, this time, he was alarmed by Foreman's appearance. True, the defense lawyer was sixty-four. True, the friend had not seen him in perhaps a year. True, it was late at night and Foreman was near the end of a grueling day. But, even so, the Percy Foreman of old had never seemed this tired. Formerly he had been able to stay up half the night—working, talking or drinking—and then show up in court as alert as if he had slept for twelve hours.

Was Foreman, as rumor had it, slipping? Was age finally slowing the old war horse? Newspapermen who had covered Foreman for years said he was growing increasingly irritable. So did other lawyers and several judges—some of them considered Foreman's close friends.

For all his charm, Foreman had always been curt. His mind was so quick, and the demands on his time so great, that he had never shown much patience with windbags or dullards. But now, his acquaintances said, he was growing "simply impossible." He was so argumentative, they said, that it was difficult to carry on a friendly conversation with him. He always wanted the last word, no matter how inconsequential the discussion.

Now, in his hotel room with his friend, it became evident why Foreman had such little patience. His phone was ringing insistently. And no sooner had he completed one conversation than it was ringing again. And again. And again. Clients, other attorneys, writers and law-book publishers all were trying to reach him simultaneously. It would be impossible to overstate the demand for Foreman's services. He spends as much time turning down cases as he does trying them. He takes a case for one of a variety of reasons—because it promises big money, because it fascinates him or because "this is a case where I'm really needed." The money is not secondary by any means, but it is not primary either. Foreman has represented indigent Negroes and Mexicans for nothing, asking reporters to keep this fact out of the press so that he will be spared requests for similar treatment from other poor defendants. He claims he hates money. But the fact remains that he is preoccupied with it.

"Like Omar Khayyam, I take the cash and let the credit go," he says.

It is a question often of whose money he decides to take—one rich man's or another's, one poor man's or another's. Take it he does, however. He once decorated a pair of his wife's dancing slippers with diamonds given him in lieu of cash fees. It was not a sign of Texas ostentation, but rather a sign of utter disdain for fancy jewelry, that prompted him to do so. He simply had nothing better to do with the diamonds, so he studded the slippers with them.

"Yes," Foreman was saying on the telephone to a client in Louisiana. "I think you'd better check into that hospital if you can. You have a doctor's recommendation that you do so, don't you? All right, you'd better check in. I'll talk to you around Memorial Day. I'm going to try to get away to Indianapolis for the race. I go every year, if I can. You can reach me there at Gasoline Alley."

At last, the phone calls stopped coming. Foreman stretched out on the bed, still fully dressed. He and his guest talked for about an hour, but his eyelids kept drooping and closing. Each time, Foreman would force himself to come awake. He was exhausted, but he just would not quit. Once he starts talking, he has to run down like a wristwatch.

"I got hurt in an automobile accident," he said. "I keep getting these pains back here [behind the neck]. Every once in a while, I have to go into a hospital or put it in a neck brace. I'd like to retire—but I just can't. I've got maybe five years' worth of cases stacked up."

"What would you do if you retired?"

"I'd go into the real-estate business. I've got all that property I own [more than forty buildings or lots taken in lieu of cash fees]. I want to have something to leave to my two children. The law practice won't be practical."

"Is your son going to college?"

"No, he's not. He's not going to be a lawyer, at any rate."

The two men talked of mutual friends, of the old days, of where the hell the world was going.

Finally, Foreman's friend urged: "Come on out to Long Island and spend a weekend with us. You know, my wife's a Southerner and, if you're getting homesick, some of my wife's Southern cooking might help."

"There's nothing in the world I'd like better than to see your lovely wife and eat some of her Southern cooking," Foreman said. "But this trial in Hartford is taking a lot of time. I'm trying to wind it up. I've been spending my weekends here in New York at the St. Regis, working."

(The defendant in the Hartford case was James Miller, forty-two-year-old owner of several Connecticut beauty shops. Miller had been arrested in 1964 on charges of being the intended purchaser of what was then the largest shipment of heroin ever seized at a U.S. border point. Seventy-two pounds of pure heroin, valued by federal authorities at $56 million, had been seized while being smuggled into the country from Mexico. Among those implicated in the case with Miller were several high-ranking Mafia figures, Canadian racketeers, a Frenchman and a Canadian. The case caused sensational publicity throughout the hemisphere —particularly in Canada. Charges of bribery in Canada caused the resignation of a Cabinet minister and a member of Parliament, and the arrest of another official. Miller was convicted of narcotics conspiracy, sentenced to twelve years in prison and freed on the unusually high appeal bond of $200,000. Foreman then dropped out of the case. In 1969 a committee that included a Yale law professor, a New Haven attorney and numerous Connecticut housewives launched a campaign to upset the conviction. The campaign succeeded. On March 14, 1969, the United States Court of Appeals for the Second Circuit ordered a new trial on the ground that the defense and jury had been kept unaware that a chief government witness had been questioned by prosecutors before the trial while under hypnosis.)

The men who were to drive Foreman back to Hartford came to the room. "Boys," Foreman said, "I'm exhausted. How about if we go back early in the morning? You get a hotel room. I'll pay for your room and meals. How long will it take us? That long? OK. I'll get up about 5:30. Pick me up at 6." At last, Foreman was alone. It was approaching 1 A.M. But, as his friend walked down the hotel corridor toward an elevator, he could hear Foreman's booming voice placing one last telephone call. Incredibly, Foreman was still working.

Since this was far from an unusual evening in Percy Foreman's life—in fact, a quite typical one—several questions naturally arise. What motivates Foreman to work so ceaselessly? What drives him? Why can't he retire?

Seemingly, he has long since conquered all the worlds open to him. He has met each challenge. He has climbed each mountain. He has savored every bit of life—at least vicariously in the courtroom—and has left untouched precious few bases outside the courtroom.

And yet he continues, year after year, fighting the battles, delivering the speeches, raking in the superfluous money. But why?

Why not accept a judgeship, as did Sam Leibowitz? Why not go into semiretirement, putting the Foreman name at the top of a prestigious law-firm letterhead? Why not write the long-awaited memoirs? Why, instead, go on playing the lone-wolf defense lawyer—living out of a suitcase, entering hostile courtrooms in hostile cities, defending clients who frequently hate his guts?

There is only one place to start in search of the answers to these questions. For the inner self of Percy Foreman has its roots in only one place. And that place is a wide spot in a narrow farm-to-market road in the piney woods of Polk County, Texas. That wide spot, and it is no more than that, is called Bold Springs, Texas. You won't even find it on the official road maps prepared by the state of Texas. All you will find is a Baptist church, with a cemetery behind it. You won't find the name Foreman on many gravestones—just one grave marker for a Foreman infant.

It has been written that Percy Foreman has something in common with Abraham Lincoln and with George Washington, but whether Foreman originated the idea is unknown. The theory is that he was born in a log cabin and that he has never told a lie. If this particular Foreman legend is self-initiated, it is a contradiction in terms. For, if he ever claimed he was born in a log cabin, he has told at least one lie.

It is not really a log cabin, but it is not far from it. What it is, in Texas terminology, is a wooden "box house." It lies a short piece down a narrow shell road (made from Gulf Coast shells and other building materials) from the church. Here now resides a stubble-bearded, lanky boondocker named Tom Marsh. And here is where Percy Foreman was born on June 21, 1902.

"Percy comes around every now and then," says Marsh. "I guess he just wants to look around at the ol' home place. He comes in, walks around and then leaves."

The house is modest even by East Texas piney-woods standards. It usually has a few hounds yipping at the heels of visitors. There are several other houses along the shell road, but this is an isolated spot that reminds one of Faulkner's Mississippi. East Texas, one of the many distinct regions in the vastness of the state, is Lady Bird country—not the Central Texas hill country of LBJ. It is also redneck country, more akin to Louisiana-Mississippi-Alabama than to the Midwestern nature of the Panhandle, the Southwestern nature of West Texas or the free-and-easy nature of the Gulf Coast. It is a section where Negroes are still called "niggers" and where it is not uncommon for policemen to be accused of beating Negro prisoners. In early 1967, a state highway patrolman admitted clubbing several Negro gospel singers after a traffic arrest. The Negroes claimed the beating took place in the Polk County Jail; the officer claimed it occurred incidental to the arrest on U.S. Highway 59.

"You know, Percy once subpoenaed me to testify in a murder trial," Tom Marsh says with a trace of pride. "It was that case over in Groveton—supposed to be the only one Percy and Zemmie ever tried together." (Zemmie Foreman, Percy's older brother, became the country lawyer of the family. He remained near the place of his birth, winning the sobriquet "The Sage of Polk County." There are those who contend Zemmie, now retired, was a better lawyer than his famed brother when it came to trying "country murder" cases.)

"The killing took place in a beer joint," Marsh says.

"Did you get to testify?" a visitor asks.

"No," he says, disappointment written all over his face. "They subpoenaed me, but never called me. I left the beer joint fifteen minutes before the killing." Marsh leaves no doubt that he would have enjoyed being a courtroom witness. But he sees no fame in residing in the home where the great Percy Foreman was born.

"Do you get any kick out of living in Percy's old house?" he is asked.

"No," he says with a puckish grin. "It's my house now."

At the cemetery it is not uncommon to encounter some of Foreman's relatives or friends, such as Mr. and Mrs. L. R. Rasberry of Livingston, the Polk County seat. "I'm Percy's cousin," Mrs. Rasberry says. "I was a Meece—Ruby Meece. We're kin to Percy's mother. I've known Percy all my life. Of course, we never called him 'Percy.' We called him 'Gene'—his middle name. All the Foreman boys were called by their middle names until they left home. Percy didn't become 'Percy' till he went to Houston."

Asked about the "log cabin," Mrs. Rasberry laughs. "That Percy, he's a mess," she says. "He wasn't born in any log cabin. Matter of fact, I don't recall him even being born in Bold Springs. I think he was born downtown in Livingston." (Mrs. Rasberry is wrong. Since she is younger than Foreman, and the Foreman family later moved to Livingston, her mistake is understandable.)

As a boy, Foreman was seemingly the brightest, most precocious youngster in Polk County. He earned more money as an eleven-year-old than most full-grown men in the county did.

Mrs. J. J. Hollenburger of Livingston, chairman of the Polk County Historical Survey, recalls hearing numerous stories about Foreman from her father, Jett Brock. "My father was a member of a grand jury that considered indicting Percy when he was a kid," she recalls. "It was amusing, really. All Percy had done was pull some Hallowe'en pranks. But this grand jury was seriously considering indicting him and some other boys for delaying the United States mails and bank burglary. You see, he and some of his friends stole the sign from the First National Bank of Livingston. They broke a window in the process. They also pulled another prank that delayed a train carrying the mail. My father cast the deciding vote against an indictment, but there were some other men on the grand jury who really were adamant about wanting an indictment. My uncle, Ray Brock, ran with Percy and the other Foreman boys when he was a kid. He knows all about it."

Ray L. Brock is nine years older than Percy Foreman. He really "ran" with Percy's brother, Zemmie. But Percy was so bright that the older boys let him tag along. Brock spends his days in retirement in a small, comfortable home a few blocks off Livingston's main drag. He is in relatively good health, and his memory is excellent. He regales listeners with stories about the old days in Polk County. As for the Hallowe'en pranks, Brock gets a twinkle in his eye and leaves the impression he is telling only those portions of the tales that will not seriously implicate himself and the others. He says, for example, that he just can't seem to recall that grand-jury investigation.

"I don't remember the business about the bank, but I remember the train all right," Brock says. "The Foreman boys got a bucket of soap suds one Hallowe'en and soaped the railroad tracks leading into Livingston. Well, there's a big hill just before you get to town. The streamliner was comin' in, on its way from Houston to Shreveport. It hit those suds halfway up the hill and started skidding. Then it just rolled back down the hill. The engineer tried it again, but he just couldn't make the hill. The tracks were too slick. Percy and the other boys got such a kick out of it that this became an annual prank. I remember another time, on Hallowe'en, they got somebody's buggy and somehow put it up on top of the general store downtown. The owner had a heck of a time getting it down again."

"Downtown" is not what cosmopolites would consider "downtown." For Livingston, even as the county seat, has a population of only about 4,200. When Percy Foreman was born, this was frontier country—if not in name, then in fact. Even today, it is a somnolent community about seventy miles north of Houston, a stopover en route through the Big Thicket between Texarkana and Houston. (The Big Thicket, revered in Texas folklore, has been described by Louis Hofferbert of the Houston *Chronicle* as not so much a geographic area as an attitude. It is backwoods Texas.)

On Highway 59, Livingston calls "neighbor" such thriving metropolises as Crosby to the south and Moscow and Corrigan to the north. Polk County, as a whole, has a population only slightly in excess of 15,000. Yet, it is not without distinctions. It boasts of having possessed the shortest railroad in the state—the 6.86-mile Moscow, Camden and San Augustine line. It also contains Texas' only remaining Indian reservation. The reservation, for members of the Alabama and Coushatta tribes, lies due east of Livingston. As in days gone by, the Anglo population of the county (seventy-one percent of the total) has little use for the Indians. On a recent day, an articulate antique-store operator stood outside his roadside shop on Highway 59 and cursed at two Indians who were erecting a sign directing tourists to the reservation. "Those goddam Indians," he snarled. "What right have they got to put up that sign across the highway from me?" The answer seemed obvious, but his customers did not contradict him.

Percy Foreman himself is part-Indian—and proud of it. He traces his lineage to the Cherokee tribe. Another part-Indian, the late Will Rogers, was his cousin. Each of the men was distinguished by a droopy-lipped grin, a shock of unruly hair and a pair of twinkling eyes. But the resemblance ended there. Foreman, even as a youth, was much larger than his cousin. Today, he dominates any room he enters—particularly a courtroom—purely by virtue of his size. He is massive. Some have said he looks like a big, friendly bear. But he really is bigger than some bears. He looks like just what he is—a huge, drawling, but fast-moving Texan. It is a chore for the average person to keep up with Foreman's long strides.

To understand Percy Foreman, it is necessary to understand the history, geography, topography and economy of Polk County. The county, one of 254 in Texas (which has far more counties than any other state), was cut off from neighboring Liberty County in 1846. It was named for James K. Polk, who was President when Texas entered the Union in 1845. Its median annual temperature (sixty-six degrees) and rainfall (forty-nine inches) make it ideal for the lumber industry. The county lies on a rolling, thickly wooded plain between the Neches and Trinity rivers. The soil, sandy in the uplands but rich in the river valleys, also is conducive to lumbering. Thus, longleaf and shortleaf pine are Polk County's chief products. Oak, walnut, sweet gum and magnolia also grow in abundance, as does cotton. It is also an oil-producing county (2,100,000 barrels a year), and has natural gas, iron ore and lignite deposits.

The Big Thicket represents a hunter's paradise—rich in deer, small game and waterfowl. There is excellent fishing in the Trinity, in Bear Creek and in several small lakes. (Percy Foreman, after becoming a national figure, once forced a chamber of commerce in nearby Hardin County to change its dinner menu from Cornish game hen to local catfish in order to entice him as a speaker. He said he had fished in a Hardin County creek as a boy and would come only if catfish were the main course. Local panjandrums conceded, resorting to everything from mass fishing parties to an illegal fishing practice called "telephoning" in order to comply.)

Without question, Polk County's most illustrious product is neither lumber, cotton nor oil—but Percy Foreman. For a man who has earned fame and fortune as a defense lawyer, frequently at the expense of lawmen and politicians, Foreman has an unlikely background. He entered life as the son of a man who was both a lawman and a politician. His father, R. P. Foreman, held various public offices, including county jailer, deputy sheriff and sheriff. Young Percy grew up around the jail. (In many Texas counties, as elsewhere, the sheriff's office and jail also serve as living quarters for the sheriff and his family.) Percy's chores as a boy included carrying meals to his father's prisoners. He got his first taste of what "justice" was all about in talking with these prisoners. He also got a taste of what jail life is like. He learned quickly that murderers are the elite of the inmate world. "They usually think they have done the right thing," he says today. He also learned that accused murderers are willing to pay almost anything to criminal lawyers—even if their families must go into hock to keep them out of the electric chair.

There was no electric chair in Texas when Foreman was a youth. The hangman's noose awaited Polk County transgressors. Today, Polk County old-timers talk about the "legal hangin'" and the "lynchin'" that took place during Foreman's boyhood. In both cases, in their words, "a nigger got hanged." The "legal hangin'"—the one witnessed by Foreman when he was eight—involved a Negro who had killed several white persons. It was carried out on the grounds adjoining the jail. The occasion resembled a celebration. Hundreds of persons came with picnic baskets to camp on the jail grounds and await the moment of public retribution. "I don't believe six people in Polk County stayed home," Foreman recalls.

The "lynchin'" involved, in one old-timer's words, "a nigger who neglected to say 'howdy' to a white man on the street." One morning, the old-timer said, "we woke up and there that nigger was—hangin' from a tree limb down near yonder bridge."

Before his father became jailer and sheriff, Percy Foreman and his family resided eight miles from the county seat in the "box house" at Bold Springs. There Foreman led the life of a typical farm boy—except that, from the start, he showed little inclination for farming.

"He never even learned to milk a cow," his mother, Mrs. Willie Foreman, complained in a 1955 newspaper interview. (Mrs. Foreman, then eighty-four, has since died.) "He was arrogant and complained of being swatted in the face by the cow's tail," Mrs. Foreman said. Once, she heard a terrible commotion in the barn and ran to investigate. She found Percy's older brother, Zemmie (pronounced "Zimmie"), milking the cow. The cow's tail was tied to a rafter with a rope. Mrs. Foreman never learned whether this was the doing of Percy or Zemmie.

The Foremans were among the first in Polk County to take advantage of such technological improvements as electric lighting. Mrs. Foreman recalled that, during one of her husband's political campaigns, the family buttered up some of his backwoods supporters by feeding and stabling eleven of their horses. "One guy from 'way back in the woods spent the night in our house," she said. "When I went to clean his room the next morning, I found he'd tied a black sock over the electric light—which was still burning. That guy didn't even know how to turn off the electricity."

Percy Foreman felt as a boy that this backwoodsman was only too typical of the ignorance prevailing in Polk County. Such ignorance, in his view, pervaded the faculty of his school. Thus, he decided at an early age to give short shrift to formal education. He started working at the age of eight as a shoeshine boy. At fifteen, he quit school "because I knew everything they could teach me." Even before giving up school, he estimates, he played hooky about eight months of every school year. In addition, he was engaged in a running public feud with the school principal. "The man incarnated education—but he wouldn't pay his laundry bill," Foreman recalls.

Young Foreman set out to collect that bill, and others, for the local laundry. His business ventures and his informal education flourished as he expanded into large-scale bill-collecting, among other enterprises. When he opened his shoeshine stand, there was one competitor in town. Soon, there was none. Foreman bought out the competitor, hired another boy and thus had two thriving stands. "I gave a better shine," he says proudly.

One job led to another. In addition to shining shoes and collecting bills, Foreman made deliveries for the laundry, the drugstore and various newspapers. At the age of eleven, he was making about eight dollars a day—a wage that exceeded most adult salaries in Livingston. Young Foreman drove a hard bargain. On bill collections, for example, he kept a fourth of the proceeds.

At age twelve he entered the low bid on a contract to load cotton aboard trains. The bid was twenty-five cents a bale. Foreman then hired a group of Negro laborers to do the work for eight cents a bale. During a seven-year period—part of which he was not even in Livingston—his workers loaded almost 200,000 bales. By the age of sixteen, he had saved $6,500 in cash and government bonds (World War I Liberty Bonds). He had, perhaps, also lost a bit of his boyhood arrogance. At any rate, he decided it was time to resume his formal education.

He set out for Houston to seek additional booklearning and to expand his fortune. He enrolled in a correspondence school, completing a one-year course in three months. The school was so ecstatic about his performance that it took a quarter-page advertisement in the Houston *Post* to brag about him. Next he won a working scholarship at the prestigious Staunton Military Academy in Staunton, Virginia, where he worked at odd jobs around the campus while compiling an outstanding academic record. His financial fortune continued to mount.

Within a year the wanderlust struck anew. Foreman persuaded the operators of a chautauqua company in Washington, D.C., that he could make himself useful on a national tour. Only seventeen, he found himself suddenly caught up in the glamour of constant travel and the intellectual stimulation of relatively "high-brow" discussion. The carnival atmosphere—the tents, the acrobats, the magicians—fascinated him. Some of the talents he picked up on the chautauqua circuit would become mainstays of his legal repertoire in later years. For example, he developed a memory trick that had long been a standard for carny magicians. Before a show Foreman would contrive to be introduced hastily to a dozen or more local celebrities. Later, from the lecture platform, he would address each man by name, point to him in the audience and make an appropriate comment. There is nothing miraculous about the trick. It involves a simple process of mental association concerning the man, his face and his occupation. Many college psychology professors teach the gimmick in their freshman classes as an example of how the mind works. However, Foreman never failed to bring down the house with the trick. And, even today, his memory is regarded as one of his most effective courtroom weapons. He frequently amazes opposing counsel, judges and jurors with his ability to recall a specific line of testimony—perhaps offered several years earlier in another case—by a recalcitrant witness.

In his initial chautauqua days, Foreman did not take the lecture platform. He acted as the company's advance man. Later he became a $30,000-a-season circuit manager. But his first love, and his enduring one, was for the limelight.

Thus, at the age of eighteen, he delivered his first public oration to an audience at Burnside, Kentucky. "If you didn't talk for two and a half hours in those days, people thought they were being cheated," Foreman says. He gave them their money's worth. Eventually he served in the dual roles of company manager and star lecturer. Before long he had raised his personal fortune to $67,000. However, he was still not a full-grown man, and his lifetime occupation had not yet been chosen. His horizons had broadened beyond Polk County, but he knew where his roots lay. He loved Texas. He still reveres it today. (During the Candy Mossler trial in Florida, he asked judicial notice of the fact that March 2 was Texas Independence Day. The judge granted Foreman's request, remarking that all Americans were indebted to the state of Texas.)

While touring with the chautauqua company from coast to coast, young Foreman did not lose touch with his family, his community, his state or his region. His ancestors had fought on the

Confederate side during the unpleasantness between the states, and Percy Foreman was not quite ready to become a Yankee. His grandfather, the original Zemmie Foreman, had fought with the famous Hood Brigade. His other grandfather, William Pinckney Rogers, carried the blood of the Georgia Rogers family and the North Carolina Pinckneys. (It was this Rogers family that produced Will Rogers, who was Percy Foreman's third cousin.) When the first Zemmie Foreman died, he was buried in his Confederate uniform, his rifle beside him, with attendant military honors. Percy recalled his grandfather's old Civil War stories, and his awe of the "progress" being made in the North did not blind him to the simple virtues of the South.

Foreman might be lecturing one night in Illinois on "The High Mission of Women in the Twentieth Century" or another night in Kentucky on "America's Social Ideal." But, as mature as he sounded on the lecture stand, he still sought his mother's counsel when trying to chart his future course. He realized he could not spend his entire life on the chautauqua circuit. "My mother thought law would be my best bet," he recalls. "Were it not for her, I would have become a professional wrestler."

Thus, at the age of nineteen, he enrolled in the institution with the best law school in his home state—the University of Texas. Some wealthy boys from Texas attended Ivy League schools. But this would have been out of character for Foreman. Though he has since lectured at Ivy League schools, they are not his cup of tea. He is a Texan through and through.

Foreman's college career was unusual, to say the least. For one thing, he attended classes only from Thanksgiving through Easter, touring with the chautauqua company during the remainder of the year. For another thing, it is difficult to tell where one class year ended for him and the next began. He somehow completed undergraduate studies and law school, with this strange schedule, by the time he was twenty-five. Moreover, he served as president of the law-school student body during his senior year. And, when the law-school administration tried to make him wait an additional year for his sheepskin, student demonstrators forced a change in policy. At the time, Foreman was not even at the university. He was touring Michigan with the chautauqua company.

While in law school, Foreman was named the first winner of what was to become an annual oratorical contest sponsored by San Antonio's Battle of Flowers Association. The contest, open to students from various colleges throughout Texas, aims to encourage interest in state history and traditions. After several preliminary rounds, the final competition takes place in San Antonio each San Jacinto Day (April 21, the anniversary of the crucial Battle of San Jacinto in Texas' war for independence.) In winning the first competition, Foreman spoke on the subject "A Tribute to Stephen F. Austin as the Father of Texas." He still relies heavily today on his knowledge of Texas history, both in formal speeches and in jury arguments. And the Battle of Flowers Association still reminds prospective orators each year that Foreman used the contest as a springboard to greater accomplishments.

In 1927, however, Foreman's major triumphs lay ahead of him. He was ready to hang up his law shingle, but he had not yet decided where to do so. During his chautauqua travels he had been offered numerous jobs with law firms and prosecutors' offices. The Cook County District Attorney's office in Chicago wanted him. So did various firms in Texas, Maine, Michigan, Ohio and California. Gradually, he narrowed the competition to two cities—San Francisco and Houston. There was much to be said for each. But the deciding factor was just one man, a highly respected Houston lawyer named J. W. Lockett. He was seventy-two by the time Foreman was ready to enter law practice. But Foreman had once watched him in the courtroom and had liked what he'd seen.

"I was so impressed with his knowledge and the way he prepared the case that I wanted to practice law with him," Foreman says. "I guess it was Lockett who sold me on Houston."

Thus, in December of 1927, a new Houston law partnership emerged—Lockett and Foreman. The old man and the novice had offices in the Binz Building, across the street from the Rice Hotel in downtown Houston. Foreman's early career was hardly spectacular. Except for helping Lockett prepare civil cases—the firm represented some of the Houston area's most wealthy and respected families—Foreman did nothing in his first three months except draw a lease on a fig orchard. The first client to call Percy Foreman his personal lawyer was a dentist, Dr. C. M. Taylor. He paid his fee for the orchard lease with a five-dollar bill. Foreman still has the bill.

Despite his respect for Lockett, Foreman quickly grew impatient with the firm's essentially civil practice. He yearned for the drama of the criminal courts. He was not getting it with Lockett. But his entry into the criminal-court arena lay just over the horizon.

3

I was Saul before I was Paul.
PERCY FOREMAN

IN THE BIBLICAL idiom that he frequently affects, Percy Foreman uses the Saul-Paul analogy to explain that he was a prosecutor before he became a defense lawyer.

Early in March of 1928, dissatisfied with the lack of trial work available in his partnership with J. W. Lockett, Foreman took steps to move into the field of criminal law. One evening, he delivered an address before a group of his fellow University of Texas alumni. Among his listeners were men from some of Texas' most prominent families. These men were split into two opposing factions. Foreman felt the dissension was hurting the University of Texas, its alumni organizations and the men themselves. He told them so from the lecture platform. "I just gave them unshirted hell," Foreman recalled in a 1959 interview with *Houston Town Magazine* writer Patrick O'Bryan. After he had finished his speech, several of the men involved in the quarreling lingered to talk with

Foreman. "They asked me if there was anything they could do for me," Foreman said. "There was. I told them I wanted to get into the [Houston] district attorney's office as a trial lawyer. The next day Horace Soule, the district attorney, called me and asked me to come in and see him. That same day I went to work for him."

Circumstances contrived to prevent Foreman from spending any more than nine months in the district attorney's office during his first tour of duty there. District Attorney Soule was defeated in a reelection campaign and left office on December 31, 1928. Foreman left with him, but would return as an assistant district attorney four years later. His nine-month gestation period as a prosecutor had served him well. By the time he reentered private practice in 1929, he had accumulated sufficient trial experience that he was able to begin specializing in criminal law.

Foreman caused his first major stir in the press by serving as defense attorney for a group of bearded Jewish peddlers who had banded together in an organization known as the Hebrew Peddlers Benevolent Association. The peddlers had enraged local merchants by wheeling their pushcarts up outside Houston groceries and selling their wares at cut prices. The established stores found business dwindling and vowed to get even. At their insistence, the police launched a massive crackdown on members of the pushcart brigade for peddling without the necessary licenses. The peddlers were hauled away to jail by the dozen.

"They finally came to see me and offered me a hundred dollars a week to represent them," Foreman recalls. "I accepted. And that may have been when I learned it could be better to fix a high fee and lose a client than to fix a low fee. Some weeks I would get thirty to fifty of these peddlers out of jail. But I finally put a stop to the mass arrests.

"I let two hundred or three hundred cases accumulate, then agreed to try them all on the same day. The crime was peddling vegetables without a license. Like any criminal case, the complaining witness had to identify the person accused of the crime. So I brought in about sixty or seventy of my clients and they sat down—all looking very much alike, with their long beards. As soon as the first officer took the stand, I asked him if he could identify the accused. He took one look at all of them, with their beards, and gave up. Ralph Fowler (now a United States commissioner in Houston) was the judge handling the cases. He turned all of my clients loose except one."

The one unlucky peddler was a man who was all too cooperative with the minions of the law. Foreman asked the arresting officer in his case: "Can you identify Muscowitz?" At this point the client stood up and announced: "Muscowitz, dot's me!" The officer promptly identified him as the defendant, and Muscowitz was convicted.

"I must have had 900 cases for those peddlers and that's the only one I lost," Foreman says.

Such courtroom strategy did not, of course, endear Foreman to the local police. Nor did his defense of a poor Negro who had, in Foreman's view, been falsely accused of a petty burglary. The chief prosecution witnesses were two well-known Houston detectives who claimed they had seen Foreman's client running from the burglary scene. But Foreman proved, through the detectives' own testimony, that they were seven blocks from the scene at the time.

"I also brought in an engineer who testified that the street curved between where the detectives were and where the burglarized store was," Foreman says. "To see my client, the detectives would have had to look through solid construction. The result was that I proved two ace detectives were liars. My client was acquitted."

Law-enforcement officers were not alone in criticizing the young defense lawyer. The members of four Baptist churches that he had helped organize accused him of being un-Christian in representing so many accused sinners. Foreman, even then a staunch advocate of the worst sinner's right to adequate counsel, asked the parishioners testily: "Does a barber cut an infidel's hair?" Picqued by the parishioners' attitude and determined to be his own man, Foreman stopped his regular churchgoing. Though remaining devout—and retaining his status as an ordained deacon—he became, in his own words, "ordained but unchurched."

In 1932 one of Foreman's friends, K. C. Barkley, was elected district attorney. When he took office on New Year's Day, 1933, Foreman rejoined the DA's staff as a prosecutor. He quickly earned a reputation as a crusading, hard-nosed assistant DA.

"I raided the gamblers and gave them hell from the day I returned to the district attorney's office," he recalls. "I wouldn't be bought. I might not have been too good to take money, but I was too smart. I wanted the gamblers to remember me. I knew they would have no respect for me if I could be bought or intimidated. I also knew that, when I went back into private practice, the same people I was raiding would someday bring me my most lucrative business. It worked out that way, too. I wound up representing for years all the old-time gamblers who were in Houston then. I still represent some of them today."

Among the most notorious gamblers driven out of Houston by Foreman were the brothers Maceo—Sam and Rosario (Rose)—who were later identified by federal agents as two of the top Southwestern chieftains of the Mafia. The Maceos ruled for decades over the gambling syndicate in Galveston, fifty miles south of Houston, which was long the "Sin City" of the Southwest—with wide-open gambling, prostitution and illegal drinking spots. In their plush Balinese Room gambling casino, built on a pier that stretched a quarter-mile into the Gulf of Mexico (to thwart raiding parties), they featured top-drawer entertainers, fine food and high-stakes roulette, dice and card tables. Their friends included many of the nation's best-known entertainers and politicians (Phil Harris and Alice Faye were married at the Balinese Room).

When the Maceos tried to take over in Houston, as they had in Galveston, Foreman drew the line. He served notice that he would keep them from carrying out their plan to operate a night spot named the Hi-Hat Club as a casino.

"I called in the great old Texas Ranger Pappy Davenport and some more of the boys to back me up," Foreman recalls. "Then I personally went to the Hi-Hat Club and led a raid. Vincent Vallone [later the victim of a gangland murder in which Foreman figured prominently as defense counsel] was manager of the place. We seized several thousand dollars' worth of gambling equipment and locked it in a warehouse. Rose and Sam Maceo lit out for Galveston and never tried to come back into Houston again."

The Maceos, however, prospered in Galveston—so much so that the federal government eventually prosecuted several members of the syndicate on charges of income-tax evasion. The federal men and Foreman showed considerably more zeal than Galveston authorities. The Galveston County sheriff, Frank Biaggne, was once called before a "Little Kefauver" committee of the Texas Legislature to explain why he had never raided the Balinese Room casino. His answer has become a classic of Texas political folklore. "The Maceos never would let me inside," the sheriff complained.

Foreman's fervor as a prosecutor almost led at least once to his own murder. Offered an $800-a-month bribe to lay off some local hoodlums, Foreman disdainfully told the mobsters to get lost. The word soon was out that Foreman was on the mob's rub-out list. One day in 1934, the attempt was made in broad daylight in downtown Houston.

After leaving the courthouse that day Foreman stepped into a beer joint called the Schlitz Grille. Only the bartender, two men and a woman were inside. "I recognized the two men," Foreman says. "They were the ones who were supposed to get me. They started closing in on me. It was a tense situation. Then I happened to see a young lawyer named William States Jacobs pass outside. I called to him and he came in. There was a slugging match, but they were afraid to kill me with a witness present. I owe my life to Jacobs. I'm certain of that."

Both men who participated in the attack were sent to prison. But Foreman held no grudge. He later served as defense attorney for one of them. It was not the last time he would make such a turnabout. He would later befriend two peace officers who beat him up in a courthouse. "I am not a vindictive man," he explains.

Perhaps this is due in part to empathy resulting from the fact that Foreman has found himself on the receiving end of criminal charges periodically throughout his career. His first brush with the law—other than his narrow escape from indictment for the boyhood Hallowe'en pranks—came in 1937. Foreman had left the district attorney's office on August 31, 1935, to resume private practice.

One of his clients was an accused bandit named Sherwood Vinson, who was charged with participating in a Wild West–style holdup. The robbery had occurred on Good Friday of 1937. Five masked men had entered a grocery—armed with machine guns, shotguns and pistols—and taken several hundred dollars. As the bandits fled, they were pursued by a police car. A ripsnorting gun battle ensued, with more than fifty shots being fired as the getaway car and the police cruiser raced through the southern and eastern sections of the city. During the chase some of the robbers abandoned their car, held up a housewife named Mrs. John T. Scott and escaped in her auto.

That night Vinson and two cohorts named Blackie Blackshear and D. L. Phifer were arrested at Vinson's home. They were charged jointly with robbery by firearms, but were later granted the right to be tried separately. Vinson's first trial, which lasted ten days, ended in a hung jury. His second trial was expected to begin two months later, on November 1, 1937.

But, before it could come to trial, the district attorney's staff unleashed a bombshell—persuading a grand jury to indict Percy Foreman on a charge of subornation of perjury. The indictment, returned on October 21, accused Foreman of bribing a witness to give false testimony in the first trial. The witness was a workman who purportedly had been a bystander during the theft of Mrs. Scott's car. The witness, Amos Hicks, had sworn at the trial that Vinson did not resemble any of the men involved in the theft.

News stories reporting the indictment pointed out that Foreman was considered a friend of the very district attorney who had brought about his indictment, Dan Jackson. "A Bible, a personal gift from Foreman, is on the desk at Jackson's office," one story said.

The indictment was based on a statement by Hicks that Foreman had paid him to testify that Vinson did not resemble any of the holdup men involved in the theft of Mrs. Scott's car. However, Hicks' credibility as a witness was soon further damaged—if not totally destroyed. At a hearing on a motion to transfer the second Vinson trial to another jurisdiction, Hicks said that Foreman did not influence his testimony in the first trial. The next day, after paying a visit to the grand-jury room, he changed his story once more. Back on the witness stand in the open hearing, he said that Foreman had, indeed, influenced him to commit perjury. By this time the district attorney's office had decided it could not make a case stand up, based on Hicks' testimony against Foreman. Assistant District Attorney A. C. Winborn filed a *nolle prosequi* motion, putting a halt to the attempt to try Foreman on the subornation charge.

Winborn, who eventually became district attorney and a criminal district-court judge, was noted as one of the few prosecutors who could give Foreman a relatively even battle over the years. The two men, though fierce antagonists in the courtroom, had a mutuality of respect. They also possessed parallel senses of humor. Once, when Winborn was presiding over a case in which Foreman was the defense lawyer, the chief prosecution witness was a prostitute. Foreman, never to be outdone, put a second prostitute on the stand to impeach the testimony of the first.

Each girl called the other a liar. Later, the two of them became engaged in a hair-pulling match outside Winborn's courtroom. They were hauled back before the bench—screaming, kicking and scratching—by a bailiff.

With a twinkle in his eye, Winborn peered down at the two prostitutes and said drily: "Mr. Foreman, you used to be a prosecutor. You've had long experience in such matters. What charge would you suggest I lodge against these two ladies for fighting and swearing outside my courtroom?" Foreman's lips curled into a wry grin.

"Your Honor, about the only thing I can think of is whores *de combat!*" he said. After the laughter had subsided, Winborn sent the girls away with a warning to have more respect for the dignity of the courts.

During the period in which he was accused of subornation, Foreman also became involved in the celebrated defense of two old antagonists—members of the Houston police force. Foreman, to this day, insists that policemen—almost congenitally—violate citizens' rights daily. He is one of the nation's most eloquent spokesmen in the fight to preserve these rights. But, at the same time, he feels equally strongly that accused policemen possess the same rights and should be provided adequate defense.

In this case, a Houstonian named Bobby Lyons originally was arrested on a charge of stealing a watch. Lyons accused two city detectives, L. M. Simpson and L. D. Hooker, of beating him in attempts to obtain a confession.

Houston's three daily newspapers—the morning *Post,* the afternoon *Chronicle* and Scripps-Howard's afternoon *Houston Press*—raised an enormous fuss over the alleged beating. The grand jury instantly launched an investigation. Sitting on the grand jury were editors of the three papers—the *Post*'s Lloyd Gregory, the *Chronicle*'s Emmett Walter and the *Press*' A. C. Bartlett. For once, all three of these highly competitive papers stood side by side in demanding indictment of the detectives. With the editors' help, they got their way.

"There's never been a time in all of Houston's scandals when the papers went so all out on a story," Foreman says. "Every criminal lawyer in town, with two exceptions, volunteered to represent the accused policemen. I was one of the exceptions. Every racketeer and gambler in town sent out runners to collect a fund for the policemen's defense. Sixteen lawyers turned out for the defense at Simpson's trial—but he was convicted just the same. He was given six months in jail and a fine of two hundred dollars."

The trial of Detective Hooker came after that of Simpson. Hooker went to see Mayor Oscar Holcombe and asked his advice on choosing a lawyer.

"If I were in trouble, I'd go to Percy Foreman," said the man who was later to become known as "The Old Gray Fox" of Texas politics. Hooker took Holcombe's advice.

"What kind of fee can you afford—without taking up collections?" Foreman asked.

"All I've got is a hundred and nine dollars," the detective replied.

"All right; that will be my fee—a hundred and nine dollars."

The jury trial of Hooker lasted nine days. For five of those days, Foreman subjected Lyons—the accused thief and purported victim of the beating—to a merciless cross-examination. On each of those days one or another of the local papers carried a headline saying Foreman would be jailed for contempt of court at trial's end.

"Every time Lyons said something, I would come back and make him admit he was a liar," Foreman recalls. "The jury was out just four minutes. It found Hooker not guilty. And I wasn't jailed for contempt, either."

Later, Foreman was retained to handle the appeal of Detective Simpson's prior conviction. He won a reversal of the case. Members of the Houston Police Department, so often tormented by Foreman in court, this time took up a collection and bought him a fancy set of matched luggage as a gift. It would not be the last time Foreman would defend an accused lawman, or the last time he would receive such a gift for his efforts.

But Foreman had not finished having his fun. An ardent needler of the Establishment, he took delight in causing embarrassment to the Houston *Chronicle* editor Walter. He discovered that Walter had served on the grand jury without paying his annual poll tax—one of several prerequisites for such service. Although the courts had held that absence of a poll-tax receipt was not necessarily cause for disqualification of a grand juror, it was held in this case that Walter had served illegally.

If a grand juror had served illegally, it stood to reason, the indictments returned by that grand jury were subject to challenge. "I must have subpoenaed Emmett one hundred and fifty times to get on the stand and admit he didn't pay his poll tax," Foreman says. "That grand jury had returned at least four hundred indictments—some on file for eight years."

As a result, many of the cases were dismissed.

Needless to say, the performance did not endear Foreman to the Houston *Chronicle*—then owned by Houston's most powerful political and business figure, Jesse Jones. The Jones interests, then as today, were bulwarks of the Establishment. And Percy Foreman rarely missed an opportunity to puncture the Establishment balloon.

On May 7, 1940, Foreman made one of his rare misjudgments of the public mood. He decided to enter politics. As a candidate for district attorney, he squared off against his old friend Dan Jackson—the incumbent who had approved his indictment on the subornation charge—and a former assistant DA named Burch Downman. "I can serve my state in that office better than I can anywhere else," Foreman said in announcing his entry into the race. He waged a typically vigorous campaign—but he lost.

Within two years, Foreman was under indictment again—this time on charges of operating a policy (numbers racket) game. Operating on the theory that "a lawyer who represents himself in court has a damned fool for a client," Foreman retained an attorney named J. J. Collins to defend him.

Collins waged a fighting defense. He claimed that District Attorney Jackson, who had won the election in which Foreman had participated, held a grudge against his onetime friend. "This is political persecution," Collins insisted. "Can it be that, for some political reason, the members of the district attorney's staff are trying to destroy Percy Foreman?" he asked in his argument to the jury that heard the case. "They want to handicap him in his career and make him roost on the ground like a whippoorwill."

The state's case rested on a contention that Foreman had aided and abetted some of his clients who were in the policy racket. Where the line between legal counsel and criminal complicity is to be drawn has long been a perplexing question for the courts and bar associations. Assistant District Attorney O'Brien Stevens denied that political persecution had prompted the district attorney's office to seek the indictment. He claimed that it was, purely and simply, a case of Foreman participating in the operation of a policy game and sharing its spoils.

The jury thought otherwise. On November 5, 1943, it found Foreman innocent.

(O'Brien Stevens had a proclivity, as Foreman did, for becoming involved in sensational cases. He would later serve as special prosecutor in a case where a district attorney was indicted on charges of operating a bawdy house across the street from the Harris County Courthouse. Foreman served for a time as counsel to the DA's codefendant, a red-haired madam—but eventually withdrew from the case. Stevens lost, anyway. The first trial ended in a hung jury, and the case against the DA was eventually dropped.)

Gradually, Foreman's fame spread beyond Houston and Texas. He began taking cases in other states. His very entry into a case was headline news. Various Texas newspapers had virtual standing headlines, in ninety-six-point type. They read: "PERCY TO DEFEND ———." All they had to do was fill in the blank and go to press. In time, even the fact that he was considering entry into a case was worth ninety-six-point type—if not one hundred and twenty point.

A basic line of criminal-court folklore became: "If you're guilty, get Percy Foreman." Not mentioned so often—but sufficiently well known—was the corollary: "Bring plenty of money." As Marshall Smith once pointed out in an article in *Life* magazine: "Foreman believes that it takes money to establish an appropriate attorney-client relationship."

"Most of my clients hate me," Foreman says. Part of this hatred, but not all, is engendered by the fees Foreman demands. He wants cash on the barrelhead if he can get it. Failing that, he takes anything of value the clients or relatives own—real estate, jewelry, furs, cars, antiques, electrical appliances. His palatial Houston home was given to him by Ervin Blum, a client who headed the Houston Housing Authority, then was indicted on corruption and fatal hit-run charges.

"It was the best home Blum had," Foreman says simply, implying he would have taken a better one if Blum had owned one. He took his part interest in the cooperative apartment on Park Avenue in New York from oilman-playboy Tom Tirado as down payment in a divorce case. He used it infrequently, but an Oriental houseboy was kept on duty full-time and the apartment was loaned to friends visiting New York. It was a rooftop Taj Mahal, with an artificial waterfall and with a pet South American monkey clambering from wall to wall.

For a time Foreman wheeled around the country in a jazzy sports car given him as a down payment by a client. But he was just too big for the tiny model, and eventually returned to driving a Cadillac with special Western-style upholstery that resembled the inside of a fancy stagecoach. Once, he accepted as his fee from a circus owner four elephants—which he later sold for five hundred dollars each.

"I don't represent wealthy clients," Foreman says. "If they aren't poor when they come to me, they are when they leave. If a case is so nefarious that a man is going to the electric chair except for my efforts, I have no compunction about charging all that the traffic will bear. My fee is my clients' punishment."

An entire Houston warehouse is filled with merchandise given to Foreman by clients. Not surprisingly, it was recently the victim of a burglary. Foreman has no idea what was taken. His inventory was not so meticulous as his courtroom files.

Nonetheless, Foreman is adamant in contending: "I hate money." How much he hates it, he says, is indicated by the fact that "I have talked myself out of at least seven million dollars by bringing about reconciliations among divorce clients." The fact remains, however, that he also won for a client the largest contested divorce bonanza in history. This was the 9.5 million dollars awarded Mrs. Cecil Blaffer Hudson, ex-wife of an enormously wealthy Texas oilman. Although Foreman's share of the proceeds is a closely guarded secret, it is reported to be more than one million dollars.

One reason Foreman is so wealthy, his friends say, is that he is close with a dollar. One federal judge tells how Foreman habitually comes to his chambers to use the telephone, in order to avoid using a pay phone. "One day he came in with a check from Mrs. Hudson hanging out of his pocket," the judge recalls. "The check was for twenty thousand dollars. And he wanted to use my phone to dun her for more of the money she owed him. I let him use the phone, but I got a big laugh out of him. He dropped the twenty-thousand-dollar check on the floor, gave it a little kick with his foot as though it was worthless and finally picked it up. All the time, he was using my phone to save a dime."

For balance, it should be pointed out that this same judge habitually orders rare books—mostly lawbooks—on his foreign vacation trips and has them sent to Foreman at Foreman's expense. Foreman has never failed to pay the bills.

Opinion on Foreman varies among judges. While all concede his obvious skill, some resent what they consider his attempts to make them look foolish. One of these is Ben C. Connally, chief judge of the United States District Court for the Southern District of Texas. Judge Connally (who, incidentally, was one of the few persons to decline to be interviewed for this book), has made no secret of his displeasure with Foreman.

Once, Foreman used the word "whore" in his court. Connally, son of the flamboyant late Senator Tom Connally, blanched at the use of the word. Judge Connally is the most solitary, stiff-necked of men. He came to the bench through his father's influence and has made scrupulous attempts to prove worthy of his position. He has done so many times over. Connally runs a tight court and is not often amused by Foreman's witticisms.

"Don't ever use that word in my court again," he told Foreman.

"Your Honor, I meant no disrespect," Foreman replied. "I've used the word 'whore' in many courts and never had any complaint before. The word 'whore,' I recall, is in the Scriptures."

Each time Foreman used the word, Connally winced. But Foreman was not finished.

"I've used the word 'whore' in Judge Winborn's court. I've used the word 'whore' in Judge [Allen B.] Hannay's court. As I say, I've never had a judge before bar me from using the word 'whore.' "

Connally lost patience. Virtually everyone in the courtroom except the judge was grinning broadly. Connally called Foreman into his chambers, reportedly read him the riot act for ten minutes and then returned to the bench. Exactly what was said in chambers is a secret to this day, but neither Connally nor Foreman has shown much warmth for the other ever since then.

Not long ago Connally addressed a meeting of the State Bar of Texas on the subject of indigent defendants. He left the meeting early, saying he had to conduct a hearing for a former client of

Foreman who now claimed he was indigent. "The judge asked me," Foreman said later, "whether I had gotten out of the case because the man was indigent. I assured him, on the contrary, that the man was indigent because I got in on the case at the start."

Again, Connally was not amused. When a visiting attorney from Cleveland, Ohio, told Connally during the bar-association meeting that Foreman's name was better known in Cleveland than those of many local lawyers, the judge replied curtly: "It's well known, too, in Leavenworth Prison."

Despite his occasional resort to judge-baiting, it is more often than not Foreman's quick mind and tongue—rather than pugnacity—that arouse a judge's ire. He has a positive talent for thinking so quickly on his feet that judges, as well as prosecutors and witnesses, are caught speechless.

Trying a case once hundreds of miles from Houston, in the Texas Panhandle, Foreman was asked to permit his bootlegger client to be prosecuted inside a Methodist Church. The local courthouse had burned down, and the church seemed the next most appropriate place to hold court. Foreman objected, on the ground that the jurors would be faced all day with religious statues and stained-glass windows.

But the prosecutor had found a precedent. Once, he said, the Dallas courthouse had burned down and a murder trial had been transferred to the city's Union Stockyards.

"What say you for the defense?" the judge asked Foreman.

"Your Honor, you take me to the Union Stockyards, let me sniff the judicial atmosphere there—and then I'll give you my answer." Foreman's client was not tried in the church.

During a federal trial, a government witness named Greenberg and his son had been subpoenaed to come all the way from New York to Houston to testify. They testified for the prosecution on the first day of the lengthy trial. Usually, in such cases, efforts are made to accommodate the witnesses by completing cross-examination, redirect and recross as quickly as possible. The witness is then permitted to return home. In this case, however, Foreman refused to go along. Each day, Greenberg or his son would ask

Foreman if he could testify and then go home. Each time Foreman would stall him off. Finally, testimony ended. Foreman did not even call Greenberg or his son back to the stand.

There was much sympathy among trial participants for the plight of the Greenbergs. But, at the same time, they had made themselves obnoxious by persistently demanding that they be permitted to leave. Their problems had become a standing joke during the trial.

At long last, the prosecutor moved that they be excused as witnesses.

"Is that all right with you, Mr. Foreman?" the judge asked.

Foreman replied casually: "Yes, Your Honor." Then he added the kicker: "As a matter of fact, Your Honor, I move that their excuses be made retroactive to the first day of the trial."

And yet—for all his seeming irreverence—Percy Foreman actually reveres the law and the judicial process. It is indicative of his nature that, despite the demands on his schedule, he once insisted on putting aside his law practice to serve on a jury panel. He explained to a judge, in asking for postponement of a client's case, that he often pleads before civic groups that members serve willingly on juries—rather than try to duck their summonses. "It's the duty of every citizen, when called, to report for jury service," he told the judge. "I consider jury service the highest privilege to which a citizen can aspire. I intend to serve. I cannot, in good conscience, spend the rest of my life before juries and attempt to escape jury service when I myself am summoned."

At this writing, Foreman still gives strong evidence that he will spend "the rest of my life" before juries.

4

Steve Mitchell's wife probably deserved killing. Steve's problem was the way he killed her. It would have been just another murder case. But poor Steve . . . he shot her while she was sitting on the toilet.

Anonymous (*uttered by so many amateur lawyers that its origin is obscure*)

Shortly before 1 p.m. on December 16, 1948, a clerk in the Houston Police Homicide office answered the telephone. The clerk, Mrs. Marie Williams, heard the voice of a distraught man.

"Send out the police and get me," the voice said. "I've just killed my wife."

Mrs. Williams, scribbling furiously, asked: "What's your name?"

"Steve Mitchell."

"Where are you?"

"Thirty-five-o-one Jensen."

Holding her hand over the receiver, she whispered to Homicide Detectives F. E. (Pappy) Melder and Joe O'Rourke to rush to that address. Meanwhile, she continued her conversation with Mitchell. A squad-car patrolman, R. W. Hope, soon heard a radio call and raced to the Jensen Drive address before the detectives could arrive. He found Steve Mitchell, in a dazed condition, holding a .32-caliber Colt pistol. Mitchell gave up the weapon without resistance.

Patrolman C. C. Outman, who entered the Mitchell place shortly after Hope, helped search the house. They found the bathroom door closed, with one bullet hole through it. Forcing open the door, they discovered the body of Mrs. Jean Mitchell, forty. Mrs. Mitchell, wearing only a housedress, was slumped on the floor of the bathroom. She had a bullet hole in her head.

Her husband, five years older than she, was taken to police headquarters and questioned. He said he operated the Steve's Drive-in Restaurant Number Seven, adjacent to his home. He had been having trouble with his wife for a long period, he said. She worked in the drive-in during the afternoon, closing it at midnight each day. Despite their troubles—Mrs. Mitchell had begun sleeping away from home—she had continued working for him.

"When she came to work today, I asked her to talk the thing over," Mitchell said. "After a few words, I told her I was through with her. She started fighting with me. I reached into a dresser drawer to get my pistol. She continued fighting with me." The brawl moved from room to room, with husband and wife fighting like wildcats. Finally, Mitchell succeeded in getting his pistol. His wife ran into the bathroom and slammed the door behind her. She was seated on the commode. Mitchell fired blindly at the door. He heard no more from inside.

Mitchell wrote out a statement for the detectives, but refused to sign it before consulting his attorney. He was arraigned before Justice of the Peace Tom Maes and ordered held without bail. Leaving the arraignment, he was interviewed briefly by newsmen.

"You wouldn't understand," he told the reporters. "It was family trouble. My wife left me. She sued me for divorce. She wanted half my property. I had a right to shoot her. . . . Don't you think I had a right to shoot her for that?"

Mitchell was right about one thing. The reporters wouldn't understand. In homicide-happy Houston, there were degrees of guilt and degrees of notoriety. Under ordinary circumstances, this would indeed have been just another murder. A drive-in operator, by Houston standards, is a nobody unless he gets his name in the gossip columns. By that measure, Steve Mitchell was a nobody. But he was about to become a somebody. Not only had he plugged his wife while she was sitting on the commode, he was to be defended by Percy Foreman.

Steve's problems, however, were magnified. For, during this period, Foreman had problems of his own. He had been ill. And he had been depressed. His own first marriage was on the rocks. (Describing that marriage today, Foreman says: "It was a mistake. I was too young, my wife too demanding." His son, William Pinckney Rogers III [called simply Bill], was adopted during this marriage. His second, and enduring, marriage has been much more successful.)

Mitchell was indicted on January 7, 1949, on a charge of murder with malice. That, of course, meant a possible death penalty upon conviction. But he had Foreman in his corner. It was one of those cases Foreman likes to describe in fun as "misdemeanor murders." Few even considered seriously the possibility that Steve Mitchell would ever draw the death sentence—much less walk the last mile on Death Row at Huntsville.

A year later Mitchell had still not come to trial. His case had been called three times, and each time Foreman had begged off on the ground that he was ill. Criminal District Judge Langston G. King lost patience. "Keep in touch with your lawyer, Mr. Foreman," King told Mitchell. "And, if he is not able to try the case, get yourself another lawyer. This is the last time this case will be reset because of the stated illness of Mr. Foreman."

Foreman, apparently irked by the term "stated illness," made a dramatic show of entering Houston's Memorial Hospital. He was admitted to the hospital for treatment of "nervous and physical exhaustion." Judge King ordered him examined and then summoned the examining physician, Dr. George W. Perdue. The physician testified that Foreman was, indeed, suffering from "a severe case of physical and nervous exhaustion." He was also running a fever. "I thought he was sick enough to be in a hospital, and I got him a room," Perdue said. He told the judge that Foreman would be hospitalized at least a week for tests and X rays, among other procedures.

The case was reset for February 27, 1950. But Foreman could not keep that date, either. He was in Polk County, attending his father's funeral. A month later, jury selection finally got under way. But even this was delayed by a threat on Foreman's life. When word was passed to Foreman that he had been threatened, he notified Judge King. A delay was grudgingly granted by the judge so that the report could be checked, but nothing substantial came of the investigation.

Prosecuting the case were two of the most formidable adversaries ever to face Foreman. They were District Attorney A. C. Winborn and Special Prosecutor Spurgeon Bell, who had been hired by the state for this case alone. (As we have seen, Winborn later became a venerable judge. So did Bell, who was known in Texas as perhaps the most successful prosecutor in cases involving Foreman. As Jack Donahue, a Houston newspaperman who later became a novelist and scenarist, once wrote: "Those who watched the Mitchell trial remember that Bell . . . matched Foreman maneuver for maneuver, yes, trick for trick.")

By March 30, all but two jurors had been chosen. Foreman is a meticulous questioner of veniremen. (A later chapter will discuss his strategy in selecting jurors.) Still another delay was prompted this day, however, when Foreman demanded a mistrial on the ground that two articles published in an afternoon newspaper were prejudicial to Mitchell. The motion was denied. White-faced and trembling, Foreman insisted that the articles had been written with deliberate intent to influence prospective jurors in favor of Mitchell's dead wife. He implied that the papers containing the articles had been distributed free among veniremen.

Judge King, a jowly, bespectacled man who had heard many a Foreman case, agreed to conduct a hearing on Foreman's claims. That done, he again denied the mistrial motion.

The last two jurors were quickly chosen, along with alternates, and the trial began in earnest. Winborn and Bell called Patrolman Hope to the stand. He told of answering the radio call and rushing to the Mitchell apartment. He found Mitchell still talking on the telephone to the Homicide office.

"He told me he had just killed his wife," Hope testified. "He had shot her. I saw a gun . . . and asked if that was what he had used. He told me it was."

Foreman was on his feet, objecting that this purported confession could not be introduced as evidence. Mitchell had steadfastly refused to sign a confession, Foreman said, and any statement made before he was given a chance to talk to his lawyer was inadmissible. King overruled him. (Later court decisions in other cases would support Foreman's contention, but they would not come for almost two decades.)

Hope said he took five live cartridges from the pistol and found one empty shell inside. The pistol, he said, had recently been fired.

Foreman took the witness for cross-examination.

Q. When you examined the body, did you find any bruises?

A. No, sir.

Q. Did you notice any scratches on the defendant?

A. No, sir.

The state's case was almost perfunctory. Justice of the Peace Maes, who had conducted the inquest in the case, testified that one bullet had struck Mrs. Mitchell in the temple, killing her before she even knew she had been hit.

At 10:47 A.M., precisely an hour after Mitchell had pleaded not guilty, the state rested its case. Foreman immediately filed three motions. One demanded a directed verdict of not guilty, chiefly on the ground that the state had failed to prove premeditation. Motion denied. A second motion asked that the charge be reduced to murder without malice. Motion denied. A third sought a verdict of not guilty on the ground that the admission of Mitchell's oral confession was a reversible error. Motion denied.

All of this was over in minutes. It had taken much less time for the state to present its case than for jury selection. That had taken four days—a new Houston record. Of the two hundred original veniremen, only thirty-three had remained when the jury had been seated.

The next day Foreman put Steve Mitchell on the stand. This is always a risky business. The defendant, of course, has the right to say nothing. But, once he takes the stand, he is subject to vigorous cross-examination not only about the crime, but also about his past and his most personal habits. In Mitchell's case, however, Foreman felt compelled to put his man on the stand.

Mitchell's story, from the witness stand, did not agree with the previous versions. He claimed he had feared for his life, that he and his wife had struggled for possession of the pistol, the weapon had discharged and a bullet had been fired into her head. But, if that were true, the bullet hole in the door still remained to be explained—unless the bullet had passed through Mrs. Mitchell's head and then the door. Prior testimony did not seem to bear out that notion.

Foreman called two employees of the drive-in restaurant—Mary Allen, forty-three, the cook; and Kathleen Riley, eighteen, a car-hop. Both testified that Mrs. Mitchell had stormed about the restaurant, screaming and cursing, shortly before the slaying. Later, they said, Mitchell had come out of the apartment and told them Mrs. Mitchell had been killed as they struggled over the gun.

Under cross-examination, Winborn pounced on this testimony. He asked Miss Riley: "Didn't both of you say in written statements, just after the killing, that you knew of no prior trouble between the Mitchells?" Miss Riley conceded that she had.

Q. Don't you call storming and cursing, which you didn't mention in your statements, trouble?

A. The parts of my statement that agree with what I've said today are true.

Winborn persisted. What about the parts that did not jibe with her trial testimony? Miss Riley claimed she had never said some of what was attributed to her in the statement.

Q. But you signed the statement, didn't you?

A. Yes, sir.

Q. No further questions.

Mrs. Allen, like Miss Riley, had not mentioned in her written statement that Mitchell bore any scars after the fight with his wife. But, on the witness stand, Foreman drew from her the statement that Mitchell's face had been marked with fingernail scratches. Winborn subjected her to close questioning, but she stuck to her later version.

The next day Foreman sprang a surprise witness. His name was Thomas Brashear, and his testimony struck hard at the credibility of a state witness. The state witness, Roy Caperton, had driven the ambulance that had taken Mrs. Mitchell's body to the morgue. He had testified, at the outset of the trial, about Mrs. Mitchell's position in the bathroom when he arrived. He said he had been accompanied to the slaying scene by a helper—but, for the life of him, he could not recall the helper's full name. He knew him only as "Red." The prosecution claimed it had tried to find "Red," but had run into a dead end.

The trail was hotter for Foreman. He not only learned the identity of "Red." He produced him in court, in the person of Thomas Brashear. Unlike Caperton, who had moved to Fort Worth since the slaying, Brashear had remained in Houston. Moreover, he had been on the city payroll—driving a bus. Foreman argued that the prosecutors had deliberately hidden Brashear's identity to keep him from testifying.

Brashear's testimony supported this contention. He could not understand Caperton's story about knowing his helper only as "Red."

"I've known Caperton for three years," he testified. "I've even slept in the same room with him. I probably know him better than anyone else in Harris County, except his wife." The two men also differed on what kind of clothing Mrs. Mitchell was wearing when her body was discovered. Brashear said she was wearing a cotton print housedress. He said she was not wearing eyeglasses. Caperton, however, said she was wearing glasses and had on a light blouse and wine-colored skirt. Initial police reports had said she was wearing a housedress.

There were differences, as well, about the position of the body. Percy Foreman made the most of these differences to imply that the body had been moved in order to bolster the police case, to the detriment of his client.

Police Captain George Seber, chief of the Homicide Squad, was called to rebut this idea. Seber insisted that the body had not been moved, that nothing in the bathroom had been disturbed, that there were no marks on Mitchell's face at the time of his arrest, and (as further refutation of the story of a struggle for the gun) that Mrs. Mitchell apparently had been smoking a cigarette when slain.

Foreman, usually the master of the courtroom demonstration, seemed to come out second best in this trial. During Mitchell's testimony the defendant was handed the murder weapon and asked to reenact the slaying. Foreman seemed pleased with this demonstration.

But he was not so pleased when District Attorney Winborn turned the tables. Directing Mitchell to play the role of his dead wife, Winborn went through a second reenactment—this one designed to show how the prosecution contended the slaying had taken place.

In the end, the case came down to that. Would the jury believe Mitchell? Was this a case of accidental shooting?

Foreman argued that it was. However, the argument seemed feeble. That bullet through the door, the cigarette found beside the body, Mitchell's initial statements to the police all seemed to belie the accident theory. Moreover, in his interview with newsmen following his arraignment, hadn't he claimed he had a right to shoot his wife?

In his final argument, Foreman hammered at seeming gaps in the state case. But they appeared to be pinholes, not craters. Winborn, Bell and a second special prosecutor, Jesse Pardue, insisted that this was a case of murder with malice and that the death penalty should be exacted.

The jury was out only three hours. Its verdict: Guilty of murder with malice.

The sentence: Death!

Percy Foreman had never lost a client to the executioner. Would Steve Mitchell—"poor" Steve, who had the misfortune to shoot his wife in the bathroom—be the first?

If so, Mitchell showed no sign upon hearing the verdict that he seriously expected to walk the last mile. He accepted the verdict stolidly. No flash of emotion crossed his swarthy face.

After all, he still had Percy Foreman in his corner. And wasn't

Percy the bane of the appellate courts? Couldn't he always find several reversible errors in a criminal trial—particularly a capital case?

Well, "always" might be an overstatement. But surely Foreman had succeeded in helping beat the rap for defendants far more culpable than Steve Mitchell. It was taken for granted by many that Mitchell, at worst, would receive a commutation of the death sentence. And a life sentence could be served in Texas, with good behavior, in eight years.

Mitchell's entire trial had lasted ten days. The appeal process, and peripheral legal battles, would take years. The jury verdict came on April 5, 1950. On May 27, the first litigation following the jury trial commenced. It was not, however, a criminal action. As if Steve Mitchell did not have enough troubles, he now found himself the target of a 100,000-dollar civil suit. His slain wife's parents, Mr. and Mrs. Jeff Bryant of Natchez, Mississippi, claimed her death would deprive them of 50,000 dollars in support payments and other benefits. In addition, they sought 50,000 dollars in exemplary damages from Mitchell "for killing his wife."

From his cell in the Harris County Jail, Mitchell disclosed that he would fight his in-laws' suit. His appeal of the murder conviction was still pending before the Texas Court of Criminal Appeals. In the end, one of his in-laws would change sides—pleading that Mitchell's life be spared.

It was not until February 20, 1951, that the appellate court got around to ruling on Foreman's appeal. It upheld the conviction and death sentence, saying it could find no reversible error. Still, there was no panic in the Mitchell camp.

There were still the federal courts. And, even if they would not upset the death sentence, there was the possibility of a clemency ruling from the governor.

A month later the question being argued in Houston courts was not the matter of Mitchell's fate, but what was happening to his slain wife's estate. Mrs. Mitchell's estate, valued at 60,000 dollars, originally was placed in the hands of a corporate administrator—the Houston Bank and Trust Company. But Probate Judge Clem

McClelland (who later went to prison himself for fraudulently manipulating estates entrusted to him) appointed a new administrator, attorney Clarence M. Wilchar, Jr.

Wilchar contended that the estate was being squandered. In particular, he objected to use of any part of the estate to pay for Mitchell's defense. Since Texas has a community-property law, half of each marriage partner's wealth belonged to the other.

"We want an accurate accounting of the estate, in order to protect Mrs. Mitchell's heirs," Wilchar told McClelland. "If the estate is being squandered, then we want to put a stop to it." McClelland ordered a show-cause hearing at which Wilchar demanded a full inventory of the community property.

It was all more than a trifle ghoulish, to say the least. It reminded one of the death scene in *Zorba the Greek*, where the harpies swoop down like vultures to steal the dying woman's belongings before she has breathed her last. Steve Mitchell, however, understood. For he himself had been born in Greece, and this was the way people in some Greek cities behaved. Certainly, Percy Foreman could not complain that the performance was in poor taste. After all, he himself was a past master at filing suits on behalf of his clients to collect on the life insurance of those they had been accused of murdering. More than once, he had collected. And, more than once, he himself had pocketed all or part of the insurance proceeds as payment toward his legal fees.

On May 24, 1951, Steve Mitchell—"Steve the Greek," as some called him—sat impassively in his county jail cell and received still another piece of bad news. The Texas Court of Criminal Appeals had refused to grant him a rehearing. Now, unless the federal courts intervened, only a pardon from the governor could save him.

Allan Shivers was governor at the time. He had long been considered an ardent advocate of tough law enforcement. As lieutenant governor, he had been closely identified with the work of the Texas Rangers and their parent, the Department of Public Safety. Mitchell, nonetheless, dared hope for mercy. (Shivers later would take a less than rigid attitude about purported wrongdoing among members of his official family. When his close friend H. H. (Pete) Coffield admitted bankrolling some gamblers, Shivers refused to disown him or remove him from the Texas Prison Board. Coffield today is the board's chairman. Shivers also served as governor during some of the state's worst scandals—administrative and legislative. Several hundred insurance companies went broke during his administration, leaving the public holding the bag for millions. Two of Shivers' insurance commissioners and numerous state legislators later were disclosed to be on payrolls of the insurance lobby. State Land Commissioner Bascom Giles went to prison in another scandal. Shivers himself eventually retired from politics. He is, at this writing, president of the United States Chamber of Commerce.)

On June 12, 1951, Steve Mitchell was taken back before Judge King for formal sentencing.

"Do you have anything to say before I pronounce sentence?"

"I never had a fair trial."

Fair or not—and there is much reason to believe Mitchell could not have been given the death sentence under today's rules of courtroom procedure—the trial had been legal. The sentence had been upheld by the highest court in the state. King had no choice but to follow the jury's wishes. He sentenced Mitchell to be taken to Death Row at the Huntsville State Prison and be executed.

The scheduled date of execution is always academic in Texas, and in some other states, because of what is known in the press as "the customary thirty-day stay of execution." This stay was granted by Governor Shivers precisely a week after the sentencing.

Still, the peripheral figures in the case were worried about other matters. Clarence Wilchar, the administrator of Mrs. Mitchell's estate, was concerned over Mitchell's own life insurance. Did he want to keep paying the premiums? Mitchell, who conceivably had other things on his mind, declined to discuss the insurance premiums. But Wilchar was not to be put off easily. A total of $198.02 in premiums was coming due on two policies, one for $1,000 and the other for $5,585. "I must make sure the cash surrender value is obtained on both policies in order to protect the estate," he said.

While Wilchar was pursuing the insurance matter, others were pursuing the question of Steve Mitchell's life and liberty. The State Board of Pardons and Paroles set a hearing to determine whether to recommend clemency to Governor Shivers.

With Mitchell scheduled to die in the electric chair shortly after midnight on August 23, 1951, the board began hearing argument on the matter on August 22. This is not unusual. Frequently, on the day before a scheduled execution, the case is argued in an emotion-charged atmosphere. Whether this is a proper way to achieve justice is for the lawyers and judges and governors to decide. But the fact is that emotion frequently runs rampant on such occasions, yielding much heat and only occasional rays of light.

Percy Foreman, in such a situation, is not the flamboyant orator one might expect. Foreman is enough of a professional to recognize well that the place for emotion is before a jury. Before a judge, or a semijudicial body such as a pardons board, he sticks mostly to facts. And the facts usually are sufficient. In this case, Foreman reviewed the facts as he saw them, the atmosphere in Houston at the time of the trial, what he considered the improper introduction of Mitchell's oral confession and other elements that he felt were persuasive.

Perhaps sensing that this would not be enough, Foreman for once made an emotional appeal. And, for once, he confessed that his defense had been less than perfect. Telling of his personal problems—his illness, the impending death of his father and (though not mentioned specifically) the breakup of his first marriage—Foreman conceded he had been unable to give Mitchell his best effort. On that ground, in addition to the others, he urged that the board commute Mitchell's sentence to life imprisonment.

He was not alone in pleading for mercy. A number of prominent Texans appeared voluntarily at the hearing to ask for clemency. Others wrote moving letters.

Among them was "The Old Gray Fox," Houston's Mayor Oscar

Holcombe. Admitting that he knew little about the facts of the slaying, Holcombe wrote: "I have known Steve Mitchell for some twenty to twenty-five years and, during that time, I know nothing of his getting into trouble of any kind. He was well thought of in his community." Similar appeals came from such persons as the Reverend S. Haginis, pastor of Houston's Hellenic Church, other members of the city's Greek-American community and prominent attorneys G. H. Stubblefield and William H. Scott. (Within four years Scott himself would be seeking both compassion and mercy. He would become the district attorney accused of operating a bawdy house across the street from the courthouse.)

The clemency hearing actually was conducted by only one member of the three-man board, Thomas B. White. The board chairman, L. C. Harris, was on vacation. The third member, R. A. (Smoot) Schmid, who was not present but was in Austin, said he had discussed the case with no one and had no intention of participating further at this stage. Moreover, both White and Schmid said they were virtually sure Chairman Harris would not interrupt his vacation for an additional hearing. Thus, in the absence of a sensational development, only a strong move for clemency by White—strong enough to bring an immediate assent from Schmid—would be sufficient to save Mitchell. For, with Harris' vacation seemingly sacrosanct, the two other members must be unanimously in favor of clemency or the execution would be carried out. A tie vote would not be sufficient.

Hopes faded when White ruled against clemency.

At the eleventh hour, though, the most unexpected sort of sensational development did occur. Jeff Bryant, the slain woman's father, who was suing Mitchell for 100,000 dollars, suddenly fired off a telegram to White, pleading for mercy on behalf of his son-in-law. White notified Governor Shivers. And the governor hastily ordered a new stay of execution, to spare Mitchell for at least thirty-two days.

Now, frantic efforts were made to find Bryant, who had sent his telegram from his Mississippi home. But there was no response. True, there was still a month until Mitchell's new date with the electrician who pulled the switch at Huntsville. But the pardons board wanted to schedule a hearing as soon as possible. Where was Bryant?

Tom White sent a telegram to Bryant, telling him that Shivers had granted the stay on the board's recommendation after receiving the wire from Mississippi. But Bryant's wire had said he wanted to appear before the board and present his position on the case. "My telegram asked him to communicate immediately with us and let us know when he could appear," White explained to newsmen on August 29. "But five days have passed now and I haven't heard anything. I traced my telegram to Mr. Bryant to be sure that he had received it and was informed by the Western Union office in Natchez that it had been signed for there by his son-in-law, Dr. Brace M. Wilson."

Next, White wrote to Dr. Wilson, explaining the importance of hearing immediately from Bryant. "I have yet had no reply," White said. "If we don't hear from him in time, I presume the execution will go ahead as scheduled September 25."

This is not, of course, the way it happens in the movies. On the screen, there is screaming, shouting, weeping, but never this kind of apparent apathy or lack of communication. Life, however, frequently is more dull—but many times more ironic—than the celluloid image would have us believe.

Once again, it became clear, Steve Mitchell was a nobody. He was no Caryl Chessman—so reprehensible and yet talented a man that his very life or death could stir international debate. He was no Julius or Ethel Rosenberg, no Sam Sheppard, no Carl Coppolino. He was just "Steve the Greek"—the poor guy who shot his wife while she was enthroned on the commode.

It would have seemed that, with all the resources at its command, the State of Texas could have tracked down Bryant and found what he planned to do about pursuing his clemency plea. But the wheels of bureaucracy grind exceedingly slow. It was left to the Fourth Estate to pursue the matter. Finally, a Houston *Chronicle* reporter reached Dr. Wilson's wife by telephone and learned part of the story. It seemed that tragedy had again entered the life of the Bryant family. A relative in Oklahoma had just died, and both Bryant and his physician son-in-law had gone there for the funeral. They were believed to be on their way back to Natchez. Mrs. Wilson would give no information on the address, or even the town, in Oklahoma where her husband and her father might be reached.

"They are both very upset by all this," she said.

Conceivably, Steve Mitchell was a trifle more upset. His life had been spared temporarily—less than twelve hours before the scheduled execution time—by his father-in-law's intercession, but what would happen next was impossible to predict.

Finally, on August 30, Tom White heard anew from Bryant. Again, it was by telegram. Bryant apologized for his tardiness in replying to White's wire, saying merely that he had been "out of town." His new telegram said he would submit a statement of his views on the case "soon."

On September 4, Bryant's promised letter arrived in Austin, accompanied by an affidavit. He asked Governor Shivers to commute Mitchell's sentence to life imprisonment. The handwritten letter and affidavit, which had been notarized September 1 in Natchez, were addressed to the pardons board.

> On August 23 you gave Steve Mitchell a stay of execution after I had requested same [Bryant wrote]. I thank you for this. Steve Mitchell was my son-in-law and his wife, Jean, was my daughter. They were married eighteen years prior to her death on December 16, 1948. My wife and I lived on their farm near Splendora, Texas, for two years preceding her death and Steve and I got along fine and he treated us well. In fact I never knew of him being in trouble prior to December 16, 1948. At the time of my daughter's death, Steve Mitchell was forty-six. He and my daughter had worked hard and Steve's health had showed strain and he appeared to be in a state of melancholia. I want to say that, after considering all the facts and circumstances in the case and our attitude toward the death penalty, we feel justice would be done and we would rest better later should he be confined to prison for life.

This turnabout by Bryant and other members of the slain woman's family—who, it was disclosed belatedly, had helped pay the salaries of the special prosecutors in Mitchell's murder trial—caused considerable puzzlement in Texas. What had brought it about?

The full answers may never be known. They lay within the minds and hearts of men and women with varying degrees of compassion and of less enviable attributes. Suffice it to say that court records disclose the following: Shortly before Bryant made his appeal for clemency, he received 25,000 dollars in cash from the proceeds of the sale of Steve Mitchell's restaurant. The restaurant was sold to a third party for 35,000 dollars. The attorney who handled the transaction received three percent of the sale price as a fee. This meant that less than 9,000 dollars remained for Mitchell. In partial exchange for the 25,000 dollars, Bryant agreed to dismiss his damage suit against Mitchell—which would probably become academic, anyway, if Mitchell went to the electric chair.

Financial matters were still preoccupying the participants on Monday, September 24. Steve Mitchell was due to enter the execution chamber shortly after midnight. But in Houston—and, indeed, inside the walls of Huntsville—the talk was mostly about Steve's remaining estate.

In Houston, Probate Judge McClelland ruled that Jean Mitchell's estate belonged to her murderer husband. "There is no precedent in the state which would allow me to name anyone but Mr. Mitchell heir to his wife's community half of their estate," the judge said. Thus, while the criminal courts were about to send Mitchell to the chair for killing his wife, the civil courts were rewarding him with her worldly goods.

Jeff Bryant and his wife never made the trip to Austin to argue personally for clemency. They pleaded advanced age, and submitted their pleas in writing. But they found sufficient energy to pursue vigorously their claim to their daughter's estate before Judge McClelland. They contended that a man who murders his wife is not entitled to her community estate. McClelland ruled otherwise, however, leaving them basically with the 25,000 dollars they had received from the restaurant sale.

Behind "The Walls" at Huntsville, Steve Mitchell made plain

his views on the financial issues in a quiet talk with the prison chaplain, the Reverend B. C. Anderson. "Money doesn't mean anything to me now," Steve said. "I had hopes of receiving a commutation of sentence. But, right now, things don't look so good." Tears slid down his cheeks, but he did not crack under the strain.

Nothing had been heard from the pardons board or the governor. Again, the movies and television shows mislead on the aura that surrounds an execution. We picture open telephone lines, the warden anxiously praying that his prisoner will be spared. Usually, it just does not happen that way. The prisoner is prepared. Hair on his head and legs is shaved to provide a place for the electrodes that will bring him a mercifully quick death. He is removed from his usual cell in the Death House and taken to a cell off the execution chamber. Then it is a matter of waiting for a call. Sometimes it comes. Sometimes it doesn't. The governor does not phone and say: "Go ahead and burn the son of a bitch!" He, or more likely one of his aides, calls only to report a stay of execution.

It is the absence of such a call that seals a doomed man's fate.

Now, as the minutes fled with the inexorable turn of the second hand in Warden H. E. Moore's office, those who knew and loved Steve Mitchell gathered at the Death House. His cousin, Mrs. Katherine Pappas, was there with her son, Emile, and four friends. Mrs. Pappas, like Mitchell, had been born in Greece. She had come to the United States as a young woman, married and settled in Louisiana. Later, she had moved to Houston. Her husband had died in 1949, less than a year after Steve had fired the fatal bullet into his own wife's head.

Mrs. Pappas, unlike Mitchell's in-laws, had made no publicized move to become his heir. If she had an interest in his remaining property, it had not come to light until this day. Now an attorney who had handled Mitchell's business affairs for fifteen years—Percy Foreman had been hired only for the murder case—disclosed that Mitchell had just signed a will in the Death House. It left his entire estate to Mrs. Pappas.

Since 1938, there has been a ritual at Huntsville. Before a condemned man walks the last mile, he is interviewed by a crusading newspaperman—Don Reid, Jr., editor of the weekly Huntsville *Item* and local stringer (correspondent) for the Associated Press. Don Reid has watched more executions than any man alive.

Unless one has watched a man die in the electric chair (as the author of this book has), it is virtually impossible to contemplate the horror of the act. It is not the dying that is so horrible. Death occurs every day, indeed every minute. But it is the sterile, ritualistic nature of the death that makes one cry out for some better system of dispensing justice.

To Don Reid, who at this writing has watched more than two hundred men meet their Maker at Huntsville, Steve Mitchell's was one of the most senseless cases he had seen come to the Death House. "I'd seen many men who deserved to die far more than Steve walk out of 'The Walls' on parole,' Reid once recalled, "I couldn't believe Steve would actually go [to the chair]."

Now Reid was led into the condemned cell for the customary interview. Steve Mitchell sat there—solemn but not bitter—in his prison denims.

"I am no more guilty than you are," he told Reid. "I shot in self-defense, the same as you would do."

Reid left to file his "hold for release" obit. Only a call from Austin could halt the execution now. The phone did not ring.

At two minutes past midnight, after refusing to make a final statement, Steve Mitchell was led into the execution chamber. Reid, Warden Moore and the technicians of death—plus a few other witnesses—were the only ones present. His relatives and friends, nearby in the prison, elected not to increase their agony by witnessing his final moments. Instead, they made frantic efforts to get another stay.

Still, the phone did not ring.

The mechanics of the execution were proceeding swiftly. Mitchell, upon entering the chamber from his cell a few steps away, approached the chair. Guards put leather straps around his waist and wrists. An electrode was attached to his leg through a slit in his trousers. Another electrode was attached to the shaved portion of his head.

"He looked like a monastery monk," Don Reid once recalled, discussing the cases of Mitchell and numerous others he had seen in the chair. "Cotton was put in his nostrils to trap the blood. A mask was put on his face."

Now, normally, you would hear the tripping of the electric switch—the switch that would send 16,000 volts coursing through Steve Mitchell's body in a half minute, two hundred more in the following half minute and still six hundred more in the last half minute.

But it did not happen that smoothly. There were some difficulties, as the technicians put it, in "adjusting the electric chair." There would be a delay—only minutes, perhaps, but enough to give Steve Mitchell that one last chance for a reprieve.

Agonizingly he waited. Agonizingly some of those in the chamber prayed for deliverance.

Once again, it did not come.

At last, at 12:08 A.M., the dreaded noise was heard. It was more than a click, the sound you hear when you cut off your lights. It was really a crunch, as the huge lever was thrown.

Steve Mitchell strained against his bonds. By the time his act could be witnessed, it was over. He was dead in a split second. Still, the executioner went through the motions. Ninety seconds' worth of juice passed through Mitchell's body. The thirty seconds in which the dynamos flicker and fade ultimately passed.

A doctor pronounced Mitchell dead. Attendants swiftly moved in, without a word, and removed the body. It was taken by ambulance to the Huntsville Funeral Home, then transferred to the Hyde Park Funeral Home in Houston. Mitchell's stunned relatives, who had hoped until the end for a reprieve, were described in the next day's newspapers as "yet to complete arrangements for the funeral."

In death, at last, Steve Mitchell was a somebody. He had made his mark. He was the first—and, to this date, only—person defended by Percy Foreman to keep a date with the executioner. (Foreman detractors are fond of noting that he once handled an appeal for another killer who wound up in the chair. But he did not represent this man in the murder trial itself. In any event, it is some sort of backhanded tribute to Foreman that his detractors are forced to search for such peripheral entries in efforts to place black marks on the debit side of his career ledger.)

Foreman was not his usual flippant self for a long spell after Mitchell's execution. He brooded. He knew, even publicly conceded, that he had not given Mitchell his best. Foreman's health was still poor. He was still mourning his father. His married life was still a mess.

There were those—not only in Texas, but in other states as well—who whispered around the courthouse corridors that Foreman was on the skids. He had finally met his match in A. C. Winborn and Spud Bell, they said. The stories still make the rounds today each time Foreman loses a case. And he loses some. You can't win 'em all. But today A. C. Winborn is dead. Spud Bell has long since mounted the bench—not the criminal bench, but the civil bench.

And Percy Foreman is still winning most of 'em—twenty years after Steve Mitchell did in his wife. The reports of the demise of Foreman's career have been slightly exaggerated. In the intervening years, he has represented James Earl Ray in Tennessee, General Edwin Walker in Mississippi, Candy Mossler and Mel Powers in Florida, Jack Ruby in Texas, purported major narcotics wholesalers in Connecticut and New York, purported pornographers in the Midwest and countless accused slayers, rapists, thieves, forgers and confidence men from coast to coast.

He is just as much at home today in the Twenty-One Club in New York as in the Cork Club in Houston. He bristles at the notion that he is a provincial. His most bitter invective is directed at those who try to tag him as "the Clarence Darrow of Texas" or even "the Clarence Darrow of the Southwest."

"Hell, I've tried more murder cases in one year than Darrow did in his entire life," Foreman snorts. But he knows Darrow—

even with his more limited practice—never lost a man to the executioner. And that sticks in his craw. It always will. Steve Mitchell has become the disturbing statistic in the Foreman legend.

5

He's ninety-nine and forty-four—
one-hundredths percent sane.
PERCY FOREMAN

ON JANUARY 10, 1962, Percy Foreman was scheduled to try four separate murder cases involving no fewer than five defendants.

Obviously, even Percy Foreman could not represent so many slayers simultaneously. But his caseload was so heavy that, in Houston alone, he had these four trials docketed for the same day. He represented a man accused of murdering an acquaintance; a teenager accused of gunning down a grocer during a robbery; a mailman who shot a fellow employee in a post-office substation for calling him "The Mole"; and one of two men accused jointly of bumping off a woman acquaintance.

None of these cases, in itself, is outstanding. Each falls into the category Foreman describes as "misdemeanor murders." What is important about them is that they illustrate the unbelievable demands on Foreman. Each of these defendants represented a potential Steve Mitchell. If Foreman shirked, any one of them—

or the whole lot—could wind up in that antiseptic chamber at Huntsville. It is to his credit that he eventually gave each of them more than adequate representation, sparing them from Mitchell's fate.

But the fact is that Foreman conducts his law practice on the run. Wherever he goes, he is trailed by a stream of clients, prospective clients, witnesses, other attorneys and assorted hangers-on. He can barely walk down a street, in Texas or California, without being recognized. It is commonplace to see a half dozen men and women—some clients, some mere admirers—dashing after him in vain attempts to keep up with his long legs and enormous drive. He sometimes goes weeks, even months, without visiting his office in Houston's South Coast Building, where one lone Girl Friday constitutes his entire staff. At his favorite Houston hangout, the Old Capitol Club (site of Texas' first capitol) in the Rice Hotel, he stashes clients in seven or eight booths, then moves from booth to booth to conduct his business. It may dismay some club members, but most find the process so fascinating that they do not complain.

Given this context, it is perhaps easier to comprehend how Foreman at least once has wound up with a client who warned in advance that he was going to commit homicide. This was not a typical Foreman client, by any means, if there is such a thing as a typical client. This was not a man reared in the wilds of the Southwest, where men were men and women carried derringers. This was a brilliant, articulate surgeon born and reared in Brooklyn, New York.

Foreman has often described the case of Dr. Harold Eidinoff as "one of the most fascinating I ever handled." It certainly was one of the most bizarre.

Harold Eidinoff, when Foreman first met him, was a slender, balding, bespectacled man with a high forehead and piercing eyes. He had an IQ of 132, well above average college level. He was born in 1909 in Brooklyn to Russian immigrant parents. After attending Brooklyn's Manual Training High School, he went on to Brooklyn College, the City College of New York and the New York Medical College.

As a young physician, he served as a general practitioner in Harlem from 1934 to 1936, ministering to the poor residents of the slums. The Depression had left a deep scar on the community and, when his patients could not afford to pay, Eidinoff treated them for nothing. In 1936 he developed an ailment of his own, a skin condition that required a dry climate. The Southwest was considered ideal. As a result, Eidinoff moved to El Paso, Texas. By the time Foreman met him, he had moved to New Mexico.

But his problems centered in El Paso, and it was there that he would kill a man. El Paso is far from a Foreman stomping ground. A dusty border city at the western tip of Texas, it is as far from Houston as Chicago is from New York. It is perhaps farther in customs and mores. Unlike cosmopolitan Houston, El Paso possesses both the charm and the ills of its Mexican heritage. Even professional men there retain some of the rough-and-ready habits of the Old West. Thus it was that Dr. Harold Eidinoff not only killed a man there; he killed one of the city's most prominent citizens—the president of the school board.

Had the Brooklyn boy, like a chameleon, taken on the characteristics of his surroundings? Only the headshrinkers, and perhaps not even they, could tell. They would get their chance—some of the leading psychoanalysts in the nation would—to try to unravel the seemingly inexplicable behavior of Harold Eidinoff. But they would have to start at the beginning.

For Harold Eidinoff's problems, if they did not stem from the womb itself, certainly stemmed from events long preceding his move to the Southwest. They began at least as early as the time he met his bride. This was in the middle 1930s.

Sylvia Polso, a beautiful blonde professional accordionist who performed in New York theaters and nightclubs under the stage name of Sylvia Reed, came to Eidinoff originally as a patient. They dated for a while, eventually decided to marry. The marriage was performed in Crown Point, Indiana. It was followed by a honeymoon trip to Sylvia's hometown, Ironwood, Michigan, and to New Hampshire and Canada. It was during the honeymoon that the Eidinoffs were to snap some pictures that eventually would lead to violence.

Sylvia and Harold went on a picnic near a lake. The details are somewhat obscure. But it is agreed by all concerned that each snapped at least one, and probably several, nude pictures of the other. Why?

"Just for laughs, I guess," Eidinoff once explained.

"The humor of that situation might have been partly stimulated by a few drinks. I don't recall the exact details. In New York, I developed and printed the 35-millimeter pictures—three of them—and gave them to my wife, just for laughs. Photography was one of my hobbies. I suppose I assumed my wife would tear the pictures up once the novelty wore off. I never asked her. I guess I simply forgot about the whole thing. For some reason that no man could fathom, but that a woman could understand, my wife put the three snapshots away in an old trunk with her keepsakes, scrapbooks and assorted junk."

Sixteen years would pass before Eidinoff would be reminded of the existence of the pictures. In the meantime, many complications would enter his personal and professional lives.

After moving to El Paso, he set up a new medical practice. He continued his studies, qualified as a surgeon and began specializing in proctology. His practice flourished. Before long he was one of the area's best-known and most wealthy physicians. But there were those in El Paso who resented him—some out of envy, some because of his religion (he was Jewish), and some because he was not the easiest man in town to get to know. By the early 1950s Eidinoff had marital problems as well. He and his wife, who had two children, began to drift apart.

In February 1953 Mrs. Eidinoff divorced her husband on grounds of mental cruelty. Her attorneys, Leo Jaffe and John F. Hawley, tried to collect a 5,000-dollar fee from Eidinoff for their services in obtaining the divorce. Eidinoff refused to pay. Jaffe and Hawley then retained perhaps the most prestigious attorney in El Paso to file suit against Eidinoff for their money. It was this man Eidinoff eventually shot.

His name was Theodore Andress, and he represented the El Paso version of The Establishment Man. Ted Andress was one of the most prominent men in the Southwest's legal and educational circles. He had been named El Paso's outstanding young man in 1941 and its outstanding citizen in 1953. In addition to serving as president of the El Paso School Board, he had headed the Texas Association of School Boards and would one day be elected to the board of directors of the National School Board Association.

His initial representation of attorneys Jaffe and Hawley for their fee was just the beginning of what was to blossom into a bitter, old-fashioned feud between Andress and Eidinoff. In the end, by Eidinoff's account, each would threaten to shoot the other on sight.

At the outset, however, the Eidinoff case was just another file folder in the Andress office. Meanwhile, Eidinoff was encountering new problems. On the rebound, he married a second time. The marriage, to an El Paso woman named Ruth Grace, was to last only three months. Then she, too, sued for divorce.

Testimony later disclosed that, while rummaging through her husband's old storage trunk, the second Mrs. Eidinoff had discovered the nude photographs. The pictures were introduced as evidence at her divorce trial. She eventually won the divorce. Later, by some undisclosed means, the photos fell into the hands of Ted Andress. And, according to sworn testimony, he proceeded to display them to a number of prominent Texans in an apparent attempt to discredit Eidinoff. His motive was obscure. But, whatever it was, it merely compounded an already volatile situation.

When Eidinoff discovered that Andress had been showing the pictures around town—once even on a street corner—he filed a series of lawsuits against Andress and other Texans. He claimed he had suffered great mental anguish and embarrassment. Eidinoff prepared the suits himself, charging that no El Paso lawyer would buck the Establishment by representing him. In each case, he lost.

Concurrently, he and his first wife patched up their differences. They were remarried on June 5, 1955. Eidinoff's second wife, about the same time, married a man named Jack Lutz. Sylvia and Harold Eidinoff then filed suit against Ruth and Jack Lutz and attorney Leo Jaffe, who had been one of Sylvia's lawyers in the original divorce case. The suit claimed that Jaffe and the Lutz couple were in possession of some copies of the nude photographs. It demanded the return of the pictures. The Eidinoffs also filed two 100,000-dollar suits against Mr. and Mrs. Lutz, charging attempted extortion and blackmail. The damage suits were dismissed. But Eidinoff attempted to have them reinstated, naming Ted Andress and Leo Jaffe as codefendants. The courts, however, overruled the petition for reinstatement.

Other suits followed. One, filed by the Eidinoffs against Andress, went all the way to the Texas Supreme Court (the state's highest court for civil matters). Again, the Eidinoffs lost. In December 1956 they filed another 100,000-dollar suit against Andress and Jaffe—accusing them of making and distributing copies of the nude pictures. Still again, the Eidinoffs lost.

In March 1957 Eidinoff tried to get Andress indicted by an El Paso grand jury. He failed. Next he drew a suit charging Andress with committing acts involving a serious breach of morals. As a result Eidinoff himself was indicted by a grand jury on a charge of criminal libel. The charge was later dismissed. But Andress filed a civil libel suit against Eidinoff and, after a trial, was awarded a judgment for 110,000 dollars. Eidinoff, who had filed a one-million-dollar libel suit of his own against Andress, appealed the 110,000-dollar judgment. It was at this point that Percy Foreman entered the case—as counsel for Eidinoff in the remaining libel actions.

Libel suits are far from Foreman's specialty. In fact, publishing-industry cases are among those he is least likely to handle (pornography cases being rare exceptions). But Eidinoff appealed to him to accept the case on the ground that he could not obtain adequate counsel locally. *There* was a challenge Foreman could not resist—a challenge to take on one his pet targets, the Establishment.

By this time Eidinoff had left El Paso for Grants, New Mexico, where he had real-estate holdings. But he returned briefly to El Paso and drew from his bank twenty-one cashier's checks totaling 105,000 dollars. Before the checks could clear, however, Andress took legal action to seize the money as security against the libel judgment he had won.

Threats of violence entered the feud at this point. "I learned that Ted Andress had carried a concealed pistol on him throughout the six days of the original libel trial," Eidinoff later recalled. "I also learned that Andress had threatened to shoot me on sight." He tried during this period, he said, to obtain a 50,000-dollar life-insurance policy. Two companies rejected his applications, without giving any reasons. "I eventually learned that I was turned down because it was the opinion of each company that this feud would result in violence," he said.

Apprised of these facts, Percy Foreman took steps to head off the impending trouble. He recognized that Eidinoff was distraught. The furor over the nude pictures, the feud and the seizure of his money had combined to upset Eidinoff sufficiently that Foreman became convinced psychiatric help was necessary. He persuaded his client to submit voluntarily to treatment at Austin State Hospital. Eidinoff agreed. After ninety days, however, hospital authorities released him—presumably as "cured."

Eidinoff returned to Grants, New Mexico. He spent most of his time supervising the construction of two apartment buildings he owned. He did not tell acquaintances that he was a physician. They accepted him merely as a builder and real-estate man. He joined the local Optimist Club, became popular with its members and was soon named editor of the club's weekly bulletin. To casual friends, Eidinoff seemed jolly and content.

But, beneath the surface, the fires of impending violence still smoldered. The manager of his apartment projects, J. O. Hoffman, said that Eidinoff had "an obsession" about the nude pictures. He later quoted Eidinoff as telling him more than once that he would have to fight a gun battle over them. From New Mexico, Eidinoff mailed to acquaintances in El Paso a lengthy tract that he said was "The Truth—the Whole Truth" of his troubles with Andress and others. The tract totaled sixteen columns of ordinary newspaper size.

Meanwhile, the legal battle with Andress continued. On December 10, 1958, Eidinoff flew to Angleton, Texas, to confer with

Percy Foreman about the court fight. Foreman was in Angleton, forty-five miles southwest of Houston, to defend a young woman accused of murdering her husband. A Fort Worth newspaperman, Blair Justice (currently science columnist for the Houston *Post*), was on hand to cover the murder trial. Foreman introduced Eidinoff to Justice. Later, the newspaperman and the physician went to a highway cafe for bacon and eggs. During the meal Eidinoff told Justice about his feud with Ted Andress. To Justice's amazement, Eidinoff confided that he intended to kill Andress.

"I have been told on good authority that Andress is carrying a gun and has said that, as soon as I return to El Paso, he is going to kill me," Eidinoff said. "I can't let that happen. I am going to have to kill him."

Justice did not report the threat to the police or to Andress. He would say later Eidinoff seemed so calm and lucid that he doubted anyone would believe his story of the threat. Besides, he would say, he figured that Eidinoff had probably made similar threats in the presence of others and that Andress undoubtedly was aware of them. On the second point he was correct. A number of persons in New Mexico and Texas had heard Eidinoff threaten Andress' life. One lawyer—not Foreman—even told of advising Eidinoff: "You're too nice a man to kill anyone."

Percy Foreman, after conferring with Eidinoff about the libel cases, plunged back into his defense of the accused murderess. He had already done just about as much as he could to prevent Eidinoff from getting deeper into trouble—short of having him arrested. He had advised him. He had tried to cool him down. He had even persuaded him to enter a mental hospital. But now Eidinoff was back on the loose, with official sanction, and Foreman's talents were engaged elsewhere.

Forty-nine days passed—forty-nine days in which Harold Eidinoff came to feel increasingly threatened. Now it was January 28, 1959. Ted Andress was aboard an airliner carrying him home from San Francisco with his wife, Lucille. He had just added a new honor to his long list, election to the board of directors of the

National School Board Association. He was in good digestion and in a euphoric mood.

In El Paso, it was a cool, pleasant evening. A festival spirit reigned at International Airport. Swarms of whooping conventioneers in Gay Nineties costumes, arriving in town for a meeting of barbershop-quartet enthusiasts, filled the terminal with a bedlam of raucous greetings. But one man, oblivious to all the hoopla, went about his business with single-minded determination. That man was Harold Eidinoff. He knew Ted Andress was scheduled to return to El Paso sometime during the evening. And he was stalking him with all the cunning of a hired gunman.

Since Eidinoff was familiar to Andress and hundreds of other El Paso citizens, he had decided upon an ingenious disguise. His acquaintances were accustomed to seeing him clean-shaven and wearing a conservative business suit. This evening, he wore a false beard and an outlandish assortment of clothing that was far from conservative. The costume was a mixture of hot-rodder and cowboy attire—a black leather jacket, black trousers, black cabbie's cap, cowboy boots and a garish orange vest. In one hand he carried an oversized 1,115-page book entitled *The Literature of the United States.*

The orange vest and the heavy book were of special interest. The vest was bulletproof. As for the book—ah, that was a masterpiece. In best pulp-mystery fashion, a section of the book concerning the works of Edgar Allan Poe (appropriately enough) had been carefully carved out to provide a secret compartment. Concealed in this hiding place was a fully loaded .38-caliber revolver.

Inside the airport terminal, Eidinoff took up a vantage point near a luggage counter. He waited there patiently as one plane after another set down and taxied to the terminal. Eidinoff carefully scanned each group of disembarking passengers, trying to pick Andress out of the crowd. Now, at last, he saw his quarry.

Ted and Lucille Andress were walking directly toward the luggage counter where Eidinoff was waiting. They paid no attention to him. His disguise had worked perfectly.

Now, suddenly, Eidinoff drew his revolver from between the pages of the hefty book. Andress looked up just in time to discover that the gun barrel was pointed straight at his chest.

"No, no!" he cried.

CRACK! CRACK! CRACK! CRACK! CRACK! CRACK!

Eidinoff had squeezed the trigger six times, and five bullets had found their mark. Two slammed into Andress' chest. One severed an artery beneath the collarbone. Another struck him over the left eye and the fifth his right wrist. As Andress lay writhing on the floor, Eidinoff threw down the revolver and calmly walked away.

"My God, stop that man!" Lucille Andress screamed. "He just shot my husband!"

While hundreds of spectators looked on in astonishment, a policeman stationed at the airport, Patrolman Servando Blanco, immediately arrested Eidinoff. The doctor offered no resistance. It was 6:12 P.M. Seventy-two minutes later, Andress died in El Paso General Hospital. Eidinoff was charged almost immediately with murder with malice.

Now, instead of representing Eidinoff merely in some civil suits, Percy Foreman found himself defending in still another capital case.

Foreman immediately had Eidinoff examined by some of the nation's leading psychiatrists. He would base his defense almost entirely on their testimony—and, in the process, show again his skill at dealing with psychiatric testimony. In addition, he moved swiftly for a change of venue. The climate of public opinion in El Paso, Foreman charged, was so violently prejudiced against Eidinoff that he could not possibly receive a fair trial there. Moreover, he contended, the El Paso Establishment was out to get Eidinoff—and had been for some time.

It should be recalled that western Texas had once been the stomping ground of Judge Roy Bean, the self-proclaimed "Law West of the Pecos." One of Bean's descendants, Woodrow Wilson Bean, was county judge (head of the governing body) in El Paso during Eidinoff's time. In fact, Eidinoff had tried to get Bean to represent him in some of his civil suits. Bean had declined. Now, curiously enough, Eidinoff found himself standing trial for murder before still another Judge Bean—Robert Bean.

But this trial was far from El Paso, and the name was merely coincidental. Foreman had won his point concerning prejudice against Eidinoff in El Paso. The trial had been moved three hundred and fifty miles, all the way to Lubbock, on the edge of the Panhandle. In many cases where changes of venue occur, the district attorney in the trial city—rather than the one from the home city—serves as the prosecutor. Not so in the Eidinoff case. The El Paso district attorney's office handled the prosecution.

Heading the prosecution team was El Paso DA William Clayton, later elevated to a judgeship. He battled Foreman every minute of every day, knowing full well that the case was a *cause célèbre* back home and that any man who depended on the electorate for his job must at least give the appearance he was tilting on even terms with the famed defense lawyer from the other side of the state.

Foreman pleaded Eidinoff not guilty by virtue of insanity. He contended throughout the trial that Eidinoff was suffering from what he described as a rare mental disorder known as "true paranoia." As described by Foreman—in what was generally taken to be an oversimplification—the victim of "true paranoia" permits a small part of his mind to build up delusions. In Eidinoff's case, Foreman argued, these delusions were triggered by the subject of the nude photographs.

"He's ninety-nine and forty-four–one-hundredths percent sane," Foreman said. "His only irrationality concerns his obsession over the nude pictures and the feud."

Thus, the nude pictures played a leading role in the trial. Several prominent Texans testified that Andress had displayed the pictures to them. One El Paso city official testified that, after attending a meeting in Andress' office one night in early 1954, he was shown the pictures by Andress.

Foreman asked: "Were you interested in seeing the nude pictures?"

The witness replied: "No."

Q. What did you do?

A. I went downstairs in the elevator and Andress came with me. We walked as far as the corner and stopped. I think the light was red.

Q. What did Andress do then?

A. He took the pictures out of his pocket and showed them to me.

Q. Did you look at them?

A. I did, at his insistence.

Q. Do you recall what they looked like?

A. I think there were two nude pictures of a man and one nude picture of a woman.

Q. Did Andress indicate to you who the pictures were supposed to represent?

A. I think he said the man was Dr. Eidinoff and the woman was his wife, Sylvia.

Q. Did Andress indicate to you why he wanted you to look at the pictures?

A. He said he wanted my opinion as to whether they were admissible evidence.

Q. Did you reply?

A. I told him that I didn't know.

This testimony, and testimony of similar character, was essential to Foreman's case. He meant to show not only that Eidinoff was insane, but also that Andress had tormented him into resorting to violence. The nude pictures, taken so many years earlier, seemed to have little or no relevance in any litigation in which Andress was originally involved. Obviously, in Foreman's view, Andress had conducted a personal vendetta against Eidinoff. Other members of the Establishment, he contended, had joined in the harassment. Ultimately, a driven man with an obsession about the nude pictures, Eidinoff abandoned a lifetime characteristic—as a healer and saver of lives—and became a life-taker.

But why? That would be for the psychiatrists to say. An impressive array of psychiatric talent, for both the prosecution and the defense, explored the intricacies of Eidinoff's mind for the jury.

The defense psychiatrists, by and large, supported Foreman's contention. They were among the psychiatrists who believe that such a condition as "true paranoia" exists. Among reputable psychiatrists, there is room for dispute on the subject. Some accept "true paranoia" as a recognizable mental illness. Others reject the concept.

It was Foreman alone, however, who subscribed to the Ivory Soap theory—the "ninety-nine and forty-four–one-hundredths percent sane" notion. That is, without question, an oversimplification. Even those analysts who believe in "true paranoia" do not, in the main, support the theory that a man can be sane on every question except one. They contend that his irrationality would manifest itself in other ways, with respect to other portions of his personality.

But Foreman—a master at dealing with psychiatric testimony—knows what will stick in the mind of a juror. And it is just such an idea as the Ivory Soap theory—not the gobbledygook jargon of a professional man.

District Attorney Clayton, meanwhile, presented witness after witness to attack Foreman's insanity defense. The basis of Clayton's case was that Eidinoff was sane at the time of the trial, sane at the time of the slaying and guilty of nothing less than premeditated, cold-blooded murder. Clayton called to the stand the superintendent of Austin State Hospital, where Eidinoff had been a patient before the slaying. The witness testified that he had discharged Eidinoff because he considered him free of mental illness.

On cross-examination, Foreman snapped: "What would you have done if someone had sent Dr. Eidinoff back to your institution before the shooting of Theodore Andress?"

The superintendent replied: "I would have discharged him again, if his condition had been the same."

This, again, was a case where the basic facts were not in dispute. Foreman made no serious attempt to deny that his client had, indeed, shot Ted Andress. The question was whether Eidinoff had been responsible for his act. Foreman argued forcefully that the evidence showed Eidinoff was insane—that, in fact, his condition was incurable. Clayton argued that the acts of Eidinoff

—carefully plotted, ingeniously conceived—were not those of a madman. Foreman countered with psychiatric evidence that a man with "true paranoia" could—indeed, probably would—behave in precisely the manner Eidinoff had.

Under Texas law, it was for the laymen on the jury to decide this knotty medicolegal question. Confronted with the conflicting psychiatric testimony, the members of the jury elected to believe Foreman's Ivory Soap theory. They found Eidinoff not guilty by virtue of insanity. From a legal standpoint, he was theoretically as free as if he had never shot Andress. He could not be tried again for the crime.

Thus, Percy Foreman had seemingly won another major victory.

But what of Harold Eidinoff? He was grateful to Foreman—and still is—for saving him from possible execution. However, today, he sees the murder trial as no triumph for his own cause.

For, virtually since the day of his acquittal, he has been confined to the maximum-security unit at Rusk State Hospital in East Texas. His fellow inmates include men *convicted* of murder. Eidinoff contends he is a political prisoner and that he will spend the remainder of his life behind the hospital's electrified fences, unless some act of Providence frees him. In effect, he says, members of the El Paso Establishment have conspired to make him serve a life sentence in a mental hospital since they failed to prove him sane and, therefore, guilty of murder.

Whether there is such a conspiracy is debatable. But the fact is that the El Paso district attorney's office—after doing everything possible to prove Eidinoff sane at his murder trial—has spent more than eight years fighting to prove him *insane* ever since his acquittal.

This flip-flop began immediately after the jury returned its verdict. District Attorney Clayton promptly abandoned his previous position, arguing instead that Eidinoff was insane and should be committed. Judge Bean agreed. He ordered Eidinoff sent to Rusk, to be confined "until he becomes sane." Foreman could hardly, in good conscience, pull a comparable flip-flop. He had argued not only that Eidinoff was insane, but that his condition was incurable. He could scarcely demand the physician's prompt return to society. After an appropriate period, Foreman withdrew from the case. He and Eidinoff still correspond frequently. Foreman occasionally sends his former client small gifts, intended to make life behind the hospital's barred windows more bearable. But he has declined Eidinoff's numerous pleas to handle various appeals of his commitment.

Eidinoff has flooded the courts with handwritten petitions. He keeps up a steady stream of correspondence with civil-liberties groups, attorneys, judges, writers—anyone he feels can help win his freedom. He contends he was only temporarily insane, that he has been cured and should go free. But hospital authorities insist he is still mentally ill. They do not use the term "insane" in referring to his case, however. And that gives him an opening to argue, with some cause, that he is being held illegally. For Judge Bean's court order committing him did not say he should be confined until free of all mental illness—only "until he becomes sane."

Today, Eidinoff refuses to blame Percy Foreman for his current confinement. But he is not altogether pleased with the representation Foreman gave him. "My case is one in which Percy neither won nor lost—but tied," Eidinoff says. "He had a choice of self-defense or insanity as a plea. He chose insanity and got an acquittal. I have never said he should have done otherwise. The district attorney and friends of my late opponent [Andress] decided to make me serve a life sentence in a mental hospital. Thus far, they have had the political influence to do it for more than eight years. That's why my friends refer to me as a 'political prisoner.'"

Eidinoff says that the psychiatrists who have treated him at Rusk have taught him how to control his emotions. Over the years since his acquittal, he has been represented by various court-appointed attorneys in unsuccessful efforts to gain his freedom. Some of these attorneys, Eidinoff's relatives and friends—and even some psychiatrists—insist he is entitled to go free.

In January of 1968 a federal district judge in Dallas, W. M. Taylor, Jr., conducted a hearing in a case in which Eidinoff's attorneys contended he should be released under a writ of habeas corpus. Two psychiatrists testified at the hearing that Eidinoff might be sane and that his petition should be seriously considered. A third psychiatrist, however, contended that he should be kept at Rusk.

Testifying on Eidinoff's behalf were Dr. D. A. Brashear of Lufkin, Texas, a former consultant at the Rusk hospital, and Dr. Julien Kennedy of Marshall, Texas, a consultant there since 1966. Both told the court they felt Eidinoff should be considered for release from the hospital. Kennedy testified that Eidinoff's case was regarded as "so touchy" that hospital authorities continued to oppose his release out of habit—rather than because of fresh observations of his mental condition.

Dr. James A. Hunter, the psychiatrist in charge of Eidinoff's hospital ward for the previous six months, testified in opposition to his release. He said Eidinoff was still displaying most of the symptoms of true paranoia and needed supervised hospital care. Among the symptoms, Hunter testified, were delusions of grandeur and a sense of persecution.

He interpreted Eidinoff's constant writing of letters in quest of his freedom as another symptom of mental illness. But, under cross-examination, he conceded that this abundant correspondence might be natural for a man who considered himself unjustly confined.

Eidinoff himself took the stand at the hearing. He pledged, if released, to leave Texas and never return. He said he had no intention of going back to El Paso and resuming the feud. Instead, he said, he hoped to return to New York and, if possible, to try to build a new medical practice.

In the end, Judge Taylor ruled against Eidinoff. A later court ruling held that Eidinoff was being confined illegally, but the decision was appealed by state authorities. At this writing, Eidinoff is still confined at Rusk.

Percy Foreman, for one, feels his former client belongs in the hospital. "There is nothing I would like better than to see Dr. Eidinoff be cured and released," Foreman says. "But the fact is that his condition is incurable. I proved that at the murder trial."

The fact remains that Eidinoff stands acquitted of murder. All that stands between him and his freedom is a decision by hospital authorities or a court that he has recovered. There are those who contend Foreman could win him such a decision.

Except for his personal kindnesses to Eidinoff, however, Foreman has taken no interest in the case in recent years. His attitude is that he did well to keep Eidinoff out of the electric chair, that Eidinoff belongs in an institution and that his services are more badly needed by other clients than by Eidinoff. Who can say he is wrong?

"I go where I'm needed the most," Foreman says.

On the other hand, a number of competent observers—including prominent judges who are friends of Foreman—feel he sometimes shortchanges clients through his constant flitting from case to case. Foreman practices law in a highly unusual manner. He will, for example, sign a contract with a client that commits him only to try the original case. Typically, his contract permits him to leave the courtroom after delivering his summation. He is not even bound to wait around for the verdict—though he usually does. Almost invariably, in any city where he tries a case, he has one of the most competent local trial lawyers at his side as co-counsel. Thus, if Foreman must be absent for a day or two (or even longer), the co-counsel is there to carry on. If they lose the initial round, and there is to be an appeal, Foreman makes a judgment at that point whether he is needed for the appeal, whether a new fee is due him and whether he can make time to handle the matter.

Thus, he is somewhat like the hired gun who once was engaged to ride shotgun on a stagecoach. He signs on only for the big ones, then moves to the next stage for his succeeding day's pay.

It is sometimes an unnerving experience to discuss the practice of law with Foreman. Anytime you mention a particularly notorious criminal case—anywhere in the United States—he is liable to tell you: "Oh, yes. I represented that man. But I had to drop him because (A) he lied to me; (B) I didn't have time to do justice to his case; or (C) he didn't need me." Often, you find, Foreman himself has hired another lawyer for the client. The second lawyer then goes on to reap a publicity bonanza. No one but Foreman's intimates realizes, in such cases, that the Texan was called into the case in the first place. Though he has no aversion to publicity—far from it—there are times when he keeps his own counsel.

Foreman probably would never concede it publicly, but there can be distinct disadvantages to being represented by Percy Foreman. These were perhaps best summed up by his longtime adversary, Erwin Ernst, the Houston prosecutor who handled the Jack Bonds murder trial.

"Percy's only weakness in court is that, in cases that are not very significant, his reputation will give the trials an added importance that they are not really worth," Ernst says. "This works to the detriment of his client. For example, let's assume Percy is representing an ordinary car thief. Normally, the case wouldn't be worth covering in the newspapers. But, because Percy's involved, the papers give it unusual coverage. The jurors know Percy's reputation. They assume, 'If this guy hired Foreman, he must be guilty.' Now, Percy gives his client a helluva good defense. I'm not denying that. But the very fact that he's defending works to the client's detriment in other ways."

Still, across the country, there are numerous local and federal district attorneys who absolutely refuse to enter the courtroom with Foreman. If they cannot dispose of a case involving Foreman through a "trade-out" agreement—a deal in which Foreman pleads his client guilty in return for a light sentence—these prosecutors assign one or more of their assistants to handle the case. Foreman is not only a superb defense lawyer; he has the capacity to make a public officeholder appear a fool or an incompetent. Thus, a man who must win reelection in order to keep his job often finds it the better part of wisdom simply to refrain from crossing swords with the hired legal gun from Texas.

Where Foreman will show up next is always a subject for conjecture. And, along with the nervous district attorneys, there are always the young, ambitious men—anxious to build reputations—who cannot wait for the chance to oppose Foreman. It is, without exaggeration, a situation analagous to the old-time gunman looking for a reputation as the fastest draw in the West. To make it to the top, all he needs is one victory over Foreman. He can then put a notch in his attaché case, rest for a while on his laurels and run for reelection on the platform that "I was the man who defeated the great Percy Foreman in the ——— case."

There is a hazard in such behavior, however. Before long, Foreman may be back in the community to try another case. And he will be doubly anxious to win the next time.

6

I'm often asked why there is such a great variation among sentences imposed by Texas judges. I can only quote the Texas judge who was asked why a killer sometimes doesn't even get indicted and a cattle thief can get ten years. The judge answered: "A lot of fellows ought to be shot, but we don't have any cows that need stealin'."

PERCY FOREMAN

IF THERE IS one thing that can be said about Percy Foreman without fear of contradiction, it is that he is no stuffed shirt.

He may be a millionaire. He may travel first class all the way. He may be rude, arrogant, hard-headed. But he is no snob. He goes through life with a smile on his face, a wisecrack on his lips and Polk County written all over him.

When he was chosen by the Houston Press Club as the patsy for one of its Gridiron Show skits—written with an instinct for the jugular—Foreman not only enjoyed every laugh at his own expense. He also agreed to become one of the performers.

A quartet of newspaperwomen singing under the name of The Cut and Shoot Cuties serenaded Foreman from the stage of a glittering hotel ballroom with the parody "King of the Court." (The quartet took its name from a storied community in Foreman's beloved Big Thicket. Cut and Shoot, Texas, became world-famous once by producing a contender for the heavyweight boxing championship, Roy Harris. A backwoodsman who claimed he trained by wrestling alligators, Harris left his Bowie knife home when he battled Floyd Patterson for the title. He got knocked out, and another Texas legend was headed toward the grave. Year in and year out, however, Cut and Shoot can be depended upon for an occasional weird headline. One Houston *Chronicle* story was headlined: "Man Beaten to Death in Cut and Shoot!")

While being serenaded by the Cut and Shoot Cuties, Percy Foreman was not in his usual place at a ringside table. Instead, he stood boldly on the stage—the crooked-lipped grin pasted on his face—with a golden crown perched at a ridiculous angle on his leonine head. Draped around his shoulders was a royal robe of scarlet and black. And in his right hand, held regally before him, was a slightly unbalanced golden scale of justice.

Foreman's sense of humor is usually directed at others. But occasionally, very occasionally, he can laugh with genuine gusto at himself. The fact was, however, that there was as much truth as jest in the ditty sung by the Cuties.

> Guilty or innocent,
> Makes no difference to this gent.

This is indisputably true. Foreman is not in practice to defend only innocent clients. The point is that they are not guilty until proved so, and Foreman often does not even ask his clients whether they are guilty. He feels they don't know enough about the law to give an accurate answer. He merely asks a client to tell his own side of the story. Then he checks on the story. If the client has lied, Foreman drops him and moves on to another case. But, if the client has told the truth, moral guilt rarely enters into his decision whether to defend.

At one time Foreman drew the line at some types of defendants. He would not, for example, represent accused confidence men and hot-check artists. But even those barriers are down today.

As "King of the Courtroom," he will travel almost anywhere to defend almost anyone—provided he feels he is needed in the case, that no one else can provide the client with adequate representation. In 1958 he defended a twenty-three-year-old man accused in California of being a "shoe fetishist." Police in San Diego charged the young man with assault, attempted rape, robbery and burglary. They said the defendant had seized more than a hundred female shoes in thirty assaults and robberies. The case, needless to say, caused a sensation. It was repugnant to most attorneys. But Foreman agreed to defend.

In various states, purported Mafia hoodlums had trouble finding competent lawyers who would take their cases. These men ranged from hired gunmen to gamblers to narcotics wholesalers. One of them, Joseph Civello, had been a delegate to the infamous Apalachin crime convention. Foreman not only agreed to defend Civello against a variety of charges; he went to New York and worked on the appeal for other Apalachin defendants as well. Their convictions ultimately were reversed. In such cases, high-class, high-priced counselors shied from being associated with the Mafia hoods. But Foreman agreed to defend.

In Louisiana, Texas and New York, a big-time gambler named Eugene Anthony Nolan was accused by the authorities of masterminding perhaps the most farflung bookmaking operation in the country. Involved in the various cases with Nolan were some of the most unsavory characters in the gambling world. Many lawyers seemed unwilling to become embroiled in the cases. But Foreman agreed to defend Nolan.

Also in various states, purveyors of racy books—the newsstand variety slapped together to appeal to the peep-show mentality—had trouble finding adequate counsel in the concrete towers inhabited by publishing-industry law firms. But Foreman agreed to defend.

The principle that a defendant is innocent until proved guilty gets more than lip service from Foreman. He lives by it, and gladly takes the heat generated by his defense of unpopular causes and clients.

In October of 1962, there were few Americans with less popularity than former Major General Edwin Walker. Except for a coterie of extremist followers, Walker was so far outside the mainstream that even many ultra-conservatives wanted nothing to do with him. As an Army general, Walker had originally hit the headlines in 1957 as commander of the federal troops sent to Little Rock, Arkansas, by President Dwight D. Eisenhower to prevent violence from interfering with court-ordered school desegregation. Walker had carried out the orders, but had not liked them. His military career had later taken numerous strange turns. He had been disciplined by the Army for indoctrinating troops under his command in Europe with John Birch Society propaganda. He had returned to the United States to testify in congressional hearings at which Defense Department officials were accused of "muzzling" military men. Next, he had quit the Army. From that time on, when referred to as "General," he had asked to be called merely "Mister Walker." He rarely got his way. Nor did he get his way when he entered politics, as a candidate for governor in that most conservative of all states—Texas. He ran dead last in a field of six.

In the fall of 1962, to Walker's chagrin, the civil-rights movement was in full swing. Racial barriers were falling throughout the South, and in many parts of the North. But Mississippi, it was thought, would stand firm in its insistence on segregation. The first major test of this theory came on September 30, 1962, when James Meredith arrived in Oxford, Mississippi, seeking to become the first Negro admitted to the University of Mississippi.

Meredith had come to Oxford before—backed by federal court orders directing his admission to Ole Miss. Three times, Governor Ross Barnett or Lieutenant Governor Paul Johnson (Barnett's eventual successor as governor) had turned him away. The fourth time, however, Meredith was accompanied by a large contingent of deputy United States marshals, Justice Department officials, White House aides and military men.

By this time General Walker had become a sort of wandering minstrel, preaching the far-right doctrine wherever he could find a suitable platform. His followers, whatever their number, were willing to fight and die for the cause. Or so they said.

Shortly before Meredith's fourth try at Ole Miss, Walker broadcast an appeal for 10,000 volunteers from all fifty states to join him in Oxford and stand shoulder to shoulder beside Ross Barnett. Hundreds of his followers—but far fewer than 10,000—were to answer the call. "It is time to move," Walker said. "We have talked, listened and been pushed around far too much by the anti-Christ Supreme Court. Now it is time to be heard—10,000 strong from every state in the union."

Walker urged all Americans who loved their freedom to join him in defense of Mississippi's sovereignty, even if it meant opposing federal troops sent into the state. "I intend to go to Mississippi if and when they use federal troops," he said as the crisis built. "Lots of people are not waiting for me. They're already going to Mississippi, from California to Carolina."

That they were. Out of the woodwork they crawled—some of the strangest creatures ever placed on public display. To see them was to marvel at them. Some were organized into paramilitary units, with battle flags and precise chains of command. Others toted weapons that looked as if they dated back to the Civil War. Others bore banners trumpeting the slogans of extremist organizations. Still others were not answering Walker's call at all. They were just rubbernecks who wanted to see the long-heralded showdown between "those damned Kennedys"—President John F. Kennedy and his brother, Attorney General Robert F. Kennedy—and the sovereign state of Mississippi.

By nightfall September 30, Oxford was crammed with thousands of outsiders—the federal contingent, Mississippi highway patrolmen, sheriff's officers, newsmen, plus agitators of virtually all races and political colorations. The story of the Ole Miss riot is sufficiently well known that there is no need to dwell on it at length. But General Walker's role during that long, bloody night is relevant and should be explored.

Walker arrived in Oxford the night before the riot with an associate, Robert A. Surrey, a printing salesman. (Surrey was the man later identified by the Warren Commission as author of the anti-Kennedy "Wanted for Treason" handbill circulated in Dallas on the day of President Kennedy's assassination.) After taking a motel room under an assumed name, Walker made himself available to the press—again emphasizing that he and his followers were in Mississippi to support Governor Barnett. Unknown to Walker and numerous other followers, however, Barnett was making his own secret deal with the Kennedys. When Barnett did not keep his end of this bargain—and when law-enforcement officers found themselves unable to cope with the mob that swarmed over the Ole Miss campus—the riot erupted. Before it was over, two men would be killed and hundreds wounded in the most serious conflict between the federal government and a state's citizens since the Civil War.

Just what part did Walker play in all this? The facts are hard to come by. Accounts given by witnesses, and by Walker himself, vary sharply. The following is what appears to be as close to the truth of these events as we shall get.

After the riot had begun, but while it consisted mainly of a series of small skirmishes between rioters and federal marshals firing tear-gas grenades, Walker crossed a roadblock and marched onto the campus. His white broad-brimmed hat set jauntily on his head, he strode purposefully to a Confederate monument near the center of the campus. A band of rioters—mainly consisting of college-age boys—was gathered before the monument.

"We want a leader!" they shouted. "We want a leader! We want a leader!"

Upon sighting Walker, they changed the chant. "We have a leader! We have a leader! We have a leader!"

Word that Walker had arrived to "take command" spread like a flame across the campus. The band around the monument swelled. Walker climbed up the base of the monument to address his "troops."

"I want to compliment you all on the protest you make tonight," he said. He contended that Barnett and state aides had betrayed the people of Mississippi. Thus, he was no longer in the state to stand shoulder to shoulder with the governor. Now, it was some vast conspiracy that he sought to combat—involving not only the Kennedys, but Barnett as well. "Don't let up now," Walker told the youths. "You may lose this battle, but you will have been heard. This is a dangerous situation. You must be prepared for possible death. If you are not, go home now."

In response to questions, Walker provided advice on how to cut off all the electric power feeding the campus and how to combat the marshals' tear-gas grenades. Ultimately, he descended from his Olympian height, paused, then strode toward the main force of marshals. Rioters gathered alongside, behind and in front of him. Someone shouted: "Charge!" Eyewitnesses later claimed it was Walker, but he denied it. In any event, there was a charge toward the marshals. Walker was among those making the advance. But the marshals drove the band off with a volley of tear gas. The rioters reformed their ranks at the monument, heard a second speech, then made a new charge. Another volley of tear gas sent them scattering. One of them was captured by the marshals, however, becoming the first prisoner taken by the federal forces.

The prisoner, Edward Joseph Horbatch, an Ole Miss student, gave the federals their first solid information about Walker's role. He told of Walker's arrival and his speeches. He quoted Walker as saying: "They're ruining the Constitution. . . . Other people [Walker followers] are coming in."

An immediate investigation of Walker's part in the riot was launched by FBI agents—even as the riot continued. Meanwhile, in Washington, Justice Department attorneys began researching the law to see what possible charges could be filed against the former general. Within hours the word was relayed to Mississippi by Assistant Attorney General Ramsey Clark (later appointed attorney general by his fellow Texan Lyndon B. Johnson). The word was: "Arrest Walker if you can; maintain surveillance if you can't." The charge to be filed: insurrection, among others.

Thus, this former military man—indoctrinated since his youth with the concept of loyalty to country—now was to stand accused of helping mount an insurrection against that country. It was an extreme charge. But the events were extreme.

The next morning, after the riot had been quelled, it was announced in Oxford that a warrant had been issued for Walker's arrest. The complaint against him charged:

> On or about September 30, 1962, Edwin Walker did forcibly assault, resist, impede, intimidate and interfere with United States marshals . . . while they were engaged in performance of their official duties. . . . Walker and other persons unknown . . . did conspire to prevent by force, intimidation and threats U.S. marshals from discharging their duties and to injure them in their person while engaged in the official discharge of their duties. . . . Walker did incite, assist and engage in an insurrection against the authority of the United States . . . [and] did conspire to oppose by force the authority of the United States and by force to prevent, hinder and delay the execution of the laws of the United States.

The complaint, signed by United States Attorney H. M. Ray of Oxford, said the charges were supported by information from an Associated Press correspondent, Van H. Savell. (It was chiefly Savell and the Associated Press who bore the brunt of defending themselves against libel suits later filed by Walker.) Walker was still in Oxford at the time the criminal complaint was filed, but he was preparing to beat a hasty retreat. Army troops had been called into Oxford in force to quell the riot. They had set up roadblocks on all main thoroughfares to prevent new demonstrators from flooding the town, to keep suspects from fleeing and to search for illegal weapons.

About 11 A.M. on October 1 a group of GIs maintaining order near the town square—the square celebrated in the late Oxford resident William Faulkner's novels—spotted Walker. Lieutenant Robert Clarke, who had been alerted to arrest Walker on sight, did so. Then, at bayonet point, the troops marched the former military man to a detention area on the campus. Two hours later Walker was arraigned in the local post office before United States Commissioner Omar D. Craig. Walker heard the charges, then asked if he could have time to obtain a lawyer.

The lawyer he wanted was Percy Foreman, though he did not say so in open court. Craig, however, refused to give him the requested time. "There are plenty of good lawyers in this state and in this county," he said. Indeed there were. John Satterfield, former president of the American Bar Association, and Hugh Cunningham, law partner of Ross Barnett, were among those who would eventually become involved in the Ole Miss litigation. But Walker did not want them, talented as they were. He wanted Foreman.

Several times Craig reemphasized that Walker could not have the time to bring in an out-of-state lawyer. He could, however, waive a hearing—in which case bond would be set and he could go on his way upon posting the bail. That idea appealed to Walker.

He was particularly concerned that his case be tried in Mississippi, where he knew he had allies, rather than in some other federal jurisdiction. Actually, he could not have been tried anywhere but in Mississippi—unless part of his purported offense had been committed elsewhere. Craig, in explaining these facts, referred to Walker first as "Colonel," then as "General."

Walker, alluding to his Army resignation, snapped: "*Mister*, please. That's one of my problems already. All right, I'll waive this hearing."

"Bail is set at 100,000 dollars," Craig said. "You'll remain in custody until bail is made."

Walker let out a long, soft whistle at the amount of the bail before he was led away. Robert Surrey immediately told newsmen that friends of Walker would try to arrange bail—denying all the while that the former general had committed any crime. "All he did was participate in a peaceable protest," Surrey said.

The wheels were soon in motion to retain Foreman as Walker's defense lawyer. But, before Foreman could enter the case officially, it took a strange turn.

After being held briefly in an Oxford jail cell, Walker was secretly removed by marshals and hustled across state lines to the United States Medical Center for federal prisoners at Springfield, Missouri. The authority for this transfer was an order from U.S. District Judge Claude F. Clayton. On a Justice Department motion, Clayton ordered Walker committed to the hospital for psychiatric examination. Before issuing the commitment order, Clayton had studied a memorandum on Walker prepared for the Federal Prison Bureau by its chief psychiatrist and medical director, Dr. Charles E. Smith.

This memorandum was a remarkable document, since Smith had never laid eyes upon Walker. Percy Foreman, who had used just such psychiatric evidence in his trial of the Jack Bonds murder case, would later rail against its use by the government in the Walker case. Smith conceded in the memorandum that his long-distance "diagnosis" of Walker's case came chiefly from news reports of the Oxford riot and of the former general's past behavior.

"Some of his described behavior reflects sensitivity and essentially unpredictable and seemingly bizarre outbursts of the types often observed in individuals suffering with paranoid mental disorders," Smith's memorandum said.

"There are also indications in his medical history of functional and psychosomatic disorders which could be precursors of the more serious disorders which his present behavior suggests . . . may be indicative of an underlying mental disturbance."

After being interviewed at Springfield by the warden, Dr. Russell Settle, Walker was given a set of hospital clothes and put to bed. The disclosure that he had been moved to the hospital touched off a national furor. His supporters argued that he had been shanghaied. But others, including two senators, speculated that Walker was indeed mentally ill. "Maybe he's a sick man," said Oregon's Wayne Morse. "If he is, he ought to be committed. He ought not to be at large." Ohio's Stephen M. Young, referring to the case, used the term "psychopath."

Soon, however, Walker was freed on bail with the understanding that he would consult a psychiatrist. He engaged Percy Foreman and an Oklahoma City attorney, Clyde Watts, to represent him. His fortunes began taking an upward turn. He went to one of the nation's best-known psychiatrists, Dr. R. L. Stubblefield. The Dallas psychiatrist later submitted a report to Judge Clayton in Mississippi, saying that Walker was "functioning currently at the superior level." The report further commented: "All psychiatric and psychological tests indicate that Mr. Walker appears to be able to deal freely and accurately with his recollections of the incident leading up to his arrest and present charges." Largely on the basis of this report, Clayton ruled at a mental-competency hearing that Walker was fully competent to stand trial.

Percy Foreman then challenged the federal prosecutors to bring Walker to trial. "I dare them to indict Walker," he said. "If he's not indicted, there won't be any trial. But I am willing to waive indictment and proceed with a trial on the basis of an information." (A criminal information is a formal complaint filed by a prosecutor, rather than by a grand jury. In certain cases, a defendant may waive indictment by a grand jury and go to trial on the charges specified in the information.)

Thus, the stage appeared to be set for a showdown on the Oxford town square. One could picture Foreman—an attaché case in each hand, looking like two saddlebags hung from his huge frame—walking across Faulkner's beloved square to do battle with the federal government. Conceivably, one of the Justice Department legal titans such as civil-rights troubleshooter John Doar would head the prosecution.

There was just one hitch. Edwin Walker might be a "villain" in the nation's press. He might be an object of scorn abroad. But in Oxford, Mississippi, he was more hero than villain. He had been standing up to the federals.

Thus, when the time came for a grand jury to consider the charges against Walker, a sufficient number of votes for indictment could not be found. The jury no-billed (failed to indict) him. And the Justice Department—refusing to rise to Foreman's challenge—elected not to proceed on the basis of an information. Instead, the department asked Judge Clayton to dismiss the charges against Walker "without prejudice." Clayton complied. This meant that, if it chose, the department could pursue the case anew and seek an indictment from some other grand jury.

Foreman was enraged by this turn of events. Once again, he challenged the federal government to put up or shut up.

Despite the dismissal of the charges, Foreman insisted: "Walker has been vilified, tried in public and condemned. He ought to have the right to have the American public know the facts with reference to his acts or conduct at Oxford and whether he or his accusers are in left field." Again, he dared the government to proceed on an information, saying he was still willing to waive indictment on Walker's behalf. "The general is entitled to have the government's case presented under oath to find if there is a right reason for the government's unprecedented action," he said. "Walker was tarnished with the tar-brush suggestion of mental incompetence, hauled across state lines with totalitarian tactics from Oxford, Mississippi, to Missouri, and kept there without bail on the unsworn testimony of a man who had never seen him."

The brashness of Percy Foreman caught many by surprise. Most lawyers would have been satisfied to get their clients off the hook. But not Foreman. He demanded satisfaction. He did not get it. Whether out of fear of confronting Foreman in court with shaky evidence or out of a belated realization that its case would never stand up in a Mississippi court, the Justice Department backed off. Nothing more was heard about a prosecution of Walker.

Foreman has never let the federal government forget the Walker case. As late as the fall of 1966, a full four years after the Ole Miss riot, he was still lambasting the Justice Department. In a newspaper interview, he cited the case as an example of the manner in which psychiatric commitments can be used to "get rid of people" whose views are unpopular.

"General Walker was ordered shipped in irons from Oxford, Mississippi, to Springfield, Missouri, and there locked in the ward of a U.S. penitentiary for mental patients on the diagnosis of a doctor selected by the then attorney general in Washington," Foreman said. "The doctor selected had never seen General Walker, and based his diagnosis on what he had 'read in the papers.' Up to this instance, such conduct on the part of a psychiatrist was deemed sufficient to suspend or cancel his right to practice medicine. A movement was instigated to hold this doctor accountable. However, the central government brought pressure to bear and reversed the prevailing procedure. I think this was a setback for the field of medicine we call psychiatry. The psychiatrists were not responsible. The pressure was from politicians."

By the time of this interview, General Walker had made the front pages many times over since the Ole Miss affair. In fact, barely three months after getting off the legal hook in Mississippi, Walker was back in the headlines.

This time Walker attained notoriety as the intended victim of a rifle attack. And Percy Foreman, true to his credo, eventually served unofficially as defender of Walker's accused attacker. Even more incredibly, he served still later as official counsel for the attacker's own attacker.

This is not nearly so complicated as it appears. For the attacker of Walker, or so the authorities say, was Lee Harvey Oswald. And the attacker of Oswald was, of course, Jack Ruby.

On the night of April 10, 1963, Walker was seated in his Dallas home, preparing his income-tax return. As he hunched over his desk, a rifle bullet whistled past his head. He escaped death by inches. The following year, after the assassination of President Kennedy, the Warren Commission concluded that this bullet had been fired by Lee Oswald, Kennedy's assassin. By that time, of course, Oswald himself was dead, shot down by Jack Ruby.

In the aftermath of this twin disaster, Percy Foreman was in much demand officially and unofficially as an expert on criminal law. Both CBS and NBC, in television documentaries exploring the assassination and its by-products, used Foreman in effect as Oswald's defense lawyer. Other television and radio organizations also called upon his expertise. His already crowded schedule of trials, speeches and public appearances became even more crowded. He did not seek such exposure. But, when it was offered, he accepted it proudly.

Foreman's friends and acquaintances throughout the country received in the mail envelopes bearing the return address "PERCY 77002"—indicating he was so well known that all one needed was his first name and zip code in order to write him.

Inside the envelopes were printed invitations. "Percy Foreman invites you to share an honor," they said. Mentioned beneath this sentence was the name of the TV program on which he was appearing. Off to the left, at the bottom, was the legend: "Consult your TV program."

For a Louis Nizer, perhaps, such a stunt would seem bush league. But, for Percy Foreman, it was entirely in character. For years he handed out engraved calling cards that identified him as a member of a law firm called Moses, Justinian, Blackstone, Webster and Foreman. The card listed his partners as Mose Moses (1297–1202 B.C.), Flavius A. Justinian (483–565 A.D.), William Blackstone (1723–1780 A.D.) and Daniel Webster (1782–1852 A.D.). Corporation lawyers turned up their noses at his audacity. But he had an answer for them. "Just about every big law firm is headed by a dead man," he said. "I thought I'd join the ranks."

On the television programs themselves, however, Foreman was deadly serious. He knew he was there not only as an eloquent spokesman for the criminal bar, but as *de facto* defense attorney for the late Lee Harvey Oswald.

On the CBS documentary *The Law and Lee Oswald,* aired December 29, 1963, moderator Dan Rather made this point clear. Addressing Foreman, Rather said: "There are those who believe that if Mr. Oswald had lived and if he had been brought to trial and had Texas [named] court-appointed attorneys, you might have been one. Do you think he could have received a fair trial?"

Rather, a perceptive reporter who had covered the Kennedy assassination and the Oswald murder, took the short-range, news-impact view in phrasing the question. Foreman approached the issue from a longer range.

"Well, Oswald didn't [get a fair trial], and it's not likely that he will," Foreman said. "He's still being tried. We used to think that a trial started with the indictment and the arraignment. But today trial starts almost with the commission of the offense, and Oswald had been tried and executed before he ever met a jury and, to that extent, he didn't receive a fair trial. So I would say that it's better that it happened as it did than as it would have happened in the courtroom because he would have been judicially executed or lynched with just a fragrance of legality. He would not have received a fair trial. He couldn't possibly have received a fair trial."

It is worth discussing in detail Foreman's appearances on both CBS and NBC. For they provided meaningful glimpses not only of his rhetorical skill, but also of his deep convictions on the subject of true justice.

Elaborating on his statement that Oswald could not have received a fair trial, Foreman said: "In the first place, he could not have had the first basic, fundamental right of a presumption of innocence by a fair-minded jury because the jury's mind was persuaded by the overweening publicity from every source. It would have been impossible to have obtained a jury. Any juror, under the circumstances, who would have testified that he could throw aside any opinion he had formed would not have been the type of man you'd want on a jury in the first place.

"In the second place, he didn't have a lawyer. He wasn't given a lawyer. He wasn't arraigned. And the assumption—the only possible defense in view of the released evidence to the public—would have been insanity. He was, I understand, examined. But I don't believe there's a competent psychiatrist in the country who would agree that, under the pressure under which he was examined, he could have made a fair appraisal of Oswald's condition."

Rather broke in. "Well, now, you've had a great deal of success in defending people who were in, to say the least, highly unpopular situations. Now, are you saying if Lee Oswald had lived and if he had been brought to trial, and you had been one of the defense attorneys, that you could not have successfully defended him?"

Foreman responded: "A man getting a fair trial and a man being successfully defended are two different points entirely. I'm satisfied if I've done all that can be done for a client, regardless of the outcome of the case. Sometimes success is not measured by acquittal. If any circumstance, any mitigating circumstance in the life, background or mental condition of Lee Oswald could have been presented properly and adequately—so as to perhaps relieve him, insofar as the law permits a man to be relieved under the M'Naghten Rule [on criminal insanity]—the man's life might have been saved. All of the evidence against Oswald is circumstantial."

Other members of the panel assembled in New York by CBS were Paul Freund, professor of law at Harvard Law School, an authority on constitutional law; Leon Douglas, state's prosecuting attorney before the Texas Court of Criminal Appeals, which would have been the court of last resort (other than federal appellate courts) in any Oswald murder trial; and Newton Minow, former chairman of the Federal Communications Commission, whose role in the documentary was primarily to assess the impact of electronic-media coverage on the Oswald case.

Douglas took issue with his fellow Texan. "I disagree with Mr. Foreman . . . that it was better that he [Oswald] was disposed of the way he was, instead of a judicial execution," Douglas said. "I was happy that the man was arrested, that he would face a trial before our courts and that due process would apply—and not compared to some foreign country where we know that they'll be killed when something happens."

Foreman, reacting as if he were facing Douglas before the bench, interrupted. "Just a minute!" he said. "I don't mean to say that I approve of the killing of Oswald. I just say that our courtroom should not be degraded by the mock trial that would have resulted due to the undue publicity—that, rather than have a man illegally executed with a quasi-legal stamp of approval, why, I'd rather not have that type of so-called justice administered in a courtroom. If a man's going to receive the lack of protection that this man would have received due to the publicity, I'm glad that at least no member of my profession had anything to do with his extermination."

Later, asked to assess the performance of the Dallas police and district attorney in protecting Oswald's civil rights, Foreman said: "I don't think . . . the conduct was any different than it would have been in any Texas city and probably in most other cities in the United States. [Because of] the impact of this offense, and the attendant publicity, there's no precedent by which we can now look back and see what should have been done. There's nothing that they [the police and prosecutors] had to guide them. And traditionally officers and people who are elected to office, in politics, are very sensitive of their public image. And self-realization of the satisfaction of seeing their pictures on the screen or hearing themselves talk . . . is carried on to a greater or lesser degree in all cases. Recently the Supreme Court has had to reverse a case out of Louisiana . . . because the confession in a twenty-minute interview with the sheriff was on the screen. That's done now too much and in all too many places."

Rather asked Foreman: "Could you be a little more specific about what mistakes you think were made on the part of the law-enforcement people and the district attorney in Dallas?"

Foreman answered: "Well, I don't like to criticize my good friend [District Attorney] Henry Wade . . . but I wonder if this man [Oswald] was ever arraigned." Actually, it was well known that Oswald had, in fact, been arraigned. What Foreman was questioning was whether he had been legally arraigned. He explained: "I wonder if he had a public arraignment. If he did, it wasn't shown. The only time he was taken away from the police station was when he was shot, as far as the news coverage was concerned. And, if he didn't have a public arraignment, he was never legally arraigned. Suppose a justice of the peace is going to advise a man of his rights to have a lawyer and there are around him fifteen or twenty booted and hatted and pistoled officers—and that they constitute the audience. What effect is that going to have on the average man in such a condition?"

Douglas disagreed once again with Foreman's position. He conceded some mistakes had been made by the Dallas authorities, but said "they were mistakes that were not harmful to Oswald."

Foreman, in his best cross-examining tone, asked Douglas: "If it had not been for these gentlemen of the Fourth Estate, don't you believe Oswald would have confessed?"

Douglas replied: "I don't think so. I think they have a fair police department there. . . ."

Foreman would not let him off the hook that easily. "I'm not challenging the accuracy of what you have just said. I'm not referring to the Dallas Police Department. But, in thirty-five years and in at least 35,000 cases, I have never seen a man in Texas fail to confess if an officer has decided he was going to confess."

The best Douglas could manage in response was: "Well, luckily, we don't have that in too many cases, Mr. Foreman."

Now Rather got to the nub of the reason for Foreman's appearance on the show. "Mr. Foreman, suppose you had to defend Lee Oswald," the commentator said. "Where would you have started?"

Foreman launched into a lengthy dissertation that went beyond the case of Lee Oswald. It told a great deal about his technique as a defense lawyer.

"Nowadays the defense lawyer doesn't usually get into the case until the confession has been signed, sealed and delivered—and obtained, as I said a moment ago, in a manner, whatever manner, either by violence or by psychological extortion. Assuming that I had come into the case immediately, assuming that I had been appointed by this theoretical attorney for the justice of the peace and for the people. . . . The district attorney was working; he was there on the scene. He was interviewing witnesses. The state was represented, but the defendant wasn't. I would have first asked for a state injunction restraining the further questioning of the defendant, except in the presence of his attorney.

"I would have advised him not to make any statement, except in the presence of his attorney. I would have insisted on a court reporter being present to take down the questions as well as the answers. Usually you get only the answers . . . and frequently, without the question, it doesn't carry the effect—the tenor of the conversation.

"I would have failed completely because it would have been an original. There would have been no authority for my doing what I tell you I would have done. I would have done it to be laying a predicate for my rights on appeal to the United States

Supreme Court. . . . I might have obtained that release. Meanwhile, the man would have been questioned at least three or four or five days. Actually, I think somebody should, in the interest of the public—not in the interest of Lee Oswald, but in the interest of the people of the United States—defend Lee Oswald before this [Warren] commission.

"The President has appointed, and properly, a group of men of unimpeachable integrity who hold the respect of all of America because the President, as we all know, is concerned that the public know and have confidence in whatever facts are behind or applicable to this homicide."

Rather broke in to ask: "What you're suggesting, then, is that Lee Oswald, the late Lee Oswald, have some sort of defense before the commission?"

"Absolutely," Foreman said. "There's no other way, in my opinion, that the evidence in this case can be properly evaluated. If we're going to accept as true the testimony of a policeman that a palmprint [of Oswald's] was found on the death weapon—the public generally thinks of a palmprint as a fingerprint. It isn't the same and doesn't have as great effect. [As for] the paraffin test, there's no competent person in America who will give any credence to the paraffin test. [A paraffin test, conducted on Oswald, purported to show that he had recently fired a gun.] Actually, the paraffin test for nitrites—that's what it is, exploded gunpowder—there are any number of household items from which you can get the same nitrites. You can get them from lighting a cigarette."

The suggestion that defense counsel represent Oswald's interests before the Warren Commission was not followed. The commission did ask Walter E. Craig, president of the American Bar Association, to participate in the commission hearings. But Craig himself made it clear that he was serving only as an adviser to the commission, not as "counsel for Lee Harvey Oswald." Had Oswald been represented before the commission, much of the furor attending issuance of the Warren Report might have been avoided.

Foreman, in his final remarks on the program, returned to a

favorite theme. "The only way that the courts can give the rights of an individual to the individual is by condemning illegal procedure on the part of the constabulary," he said.

"They have no way to go back and undo it any other way, and they send the message down again and again until it eventually seeps down to the reckless individual. The manner in which a case is tried, the procedure by which it is tried, is as much a part of the law of the land as the statute making murder an offense. And two wrongs *don't* make a right. And the only way the rights of an individual can be given him is for an appellate court to reverse and say, 'Try this case in a different manner next time.' "

The CBS program had been presented barely more than a month after the Kennedy assassination, when the horror of the act itself was still fresh. NBC, however, waited fifteen months after the assassination before presenting its White Paper entitled *Oswald and the Law*. Chet Huntley was the narrator. And, once again, Percy Foreman was called upon to serve as unofficial defense attorney for Lee Oswald.

Some of the points made by Foreman on NBC echoed his earlier views on CBS. His ideas had not changed in the intervening months. On the NBC program, however, he had the opportunity to elaborate on the broad legal problems brought into focus by the Oswald case.

One such subject was the matter of prolonged police interrogation of a suspect. As Huntley put it in introducing Foreman: "Many times, when a suspect is arrested and brought into a police station to be booked, the evidence against him is by no means conclusive. . . . In this kind of situation the suspect himself becomes an important source of information, and questioning is legitimate. But there is a danger that police interrogation may become coercive."

Foreman agreed. "I haven't yet found the individual who could withstand a prolonged persuasion," he said. "Sometimes it's just psychological. They [the police] are adept at psychology. They arrest a man's wife, his sweetheart, his daughter. [They tell him] 'You don't want her to go to the penitentiary with you, do you?'

They let him see her, get glimpses of her sitting outside all night long. 'We'll let her go just as soon as you tell us the story.' "

As for police investigative techniques, Foreman said: "Policemen are taught in police schools to believe every possible suspect guilty and to start with that premise and eliminate. They don't start with the idea of finding the facts that will point to the guilt of a defendant; they assume it and let him prove his innocence—that is, in the police interrogation. That's universal. It's true in all countries and it's not objectionable. It's good policemanship. But it's poor trial tactics; it's poor justice. It's the antithesis of our concept of the presumption of innocence."

Foreman also spoke out against the reliability of so-called eyewitness testimony. "Particularly in a crime of violence, with the excitement attendant upon such an offense, people are not calculated to have the ability to examine and to identify as they would, say, in a case where an individual gives a check or some other offense that doesn't carry with it the excitement. To me, eyewitness identification is one of the weakest of all the links of incriminating evidence."

As Huntley pointed out in discussing what he called a "judicial lynching" (a rape trial purportedly rigged by the Ku Klux Klan): "Even under the *normal* circumstances of a trial, justice is not always easy to obtain." Again, Foreman agreed. "One of the fallacies of the prosecution of criminal cases is the so-called presumption of innocence," Foreman said. "The court will instruct the jury both before and during the trial that the defendant is presumed to be innocent. But, actually, the average juror is going to assume from the fact of an indictment that the defendant is guilty and require subconsciously proof of that innocence."

Foreman also struck hard against the use made by prosecutors of testimony provided by underworld informers, particularly in cases where the informers themselves are parties to the alleged crime. "It's testimony that is purchased," Foreman said. (Frequently, in return for such testimony, an informer is granted immunity from prosecution or, at worst, a light sentence.) "If a defendant in the trial of a case offered one dollar or one hundred dollars to a witness, that defendant would be put away and his lawyer likewise—probably into a penitentiary—for a long, long time," Foreman continued. "Yet the prosecution does this as a matter of practice—buying testimony with liberty."

Huntley ended the program with a quotation from Supreme Court Justice Felix Frankfurter, a quotation with which Foreman concurs: "Not the least significant test of the quality of a civilization is its treament of those charged with crime, particularly with offenses which arouse the passions of a community."

No offense in our time had "aroused the passions of a community" more than the assassination of President Kennedy and the subsequent murder of Lee Oswald. It was typical of Percy Foreman that, having eloquently defended the rights of the slain Oswald, he then turned his attention to defending similarly the rights of Oswald's killer.

Though it is not generally known, it was Foreman—not Melvin Belli—who was first asked by Ruby's relatives to serve as chief defense lawyer in the celebrated Dallas murder trial. The initial approach was made to Foreman only four days after the Oswald slaying. Ruby's sister Mrs. Eileen Kaminsky later explained: "We wanted Foreman in the first place. We preferred Foreman to Belli. But Foreman was called by another lawyer [representing the Ruby family] and there was some misunderstanding about what part Foreman would take in the case. So we went with Belli."

Foreman himself explained that the intermediary, whom he declined to identify, called him four days after the slaying and asked him to defend Ruby. "I agreed to accept the case," he said. "But I made certain conditions. I was to be in complete charge. I was to be paid a reasonable fee. And I must be told where every dime came from. But the man told the Ruby family that I wanted four times the amount I cited to him, and the family decided they could not afford me. There seemed to be some feeling that I might represent Ruby for the publicity value of the case. But I told the family that I don't try cases for publicity; I try them for money."

In the next breath, however, Foreman made clear that financial arrangements were not paramount in his decision whether to accept a case. "I can afford to be choosy about my clients," he said. "If a case interests me, I'll take it—regardless of the money. If not, money will have to substitute for my interest."

The Ruby case clearly intrigued Foreman. But, because of the misunderstanding, it was Belli who served as chief counsel in the murder trial. And Belli, of course, lost the case. He not only lost; he infuriated Ruby and Ruby's relatives in the process. The family tried to fire him, but he resisted. Belli's trial tactics were subjected to heavy criticism not only by Ruby and his relatives, but also by bar-association officials, Texas Governor John Connally, State Attorney General Waggoner Carr and others. They objected particularly to Belli's use of the term "kangaroo court" in a tirade delivered after Ruby was convicted and sentenced to death. "Now we see the shame of Dallas in all its glory," Belli had cried in the courtroom. "Dallas is a festering sore."

This was the final straw for the Ruby family. On March 19, 1964, six days after the end of the trial, Ruby and his relatives dismissed Belli as chief counsel. In a letter sent to the California civil lawyer—the so-called "King of Torts"—Ruby charged that Belli had forced his way into the case in the first place. The letter, signed by Ruby and mailed by his sister Mrs. Eva Grant, criticized Belli's defense strategy—which relied chiefly on the theory that Ruby was suffering from epilepsy and was not in control of his senses when he shot Oswald.

Mrs. Grant told newsmen in Dallas: "We were dissatisfied with the defense presented by Mr. Belli and expressed shock [in the dismissal letter] at the tirade he delivered after the verdict." From Mexico City, where Belli was resting from his labors, came word that he felt he was being done an injustice. "I feel I did everything that could be done," he said. "I am not repentant. I did my utmost."

Meanwhile, in Houston, four members of the Ruby family were calling upon Percy Foreman. Mrs. Kaminsky and her brothers—Earl, Sam and Hyman—appealed to Foreman, at this late date, to take their brother's case on appeal. Foreman agreed. "I go where I'm needed most," he said. "And, right now, I can't think of anyone who needs my services more than Jack Ruby."

The problem presented him was more difficult than usual. Not only was this the murder case of the century, with all the attendant problems created by enormous publicity and hostility toward Ruby. More important was the fact that Foreman himself had not tried the case. Because of his almost flawless knowledge of the law, his trial work leans heavily on painstaking efforts to set up possible grounds for an appeal in case the client should be convicted. If the case comes up on appeal, Foreman stands a better than even chance of getting the conviction reversed. In this case, however, Foreman was faced with the problem of trying to pull Melvin Belli's chestnuts—not his own—out of the fire. And there were those who felt Belli had presented the case rather poorly.

If the Ruby family thought it was getting an attorney who would be easier to handle than Belli, it had another think coming. Foreman refused to criticize Belli's conduct of the case. And, when bar-association officials called for an investigation of Belli's performance in Dallas, Foreman responded that perhaps the bar officials should be investigated—for violating the legal canon that forbids attorneys to criticize each other's work.

Moreover, Foreman echoed Belli's criticism of the trial judge, Joe Brown. He called the trial "a comedy of errors." Speaking of Judge Brown, he said: "In one day he kept all the lawyers working thirteen and a half hours. Under California standards, that is three [trial] days in one. And, under Texas standards, it is two days in one. It was an exercise of ego of that judge. He wants to hold a hoop and make the lawyers jump through it. He's the ringmaster of the circus. Something ought to be done about it."

Something was being done about it. Percy Foreman was handling the appeal and he wasn't going to jump through a hoop for anybody. The Ruby family should have sensed that. Immediately after agreeing to take the case on appeal, Foreman served notice that he intended to be in complete charge. "I haven't been hired to work with anybody," he said. "I was hired to take charge of the appeal. If I think I can work with other lawyers [Belli's co-counsel], I will keep them."

Even before studying the trial transcript or meeting with his client, Foreman expressed confidence that the verdict could be overturned. "I wouldn't have taken the case if I didn't think I could reverse it," he said. "All I know about the case so far is what I have read in the papers. But, if I can get a new trial for Ruby, I don't think he will be electrocuted."

At first glance, Foreman saw at least two possible reversible errors in the case. "First of all, the court permitted people to sit on the jury who had seen the alleged homicide on television," he said. "Those people should have been stricken from the jury panel." (It is difficult to imagine how a jury could have been chosen by this criterion, since virtually every venireman had seen the slaying on TV—either "live" or by videotape. But that did not deter Foreman from arguing that Judge Brown had committed reversible error.) Moreover, Foreman contended the trial should have been moved from Dallas on a change of venue because of community hostility toward Ruby, though he conceded that this hostility was also strong in other parts of Texas and the nation.

"In the second place, Judge Brown admitted into evidence an oral statement made by Ruby while in jail," Foreman said. "That was a clear reversible error, in my judgment. Article 727 of the Texas Penal Code forbids introduction of such a statement unless it is in writing, signed by the defendant and witnessed. Ruby's statement was not in writing, was not signed by him and was not witnessed." (The statement, as quoted during the trial by a policeman, was a confession by Ruby that he had shot Oswald in order to prove that "Jews have guts.")

Foreman's entry into the Ruby case brought immediate predictions that the conviction would be reversed. Syndicated columnist Robert Ruark, a Foreman admirer, was among the leading forecasters.

> Jack Ruby is as good as out, the wise money says, because Percy Foreman is in [Ruark wrote]. Foreman is about as much of

> a cinch to spring the man who killed the man who was accused of killing Jack Kennedy as there is the possibility that bluebonnets will be blooming momentarily in Texas. . . . Foreman is the closest thing to William Fallon or, perhaps, Perry Mason, that exists today. And he is a Texan, a Bible-belter and a Confucius-quoter. He also drives the opposition up the wall. . . . The recently sacked Mr. Belli is a fine tort swinger, but he just doesn't swing like Percy. Mr. Foreman pays five dollars a copy for handkerchiefs as big as bathmats and, when Percy mops that leonine brow, the jury digs the anguish. It is doubtful that Jack Ruby will even be bothered by a lengthy second trial. Foreman is moving for a reversal, and even a lesser lawyer shouldn't have much trouble with that tiny detail.

Other commentators around the world were equally laudatory. In London, where Foreman had been given front-page treatment in a newspaper series several years earlier, there were new raves. Newspapers everywhere were particularly impressed with Foreman's record in defending women who had slain their husbands. As one paper noted: "During 1943, Foreman defended thirteen women clients accused of capital crimes. Of these, the maximum punishment assessed was a five-year suspended sentence."

However, these were "misdemeanor murders" in Foreman's book. The Ruby case was something else again. He immediately set to work on the preparation of a motion for a new trial. He flew to Dallas, conferred with Ruby at the jail, then began thirty-six hours of conferences with Melvin Belli's co-counsel, Joe Tonahill and Phil Burleson. (the Houston *Chronicle* dutifully noted that, if Foreman kept Tonahill in the case, Ruby would have "a huge defense," since Tonahill and Foreman each stood six foot four and weighed in the neighborhood of two hundred and fifty pounds.)

The basic strategy outlined by Foreman eventually was to result in a reversal of Ruby's conviction. But, by the time the appellate court ruled, Foreman had long since departed the scene. As a matter of fact, he served officially as Ruby's lawyer for a grand total of four days.

During those four days he became entangled in a bitter dispute with members of the Ruby family, though not Ruby himself, over the handling of the case. Apparently, the relatives had not taken seriously Foreman's demand that he be placed in sole charge of the case. The relatives wanted some control over Foreman. In addition, they wanted him to heed the counsel of a Dallas civil lawyer, Stanley Kaufman.

Rather than agree on a compromise, which he felt would work to his client's detriment, Foreman quit. Despite his statement four days earlier that Ruby needed him more than anyone else, Foreman now announced: "I just think I could make my time more valuable elsewhere."

Foreman said he had reached his decision to quit after his lengthy conferences with Tonahill and Burleson. Exhausted from working two days with hardly any sleep, and from arguing with Ruby's relatives, he had sagged into bed. "As I lay in bed, it suggested itself to me that I ought to withdraw from the case," he told reporters. He said he could never accept the system of split control insisted upon by the family. "I'm not accustomed to representing five or six people," he said. "Jack Ruby and I get along fine. But . . . the family is a close-knit corporation. I will not criticize my client or his family. I only criticize the system of divided authority. No criminal lawyer with integrity can let a civil lawyer or a layman tell him what to do, especially when a man's life is at stake."

After conferring with Ruby initially, Foreman had said: "I certainly hope to reverse the sentence. But it would be presumptuous of me to make a prediction. . . . I am no miracle man. I carry no script and no bag of tricks." Now, he said that he felt Ruby had been "barbecued" in the murder trial, that he thought the conviction could be upset, that he wanted to help upset it, but that he could not remain in the case under the prevailing conditions. "When I get into a case, I represent the client," he said. "I don't represent five or six people."

He could not bring himself to tell Ruby in person of his resignation. "I couldn't take it to see that poor wretched person I saw yesterday up there in the jail, with the inability to understand why he's there," Foreman said. Instead, he sent Ruby a letter explaining his decision to withdraw:

> Your sister, Mrs. Eva Grant, insists on retaining and exercising the general power of attorney [obtained] from you. Attorney Kaufman . . . thinks criminal cases should be tried as he tries civil cases. I do not agree with his opinion. Both attorney Kaufman and Mrs. Grant believe that your attorney should not answer questions of the news media except with "no comment." I do not agree with this, especially in your case. The peculiar facts of your case make it necessary that the public know whatever facts might mitigate the offense. You were tried and convicted in the news media before you were in court. Both convictions ought to be set aside. Change in public opinion may help bring about a reversal in the appellate courts.

Foreman made it clear that money matters had nothing to do with his decision to quit. "You don't owe me a cent," he wrote Ruby. "There is no possibility that you and I could not agree on a fee and a method of payment. When a human life is at stake, there should be no quibbling about money."

The announcement of Foreman's resignation set off a panic in the Ruby camp. Ruby's brother Earl telephoned Foreman from Detroit and said he was flying back to Texas to try to straighten out the dispute. Jack Ruby himself asked Foreman to reconsider. Others echoed this plea. But Foreman held fast. He said he could not work in the type of "double harness" proposed by the family. "I cannot change my position," he insisted.

He kept his word. Despite numerous appeals, he refused to return as chief counsel. He emphasized, however, that he was willing to serve unofficially as an adviser to the attorneys eventually assigned to carry the appeal through the courts. In the end, he did make suggestions on the handling of the appeal—suggestions that were to help upset the conviction and death sentence. Ruby, of course, was never retried. He died of natural causes before his second trial could begin.

It was a measure of Percy Foreman's stature that he could afford to walk out on a case as important as Ruby's. But it was also characteristic of the man. He had quit celebrated cases before and would do so again.

What was perhaps more significant was the fact that Foreman would be remembered by many for his participation in the cases of General Walker, Lee Oswald and Jack Ruby, although he had been involved only briefly with all three. Like the hired gun of the Old West, Foreman has time only for the major assignments. He does not, as a rule, mess around with small fry. He does not, as a rule, sign on for the long haul. He comes in, does the job he is hired to do, then moves on to fresh pastures. He sometimes leaves in his wake difficult appeals—to be handled by other lawyers.

This practice does not always endear him to judges, clients and fellow attorneys. But Foreman has never tried to win any popularity contests. He accepts each case as a challenge. The bigger the challenge, the better he likes it.

And, when he says, "I go where I'm needed most," he is not merely boasting. He means every word of it.

7

> A criminal lawyer is like an eminent surgeon performing a delicate brain operation. The surgeon is concerned with technique—not the individual on the table. The patient is incidental. This stuff about a lawyer wanting to save an innocent man from the electric chair is bunk. He's worrying about technique, the same as the surgeon is concerned with where to put the knife without severing an artery. The satisfaction comes from doing the job well—not from saving the man from the electric chair.
>
> JUDGE SAMUEL S. LEIBOWITZ

JUST WHAT is the Percy Foreman technique? What is it that sets him apart not only from run-of-the-mill defense lawyers, but even from the other great ones?

There are nearly as many answers to these questions as there are persons to be interviewed on the subject. Though he has many of the attributes of other famed trial lawyers—the hard-boiled nature of Sam Leibowitz himself, the fantastic memory of Edward Bennett Williams, the flamboyance of Bill Fallon, the homespun-philosopher style of Clarence Darrow and the quiet confidentiality of Max Steuer (who whispered into jurors' ears)—Foreman has not consciously copied any of these men.

Almost any expert questioned about Foreman invariably mentions one elementary ingredient of his style: when he enters the courtroom, he knows more about the case than anyone else. It is this knowledge—the result of hour upon hour of behind-the-scenes preparation—which enables Foreman to be such a tiger at cross-examination. His quick mind helps, of course. But far more important is his awareness of the background of every witness, every officer, every attorney, every judge, every juror involved in the case. Such awareness, coupled with a sixth sense that is the trademark of every fine trial lawyer, enables him to gauge almost instinctively when to hammer, when to coddle, when to feign boredom.

At the heart of each Foreman case is his pretrial work. Whenever possible, he rushes to his client's side immediately after the purported offense is committed. If he arrives sufficiently early, he reasons, he can prevent the client from making incriminating statements to investigating officers. In addition, Foreman himself wants to view the evidence—the crime scene, the blood (if necessary) and the exhibits—while they are fresh. He also wants to get his client out on bail, if possible, at the earliest possible time. He sometimes manages to arrive on the scene before the police. It is not uncommon for him—*à la* Perry Mason—to surrender a client who has somehow eluded capture.

Once the preliminary matters such as bail are arranged, Foreman may take only a passing personal interest in the case for weeks or months. He may be in another state. But his people—private investigators, attorneys hired by Foreman and others—are working and keeping him posted. Necessary pretrial motions are filed. Finally, the preparations are finished. The trial begins.

As any law student knows, jury selection is at once among the most boring and yet most important aspects of trial work. Foreman is a master of the art. He leaves no base uncovered in his search for the perfect juror—that is, the juror most likely to acquit. He spares his client no expense in investigating the background of each likely prospect. He questions each closely, maintaining his interest long after opposing attorneys have grown weary of the examination.

As he explained in 1965 to a Houston *Post* reporter, Harold Scarlett, Foreman even makes use of his old shoeshine-boy experience when assessing prospective jurors. Since the days when he was shining shoes in Livingston, Foreman has believed that a man's shoes say something about his character. "I still look at the shoes when a juror passes my chair going to the witness stand," he told Scarlett. "I look for comfortable shoes—not tight shoes with sharp toes." He also makes careful notes on prospective jurors' mannerisms, such as the way they walk. "I like easygoing walkers—not those who march in like Prussian generals," he says.

To learn how jurors think, Foreman made it a practice as a young lawyer to sit in a clerk's office adjoining the jury room during deliberation periods. Since the walls were paper thin, he could hear what was being said next door. On the basis of such eavesdropping, he drew conclusions on how to pick jurors the next time and how to avoid making the same trial mistake twice.

Once, Foreman went so far as to sit in a men's room next door to a jury chamber for hours, taking shorthand notes on the deliberations. (Among other ways in which he earned pocket money during his early years was as a shorthand stenographer and typist. He remains proficient at both skills today and takes pride in them. They also come in handy to a man who has only one girl Friday as his entire permanent staff.)

Foreman's theories on jury selection vary with the particular defense strategy he plans to employ. For example, in choosing a jury in a murder case where self-defense will be the plea, he looks for people who have come up through the school of hard knocks. "I want jurors in such cases who have worked with people, rather than things—people who can look behind the facts and understand what makes a man do what he does," Foreman says. Thus, in such a case, he would choose a truck driver, waiter or salesman over an engineer, accountant or draftsman. "If a man has never been in a bar—or was brought up in a home where a deck of cards wasn't allowed—he may not be able to understand some bully who gets full of beer and then gets killed when he tries to whip the biggest man in the place."

However, when the case involves such matters as an insanity plea, complex psychiatric testimony or a delicate legal question, Foreman prefers college graduates as jurors. His reason is based on simple logic. The college graduates are better able to understand the evidence in such cases.

Under no circumstances will Foreman knowingly choose as a juror anyone who has ever served as a member of what he describes as "the constabulary." He explains: "What makes a good law-enforcement officer, of itself and necessarily, makes a poor juror. A good officer is taught and trained to believe that anybody can be guilty until he proves himself innocent." The reason Foreman is so adamant on this point is that he once violated his own rule, and his client paid the price—albeit a light one—for the miscalculation. In this case Foreman, against his better judgment, permitted a former sheriff to sit on the jury. He had been told the ex-officer was the most humane man in the community—a man who went so far as to post bonds for indigent prisoners he arrested. When the jury began its deliberations, everyone except the former sheriff voted for acquittal. Several more votes were taken, each eleven to one for acquittal. But the ex-lawman was insistent. He would vote for nothing except conviction. In the end the other eleven swung around to his way of thinking, although they did persuade him to let Foreman's client off with a suspended sentence. Nonetheless, the client went through life with that felony conviction on his record.

As a rule, Foreman prefers married persons as jurors. He feels that bachelors and spinsters lack compassion. "Often they are single because they just don't like mankind, especially the spinsters," he says. "And, in a trial, there's nobody they can hurt except the defendant."

Conversely, Foreman feels, someone who has been divorced once or more may be more sympathetic than the average juror to a defendant accused of bumping off his or her spouse. In a murder case—or any case where a long prison term is possible—he prefers older jurors to youths. "A young man or woman is apt to give a much longer sentence than a person to whom time means more," he explains. "You rarely find a seventy-year-old juror giving a thirty-year or forty-year prison term."

National origin and religion also play important roles in Foreman's jury-selecting strategy. "Religion is important as an indicator of the juror's genealogical concepts—his racial and tribal characteristics," Foreman says. "It's not the religion itself. I would challenge Hans Sternberg, a Lutheran, just as quickly if he were a Baptist or a Methodist—just because of his Teutonic name." He feels Germans, because of their history of devotion to authority (even totalitarian authority), make poor jurors for the defense cause.

Foreman's favorite jurors are members of long-oppressed minorities. He particularly favors Jewish jurors, saying their "long history as the underdog" makes them sympathetic to underdog defendants. He also likes Negro jurors, except when the defendant is a Negro—the theory being that Negroes sometimes show less compassion for their outlaw brethren than white jurors might. The Irish (described by Foreman as generally "tolerant, long-suffering, able to identify") and various Latins such as Mexican-Americans, Italians, Spaniards and Frenchmen ("most are warm-blooded and sympathetic") are other Foreman favorites.

Beyond his general prejudices, Foreman depends heavily on his questioning of veniremen in choosing those privileged few who will be permitted to sit in judgment on his client. He strives to get inside each prospect, to take him apart and find out what makes him angry, sad, ecstatic or bored.

"The way a man answers a question is a helluva lot more important than what he says," Foreman explains. "For example, in a case that involves drinking, you may ask whether he's ever belonged to the WCTU—and there are some male members—and his smile may tell you that he takes a drink himself now and then."

In almost every case, Foreman asks the question, "Would the fact that I am the defense attorney in this case prejudice you or influence your verdict in any way?" Not infrequently, the prospective juror answers in the affirmative. But that does not always mean Foreman will excuse him. In one celebrated murder case, Foreman asked a man if he knew him by reputation.

"Yes," the veniremen said.

"Would you be prejudiced by what you know about me?"

"Yes, because you are a shyster. They wouldn't hire you unless they were guilty."

"I'll accept this juror," Foreman announced to a stunned audience. "He's an honest man."

In the end, this juror held out—against others who favored a stiffer penalty—for a five-year suspended sentence. His view prevailed. The defendant walked out of court a free man, subject only to probation conditions.

When the jurors have been seated, Foreman affects a disinterested attitude during presentation of the prosecution opening statement. He has heard it all before, he implies, and it is not only false but dull. Often, he does not make an opening statement, preferring to save it until the conclusion of the state's case.

During the presentation of state's evidence, once again, he seems bored by it all. He has been rumored to doze off from time to time. Whether he is actually asleep, or just pretending, is a secret known only to himself. But let the prosecutor stray from established procedure just once and Foreman is on his feet with an objection. Sometimes he leaps up. More often he pulls himself aloft, as if it is a great struggle to drag his huge frame out of the chair. He stands patiently, arms crossed, waiting to be recognized. Occasionally, his hand sweeps through his unkempt hair, struggling to keep it out of his eyes. By the time he is ready to speak, he has achieved the desired effect. All eyes are on him.

Most often his objection is: "Your Honor, we don't object to the question, but we do object to the form of the question." Translation: Mr. Prosecutor, won't you ever learn your trade?

Sometimes Foreman even becomes so helpful as to suggest the proper way to ask the question. "Now, if he wanted to ask it this way, we'd have no objection," he tells the judge on such occasions. Usually, out of sheer obstinacy and/or self-pride, the prosecutor will refuse. But there have been times when a grateful prosecutor has accepted Foreman's suggestion word for word. Once, in a case where a prosecutor was posing a delicate question of a woman who had mutilated herself in order to make it appear that she had given birth, Foreman's objections got the DA so befuddled that he was forced to ask for a recess. After taking a breather, he sent for a law book and then proceeded to read his question verbatim from the text.

It is as a cross-examiner of opposition witnesses that Foreman reaches the heights of brilliance. As many prosecutors put it: "Percy does everything well in the courtroom—but he's just the best goddam cross-examiner in the business."

In one case, Foreman was confronted by a prosecution witness who was a convict. The convict claimed he had "discovered God" while in the Arkansas State Penitentiary, had taken seventy correspondence courses in the Scriptures and been ordained by a ministerial school in Ohio. His testimony, unless rebutted, would have been particularly damaging to Foreman's defense.

On cross-examination, Foreman asked: "You say you are now a student of the Holy Writ?"

"Sir, I don't understand this," the convict replied.

Q. You are a student of the Bible?

A. Yes, sir.

Q. Have you studied about a character in there by the name of Ananias?

A. I certainly have.

Q. Have you or not modeled your ministry after the individual?

A. No, sir, I have not.

Q. Who was Ananias?

A. Sir, I will preach you a sermon if you would like to hear one.

Q. Preach it on Ananias.

The judge interrupted: "Just answer the question. We do not want a sermon. Just answer the question." By this time the witness had forgotten the question—or pretended to—but Foreman had not.

Q. Tell the jury who was Ananias.

A. At this time, sir, I couldn't tell you.

This was the answer Foreman had been seeking. He stood straight up, as if shocked by the ignorance of this "minister." Then, in a booming voice aimed at the jury box, he proclaimed: "He is the biggest liar in all antiquity! Does that help you any?"

"No, sir," the witness said.

Q. How old are you?

A. I am forty-four years old.

Q. How many crimes have you been convicted of?

A. Approximately eight.

Q. Do you mean eight felonies?

A. No, sir.

Q. Eight crimes?

A. Eight crimes.

Q. In how many states?

A. Most all—I have been convicted in Oklahoma, Oregon. I was in Leavenworth, Kansas. . . .

Q. Wait just a minute. You were convicted in Oklahoma? You were convicted in Oregon?

A. Yes.

Q. Is Leavenworth another distinct . . . ?

A. Yes, this is [a federal case originating] in Arkansas.

Q. Go ahead.

A. In New Orleans, St. Louis, New York, in Arkansas two different times and Oklahoma two different times.

Q. That would be at least ten, would it not?

A. I said approximately eight convictions.

Q. Does approximately eight mean anywhere from eight to eighteen?

The prosecutor broke in to say: "That is argumentative." But the judge directed the witness to answer. The witness hesitated, as if ashamed to reply.

But Foreman hammered at him again: "Would you tell us, does approximately eight mean anywhere from eight to eighteen?"

The witness flushed, then conceded: "Sir, I have been arrested some fifty times, but not convicted . . . [in all fifty cases]."

That was what Foreman had been seeking. He knew in advance the man's criminal record. The fifty arrests, with at least ten convictions, plus his efforts to pass himself off as a man who had "found God" in the penitentiary, destroyed his credibility as a witness. Foreman's client was acquitted.

Not only witnesses, but prosecutors as well, fall into traps set for them by Foreman. As previously pointed out, Foreman considered A. C. Winborn—the Houston DA who later became a judge—as one of his most talented adversaries. Winborn was a tough trial lawyer, but his jury speeches were so lyrical that they moved spectators to tears. During one such speech, in a case against Foreman, the defense lawyer brought a stenographer into court to take down in shorthand every word uttered by Winborn.

Foreman lost that case. But, a few months later, he got another chance against Winborn. He had the stenographer type up a transcript of Winborn's previous jury speech. He then proceeded to memorize it. In the second trial, after all the evidence had been offered, Foreman rose to address the jury.

"Gentlemen, the district attorney has a wonderful speech he always uses at what are considered big trials," Foreman told the jurors. "It goes this way. . . ." He then delivered, verbatim, Winborn's pet speech.

Sure enough, Winborn had planned to use that very speech again. He was left without a closing argument and with egg on his face. He made a courageous effort to improvise, but it fell flat. As one Houston newspaperman, Jack Donahue (now a novelist and scenarist), wrote: "Mr. Winborn had to start from scratch, and scratch ain't quite good enough when Percy is your opponent." Foreman, needless to say, won the case.

Foreman, like Bill Fallon and indeed Perry Mason, is a master at the courtroom demonstration. Once, he defended a woman liquor-store operator accused of murdering a policeman. At the outset of the trial there seemed little doubt the woman would be convicted. The only question seemed to be whether she would go to the electric chair or get off with a life sentence.

Foreman did not dispute the prosecution's contention that his client had shot the policeman to death. But he claimed that the shooting had been a case of self-defense—that the woman had been involved in a struggle with several officers at the time the fatal shot was fired. He brought in two detectives who had been involved in the struggle. He got them to demonstrate, using Foreman himself to represent the woman, how they had pulled her hands behind her back during the fracas. It made a vivid scene. But that was only the beginning.

Throughout the trial, Foreman had referred frequently to a plaster mould of a woman's head. His objective was to show that his client had been clubbed on the head during the brawl. Finally, he put on the stand a detective who had clubbed the woman. The detective admitted striking her in the head with his gun butt.

"Show us how you did it," Foreman directed.

The detective hesitated. But Foreman persisted. Pointing at the plaster mould, he repeated: "Show us how you did it."

The detective drew his pistol from his holster, approached the mould and tapped it ever so gingerly. Of course, as Foreman had known it would, the mould broke apart and clattered to the floor in hundreds of pieces.

When the jury retired, it took only minutes to bring in a verdict: Not guilty!

On another occasion, Foreman represented a one-legged safecracker. The man's missing leg had been shot off in a gun battle. Between safecracking engagements, the client appeared as a spectator at prizefights and other sporting events—wearing an artificial leg and a dazzling array of clothing. He showed few signs that the artificial leg interfered with his social life. But, when Foreman represented him in court, the safecracker showed up in tattered clothing—minus the artificial leg. Most days, he hobbled into court on crutches. One day, Foreman even went so far as to carry him into court and place him in his chair. A sympathetic jury acquitted him.

Those who say Foreman will stop at virtually nothing to win a case invariably point to his representation of an accused pimp named Michael S. Coury. On October 6, 1961, a pretty, nineteen-year-old bookkeeper named Carol Jean Joseph signed a written statement for Houston police, accusing Coury of operating a call-girl service, forcing her to work as a fifty-dollar-a-day prostitute and beating her when she tried to quit. Coury, twenty-seven, was later indicted on charges of pandering and aggravated assault. Miss Joseph, of course, was scheduled to be the chief prosecution witness at his trial. Coury retained Foreman to defend him.

On December 29, however, the state's case fell apart. For on that date, with Foreman's blessing, Coury married Miss Joseph. And, of course, a wife cannot be compelled to testify against her husband.

"CALL GIRL CAN'T BE USED AS WITNESS; MARRIES ACCUSED MAN," summed up the Houston *Chronicle* headline. The accompanying story pointed out that Percy Foreman, smiling "like a father at a wedding reception," had announced the nuptials. Foreman adamantly denied that the marriage had been contrived to circumvent the law. "I'm sure they didn't give any thought to the legal consequences," he said. "This was simply a case of true love taking its course."

True love or not, the wedding got Coury off the legal hook.

It is episodes such as the Coury-Joseph wedding that put Foreman in the headlines as often as not. But the basic secret to his success as a trial lawyer rests neither in tricks nor in histrionics. It rests in ordinary hard work. Men half his age marvel at his stamina.

"He has more energy than any living man I ever saw," says one of Foreman's most frequent opponents, Assistant DA Conrad Castles of Houston. "He can wear out a prosecutor and wear out a judge. Then he goes across the street to the Old Capitol Club—where he has clients stashed away in almost every booth—and goes right on working on other cases. You've got to battle him. If you don't draw a line, he'll run you right out of the courtroom."

Foreman's aggressive courtroom tactics frequently arouse the ire of relatives and friends of his clients' purported victims. Such was the case in the fall of 1960 when he represented Jessie Glenwood Turner, a fifty-seven-year-old truck driver from Foreman's hometown. Turner stood accused of murder with malice in the slaying of Earl Albert Smith, fifty, during a fracas at a roadside fireworks stand just north of Houston. The slaying had occurred on Christmas Eve, 1957.

All the pathos of a holiday-season tragedy was spelled out by the prosecution. Adding to the drama was the presence in the courtroom of Smith's widow, Mrs. Katherine Smith Ainsworth (she had remarried following the slaying), and his nine-year-old son, Darty. Foreman did not dispute the fact that Smith had, indeed, been shot to death by Turner. In fact, he agreed to enter a plea of guilty on Turner's behalf to a reduced charge of murder without malice. The prosecution, rather than take the chance of losing the case to Foreman, consented to reduce the charge. Thus, the issue became not whether Turner was guilty, but how he should be punished.

Both the prosecution and the defense produced evidence aimed at helping Judge Sam Davis decide on a proper sentence. The presence of the victim's widow and son did not deter Foreman from presenting a rock'em-sock'em case. In typical fashion, he attempted to put someone other than his client—namely the victim—"on trial."

He produced evidence that Smith, during an argument with Turner at the fireworks stand, had taken off Turner's eyeglasses and slapped him across the face. Only then, according to the evidence, did Turner pull a .22-caliber pistol. At sight of the weapon, Smith fled across a plowed field. Turner chased him. As they ran, Smith turned to look back at his pursuer. Just then, Turner fired. The bullet struck Smith in the chest, killing him.

Foreman called numerous witnesses who testified to the good character of the defendant. By contrast, he introduced evidence that Smith had a substantial police record, including three prison sentences. When this evidence was offered, Smith's son turned to his mother and said plaintively: "You never told me, Mama."

The introduction of her late husband's criminal record infuriated Mrs. Ainsworth. She grew even more irate when she heard the sentence decided upon by Judge Davis—a five-year suspended term that permitted Turner to avoid serving even a day of prison time.

As Percy Foreman walked from the courtroom, Mrs. Ainsworth rushed up to him and shouted: "You may be a great lawyer, Mr. Foreman, but you have turned a killer free! There was no justice here today!"

Foreman heard her out, then asked: "Are you through?"

"The only thing I have to say to you is that you won't get to heaven," Mrs. Ainsworth sobbed.

"Well, if you get there before I do, tell 'em I'm coming, too, whether they let me in or not," Foreman retorted. As usual, he got the last word.

Actually, the verbal abuse Foreman received from Mrs. Ainsworth was mild compared with the treatment he sometimes gets from angry litigants. Less than a year after the Turner trial, for example, he had a heavy plastic pocketbook hurled at him by the former wife of one of his clients. Foreman was in the process of arranging a property settlement in their divorce case when the woman—furious because she was losing custody of her two daughters—threw the purse at Foreman in a courtroom. It hit Foreman's shoulder, then dropped to a table. Foreman picked it up, smashed it against the table and walked out of the courtroom holding the remnants.

Someone asked: "What are you going to do with those?"

"Keep them for mementoes," he replied.

Even this incident was mild compared to some. As will be discussed in a later chapter, Foreman has been physically attacked more than once for his spirited defense tactics, suffering at least one beating at the hands of peace officers in a courthouse. His tart tongue is simply more than some men can bear.

Once, when a prosecutor named Lee Ward complained to a judge that "someone has been tampering with my witness," Foreman challenged him to present to a grand jury any evidence he had of such tampering.

"I would if I could," Ward replied. "But some people are just too slick."

Foreman turned to face the packed courtroom, smiled and replied in a booming voice: "Mr. Ward, most anybody is too slick for you."

Bedlam erupted. It seemed that a brawl was imminent. But the judge restored order by threatening to clear the courtroom. Ward lost his cool and later lost his case.

Sometimes a witness will try to joust with Foreman. Invariably, the witness winds up on the short end of the joust. A onetime Agriculture Department employee, Mrs. Mona Jean Craft, found that out when she matched wits with Foreman in a trial resulting from a series of acreage-allotment scandals. This exchange summed up her problem.

Foreman: Did you talk with any government attorneys during the lunch break?

Mrs. Craft: Yes.

Foreman: Well, did Mr. Jackson [federal prosecutor William Jackson] tell you not to make faces at me? Did he tell you not to be so arrogant, not to be so smart-alecky and not to answer questions in a manner so as to alienate the jury—as you were doing this morning?

Mrs. Craft (tartly): Well, he told me to be calm and to control my temper because "you can't outsmart that guy."

Her answer brought down the house. Foreman, satisfied, moved on to question her on the matters at hand. Mrs. Craft, though it seemed an effort, followed the prosecutor's advice.

On more than one occasion, Foreman has been accused by a witness of "trying to make a fool of me." He has a pat answer. "You're wrong," he says. "I'm not making a fool of you. I merely ask the questions. You answer them. And the jury draws its own conclusions."

Such repartee, while entertaining, has a serious place in the Foreman style. If he can draw attention away from his client or the crime, he is ahead of the game. The more the prosecution emphasizes the heinousness of the crime, the more Foreman tries to bring other matters to the fore. The more the prosecution hammers at his client, the more he bombards the state's witnesses. Sarcasm is one of his most effective weapons.

However, when the time comes for his jury summation, levity becomes a sometime thing. By and large, he prefers to affect a solemn air. A man's life is at stake, he emphasizes, and lives are not to be played with like toys.

As previously pointed out, Foreman faces the jury holding a legal pad that is either bare or carries only a few notes. He looks directly into the jury box, staring in turn into the eyes of one juror after another. Usually, he has decided in advance how each juror is likely to vote—and he patterns his performance accordingly. He "plays" to those jurors he believes need the most persuasion.

His assessment of juror attitudes is based on a close scrutiny of the jury box throughout the trial. Just as he could tell in his chautauqua days whether an audience was friendly or hostile, he can usually tell after forty years before the bar whether a juror is sympathetic or unsympathetic. (On those rare occasions when he learns he has guessed wrong, he is noticeably upset. One such error, *Life* magazine correspondent Marshall Smith wrote in 1966, made Foreman feel as badly "as he had the time years before when he mixed his Biblical references and pictured Abel killing Cain." The miscalculation to which Smith referred, however, was a happy one for Foreman's client. Foreman had feared a certain juror would vote for conviction. But the juror had argued for acquittal from the beginning and had helped win Foreman's case for him.)

In his summation, Foreman begins with a recapitulation of the evidence. He recalls the testimony of both the prosecution and the defense witnesses. Though he presents it in the best possible light for his client, he does not disregard the damaging testimony. Instead, he rebuts it. The witness was mistaken, lying or both, he implies. Eyewitness testimony, in particular, is a pet target of his scorn. Could the witness really have seen what he said he saw? Wasn't the lighting poor? Didn't the witness have poor eyesight? And what about the other witnesses? Their testimony didn't jibe with that of the key prosecution witness, did it?

Another favorite target is his client's confession, if there has been one. The confession was not a confession at all, Foreman will insist. It certainly was not a legal confession, for it was coerced, through physical or mental torture. Or it was fabricated. Or it was not in writing. Or it was not signed. Or it was not witnessed. Or it was taken before the client was permitted to call an attorney.

These are not capricious claims. Foreman, as has been pointed out previously, believes the taking of purported confessions from defendants is rarely done in accordance with either the Constitution or pertinent court decisions. Even when it is done in such manner, however, he attacks the confession. If he cannot find any other way, he will try to persuade the jury that the purported crime was not carried out in the way it was described in the confession. Therefore, the confession must be disregarded. Or so he says.

The police are almost always on the receiving end of Foreman's tongue-lashings before the jury. He is careful not to attack law-enforcement agencies as institutions. He makes clear his respect for the law and its representatives. But the incompetence, brutality and venality of individual officers are something else. He attacks them with all the vigor at his command.

"Who wouldn't have confessed if faced with these men in a small room?" he will ask. "Who wouldn't have confessed—even to something he did not do—to keep these men from 'persuading' him?"

As he approaches the end of his summation, Foreman usually turns from the specific facts of the case to the more general facts—and emotions—responsible for bringing his client before the bar. Did the client come from an impoverished background? Did he fight his way up through the rough-and-tumble of life, only to meet prejudice because of his humble beginnings? Did he hold his frustrations in check for years, then lash out at society in one irrational burst of emotion? Was he tormented by his wife, employer, community? Was he deranged? Did he act to protect himself, his family, his home? In short, was his crime—if a crime at all—justifiable or understandable?

Foreman's argument is aimed at creating more than the "reasonable doubt" required by law. He wants not only legal, but moral, doubts in the jurors' minds. And it is most commonly an emotional, rather than an intellectual, appeal that will place such doubts there.

Thus, Foreman's final words usually are highly emotional. Typically, they will sound the theme: "Send this poor, unfortunate man back where he belongs—with his wife and children."

More often than not, jurors heed Foreman's plea. When they do not, all is not lost. For the trial is only the first round. And, whether Foreman handles the appeal himself or passes that chore on to another lawyer, he ordinarily has seen to it that the record contains at least one error—and frequently dozens—that can bring a reversal. In that case, barring an outright dismissal of the charges, a new trial is set.

Years may pass in the meantime. Prosecutors, judges, witnesses may come and go. But, even if he does not handle the appeal personally, the chances are that Foreman will be back at the defense table when the second trial begins—a little older, perhaps a little more cranky, but also a little wiser. The mistakes he made the first time, if any, will not be repeated.

And the prosecutor will have to battle him every step of the way. For Conrad Castles' warning that you must draw the line or Foreman "will run you out of the courtroom" becomes even more true the second time around.

8

Candy is dandy;
But, for mercy, yells: "Percy."
ANONYMOUS
(*with apologies to Ogden Nash*)

"IT WAS JUST a li'l ole misdemeanor-murder case down in Florida," Percy Foreman said more than once. It was hardly that. It was, in fact, the case that brought Foreman as much national and international fame as nearly any other.

Officially, it went by the prosaic heading of Criminal Proceeding 2244 in the Dade County Courthouse in Miami. But, to millions, it was simply "The Candy Case." Mrs. Candace (Candy) Mossler and her nephew Melvin Lane Powers stood accused of murdering Candy's multimillionaire husband in order to spend their post-slaying years making whoopee with his money. It was a lurid, messy, sensational case. It had all the elements essential for fascinating the public—sex, violence, money, conflict. And, beyond that, it had Percy Foreman.

How did it all begin? Except for Candy and Mel, who were not saying, nobody could be sure. And, to hear their side of it from

Foreman and others, even they did not know. That being neither here nor there, nobody could hope to understand this God-awful case without first attempting to understand its enigmatic major characters—Candy and Mel. Of the two, the more intriguing was clearly Candy.

Just who was Candy Mossler? Whence did she spring? How high did she rise? How low did she sink? And why? Always, the elusive why? These were the questions that were most pertinent—and most often unanswered—about the case.

Even the most fundamental questions about Candy posed riddles. For example, there was the matter of her age. Birth records indicated that she was born Candace Grace Weatherby on February 18, 1920, in Buchanan, Georgia. But Candy insisted that the records were wrong and that she was really born on February 18, 1927—which would have made her only thirty-nine when she stood trial.

With the date thus remaining in a state of limbo, it is agreed that Candy was indeed born at Buchanan, the sixth of twelve children. Her father, L. S. (Lonny) Weatherby, was a farmer.

Candy endured a difficult childhood. When she was eight, her mother died during childbirth. Her father later suffered a breakdown and drifted out of her life. As a result, she was reared by her grandfathers. One of them was a local banker. The other, who made a greater mark on her upbringing, was the Reverend Cary Brennan, the local bishop of the Mormon Church. Bishop Brennan took major responsibility for rearing Candy, who even then was a beautiful girl with long golden hair.

A year after her mother's death, Candy was stricken with polio. She was unconscious for several weeks. And, when she came to, she found herself paralyzed below the waist. For a little girl who had begun ballet lessons and dreamed of being a dancer, the paralysis was heartbreaking. It was during this period, as an underdog battling the vicissitudes of life, that Candy developed a sense of compassion for the beleaguered. It would remain with her in later life, no matter how warped her sense of values would become.

With the help of Bishop Brennan, Candy made a slow recovery.

But one leg remained crippled and twisted for a long period. "One day my grandfather came into my room with a pair of ballet slippers he had bought me," she recalls. "He had got them two sizes too big because he figured my feet would grow that much before I could wear them. He put them on a shelf where I could see them from my bed. And he told me, 'Candy, you'll dance again.' "

Each day Candy stared at those slippers and became increasingly determined to make her grandfather's prediction come true. It would be five years before she could walk normally again, much less dance. But, in the meantime, she returned to school. Her brothers took turns carrying her to school on their backs. When she was fourteen, she put on the ballet slippers and began dancing again. Her leg grew stronger and straighter. Eventually, it would be virtually impossible to detect a limp.

Candy never finished high school. At the urging of Bishop Brennan and other relatives, she dropped out of school after the eleventh grade to marry a civil engineer named Norman A. Johnson. The wedding took place in 1939. (Thus, if one accepts Candy's version of her age, she would have been married at the age of twelve.) She and her husband soon moved to his hometown of Anniston, Alabama. Their first child, Norman, Jr., was born four years after the wedding. Their second, Rita, was born a year after that.

Again, illness struck—this time immobilizing Candy's husband. When Johnson was unable to work, Candy supported the family. She went to New York, studied fashion designing and became one of the youngest fashion designers in the city. Later, she turned to modeling for photographers, specializing in advertising assignments that capitalized on her dazzling smile. Her good looks carried her a long way, long enough to pay her husband's medical bills and care for the children.

The marriage, however, was doomed to failure. Candy had been too young to marry, and Johnson was a good deal older. In 1947, after her husband had recuperated and moved to Canada to take an engineering assignment, he and Candy agreed upon a friendly divorce. Candy kept the children.

She moved next to New Orleans, where she figured the lower cost of living would enable her to rear the children in better style. Within two years she had several flourishing businesses and was making her mark on the social life of the swinging Crescent City. Her business ventures included a finishing school, a modeling school and a modeling agency.

"I was doing so well I had time for art and culture," Candy recalls. Thus, she offered to help raise funds for the New Orleans Grand Opera Company. She was given a list of prominent New Orleans executives and was asked to call upon them. One of those on the list was Jacques Mossler.

Mossler originally came from much more deprived circumstances than the woman who would become his wife and eventually would be accused of participating in his murder. He was born in 1895 to an impoverished couple in a Jewish ghetto in Rumania. His real name, Jakella Moscovitz, was changed to Jacques Mossler after the family emigrated to the United States. Settling first in Buffalo, New York, the family later moved to the lower East Side of Manhattan and still later to Chicago.

It was after the move to Chicago in 1910 that Mossler first started earning money. He worked initially as a candy salesman on commuter trains. Later, he bought a used car for 125 dollars. He repaired it and sold it for 200 dollars. That was the start of a career—selling and financing the sale of automobiles—that would make him a millionaire by the time he met Candy.

At the age of seventeen, Mossler moved to New Orleans and opened a used-car lot. He prospered. When the United States entered World War I, he was drafted. But he did not let his military service interfere with the operation of his business. He married his girl friend, gave her a twenty-percent share of the business, gave another twenty percent to his older brother Marcu (who temporarily abandoned an engineering career to help run the car lot) and kept sixty percent for himself. Thus, when he returned from the war, Mossler had an even bigger business waiting for him

From selling cars, he branched into financing their sale. He opened a loan company designed to facilitate installment-plan auto sales. Next came commercial-banking ventures.

His first marriage broke up, leaving him with memories, four daughters and a lot of money. He expanded his operations to Texas, establishing the Mossler Acceptance Corporation in Houston. Money begat money and companies begat other companies. Mossler bought large blocks of stock in two of Texas' major insurance companies, then bought controlling interest in the Allen-Parker Company, a leading auto-finance firm. From Texas he moved into Florida, acquiring control of a Miami bank. Next came control of an Indiana bank and major stock ownership in a Chicago bank. The lure of further profits carried him abroad, where he bought a loan company in Frankfurt, Germany.

But Mossler could not get by on money alone. He was lonely. He yearned for companionship. This yearning was at its height when he met Candy Weatherby Johnson.

Candy had the figure "$350" next to Mossler's name on her list of potential contributors to the grand-opera company. But, when she visited his office, she found him reluctant to make a donation. He said he gave generously to his favorite causes, but that opera was not one of them. "I've gone to the opera twice in my life and fallen asleep both times," he said. Candy did her best to persuade him to give at least the 350 dollars mentioned on her list, but all she could squeeze out of him was a check for twenty-five dollars.

About a month later, Candy took her two children to the New Orleans zoo. Little Norman and Rita were peering through the bars of a fence at the animals when Candy noticed a man taking their picture.

"He looked familiar," Candy says. "I finally recognized him as the man who had given me the twenty-five-dollar check. He walked up to me, smiling, with a camera on a strap around his neck. He said the children had looked so appealing that he just had to snap their pictures. Then he looked at me more closely and asked me, as though surprised, 'Aren't you the girl who came to see me about the opera?' "

Candy allowed that she was, indeed, the opera solicitor. A friendly conversation ensued—about "opera and culture and other things," Candy recalls. "Naturally, he asked for my address, so he could send me prints of the pictures," she says. "But he didn't send them. He delivered them in person. We were married five months later."

The marriage was performed in a Presbyterian church at Fort Lauderdale, Florida, on May 24, 1949. Shortly after the ceremony, Candy says, she got a jolt. As she described it to newspaperman Paul Holmes (author of the book *The Candy Murder Case*): "He [Mossler] told me we could never have children."

Candy told Holmes: "He said he hadn't been living with his former wife for some time before the divorce and that women had made trouble for him—tried to blackmail him. So, to protect himself, he had undergone a sterilization operation. He could never be victimized by a paternity suit."

However, Mossler told his bride that they could adopt children. "He promised me we would do so," she says. It took Mossler eight years to fulfill that promise. But, when he did so, he did it in spades, making headline news across the nation.

By that time, the Mosslers had homes in several parts of the country, but spent most of their time in Houston. In 1957, while in Chicago on a business trip, Mossler read a tragic story in a newspaper. It concerned a mentally unbalanced war veteran who, under the delusion that his wife "contained the evil spirits of the Sahara Desert," had shot her to death, then stabbed the youngest of his five children. With the child dying and his four other children in the home, the father made no move to obtain medical help. For three days the four unhurt youngsters—the oldest of whom was six—cared for their father and brother, performed household chores and prepared meals. On the fourth day the father bundled them all in his car and tried to flee to "somewhere in the South." He got as far as Melrose Park, then got stuck in a snowbank and was captured by police.

Mossler called Candy and told her about the plight of the four surviving youngsters. "What are you going to do about it?" she asked. Mossler proposed adopting all four of them, rearing them as his own and even cutting them in for a share of his estate. Candy was ecstatic.

Confronted with the life of plenty that the Mosslers were able to provide the children, an Illinois judge approved the adoption. Newspapers, radio and TV stations gave the case enormous publicity, playing it up as a rags-to-riches, tragedy-to-triumph story. The children's father was sent to a mental institution. And the children—Martha, six; Dan, five; Chris, three; and Eddie, two—went with the Mosslers. "They're my life, my world," Candy said. And, though they may not have become quite that, they were to become central figures in her life. Through thick and thin, they have stuck with her. That thick and thin has, of course, seen them lose still another parent—Jacques Mossler—to a murderer.

But there would be idyllic years before the second tragedy. The Chicago youngsters moved into the luxurious life at the Mosslers' twenty-eight room mansion on millionaire row in Houston's River Oaks section. Candy seemed a good mother not only to them, but to her own two children and Mossler's daughters.

The older children eventually grew up, married and moved to other cities. With more time on her hands, Candy grew increasingly active in social and civic activities. She never really cracked high society—she was a little much even for the swinging matrons in Texas—but she became a fixture of the cafe-society crowd. She also became a leader of various charitable organizations.

Money was piling upon money for the Mosslers. "Every month my husband would give me 5,700 dollars with which to run the house," Candy recalls. "On special occasions such as our anniversary or my birthday he would give me an extra 5,000 dollars." Candy also helped run the businesses. Jacques began leaning on her increasingly in making decisions.

Just how all this started coming apart at the seams is hard to tell. But there were some danger signals. Candy started adopting offbeat causes involving offbeat people.

There was, for example, Howard Stickney, a handsome young draftsman. When Candy first heard of Stickney, she was serving as a member of a Houston grand jury considering two murder charges against him. He was accused of murdering his best friend and his friend's wife, then taking the woman's body back to his apartment and mutilating it. The grand jury indicted him on double-murder charges.

Stickney was convicted and sentenced to die in the electric chair at Huntsville. Candy, who detested capital punishment, came to his aid. She visited him numerous times in the Death House, proclaimed his innocence and raised a sizable defense fund among Houston matrons to pay for a series of appeals. (By coincidence, Percy Foreman was involved peripherally in one of these appeals. He was not the counsel for Stickney, but was working to prevent the execution. Curiously enough, Foreman was representing a judge. The judge, Cullen Briggs of Corpus Christi, had granted two eleventh-hour stays of execution. His jurisdiction in the case was cloudy, and higher courts challenged his authority. He hired Foreman to represent him before the Court of Criminal Appeals. Foreman argued on behalf of Briggs' right to grant the stays, but did not prevail.)

Eventually, after receiving thirteen stays of execution, Stickney died in the electric chair. Candy, however, had not heard the last of him. One of Stickney's former prison buddies later would be a key witness against her in her own murder trial.

The Stickney case was only one of several criminal episodes with which Candy became involved prior to the murder of her husband. Another involved her own brother, DeWitt Weatherby, who also was charged with murder. In the late 1950s, DeWitt was operating a gambling joint back in Buchanan. He was accused of shooting another man to death during a poker game. He claimed it was self-defense—that the other man had been coming at him with a knife when he fired. But the investigating officers dismissed his claim and arrested him. He was subsequently indicted and tried for murder.

Candy rushed to his side, attending every trial session and becoming the center of attention in the courtroom. There was little thought given at the time to bringing in high-priced defense lawyers. Candy felt her brother's defense was so ironclad that local lawyers could get him off without much trouble. She was wrong. He was not only convicted; he was handed a life sentence.

Candy was outraged. No brother of hers was going to spend the remainder of his life behind bars. With her husband's consent, she launched an all-out campaign to spring DeWitt.

This campaign included high-pressure appeals by various influential persons to Georgia's Governor Marvin Griffin, urging him to intercede in the case and pardon Candy's brother. But Griffin refused. He later claimed that at least fifty lawyers were put to work on freeing DeWitt Weatherby—including a former member of Congress, the president pro tem of the Georgia State Senate, the secretary of the state Democratic committee and numerous other public figures. The president pro tem to whom Griffin referred was one of his political opponents, Carl E. Sanders. Prior to the Weatherby trial, Sanders had been placed on a retainer to represent the Mossler business interests in Georgia. After the murder trial, he made several appearances on DeWitt's behalf before the State Board of Pardons and Paroles. DeWitt later went free, after serving one of the shortest "life" sentences in Georgia history—four years.

The case became a hot political issue the following year, when Sanders ran for governor, with heavy financial backing from the Mosslers, against Griffin's hand-picked candidate, Garland Byrd. (Griffin was barred by state law from seeking another term.) Candy takes credit for persuading Sanders to enter the gubernatorial race. The parole given her brother, and Sanders' role in seeking the parole, came under heavy fire from the Byrd forces in the campaign. But Sanders coasted to victory after Byrd suffered a heart attack that restricted his personal campaigning.

Emboldened by her success in promoting a gubernatorial candidate in Georgia, Candy plunged next into the murky waters of Texas politics. Texas Governor Price Daniel was running for reelection in 1962, and Candy had personal reasons for wanting him defeated. Once again, these reasons involved the handling of a parole matter.

In this case, the defendant was Johnny Will Ford, a longtime employee of the Mosslers. He had been arrested on a charge of habitually carrying a concealed weapon, had been convicted and sentenced to three years in prison. Candy and Jacques Mossler then went to see Governor Daniel, told him of Ford's long and loyal service to them, and appealed for his release. They won a temporary victory. Ford was turned loose.

However, a newspaper reporter soon learned of Ford's release and asked Daniel why preferential treatment was being given to an employee of the millionaire Mosslers. Daniel, under pressure from the newspaperman, accused the Mosslers of misrepresenting the case to him. He revoked the order releasing Ford. By that time Ford had disappeared. Sheriff's officers received information that he had been seen hunting with Candy's son Norman. Before long a deputy showed up at the Mossler mansion, asking about both Ford and Norman. He said Norman had been reported hunting on someone's property without permission.

Candy accused the deputy of being rude and aggressive. He grabbed her maid and one of her children, she claimed, and shook them up. "That's when I hit him," she says. "I knocked his glasses clear across the room and told him to get out."

Ford eventually turned himself in, served part of his prison term and then went back to work for the Mosslers. Meanwhile, Candy and Jacques had determined to do everything possible to thwart Daniel's reelection bid. His campaign opponents were Senator Ralph Yarborough and former Navy Secretary John Connally, a longtime aide of then Vice-President Lyndon B. Johnson. The Mosslers offered 30,000 dollars' worth of television time toward the defeat of Daniel. "We didn't care whether Yarborough or Connally got elected," Candy says. "We just wanted to beat Daniel."

Actually, most of the Mossler suport went to Yarborough. In addition to contributing their own money, the Mosslers organized volunteer workers, raised money among their friends and waged a vigorous propaganda campaign on his behalf. He did not win. But neither did Daniel. When John Connally was inaugurated as governor, the Mosslers—rightly or wrongly—claimed they had helped put him in office.

By now Candy wanted her way about almost everything. And she had found that money, good looks, a keen mind and powerful friends could usually see that her demands were met. At the same time, her increasing interest in the criminal world had brought her into contact with numerous unsavory characters. Whether their warped notions of morality had rubbed off on her is unknown. Nor is it known for certain just what led to the development of marital troubles between Candy and Jacques Mossler. But it is clear that these troubles coincided with the arrival on the scene of Candy's nephew, Mel Powers.

Mel Powers was no babe in the woods when he came under his aunt's influence. Though only twenty, he had already been through the mill. According to one version, he actually met her in a Chicago jail, where he was being held on a swindle charge. A witness in a subsequent court action testified that Powers told him Candy came to the jail "to visit him or visit his cellmate, and that's how he got acquainted with her."

Powers' background is obscure. This much is known about him. He was the son of one of Candy's older sisters, Elizabeth Weatherby Powers. He was reared in the western United States, then began knocking around with various shady characters. In 1961, shortly before Candy took him under her wing, he had been working as a magazine salesman in Arkansas with an ex-convict named Arthur Grimsley. More would be heard of Grimsley later. By 1962 Mel had been welcomed into the bosom of the Mossler family—residing in the Houston mansion and working for the Mossler interests. About this time, Candy and Jacques Mossler began having marital troubles.

By Candy's account, Jacques became seriously ill during 1962 and, upon recovering, took to behaving in a peculiar manner. She claimed he developed homosexual tendencies, picked up male strangers in bizarre places and brought them home with him. Other problems developed. Candy and Jacques started quarreling about money matters. Candy particularly resented the fact that, after promising that all the children (his own, Candy's and the adopted youngsters) would share equally in his estate, he had created 2.5-million-dollar trust funds for each of his daughters—but not for the others.

During this period, law-enforcement authorities would later charge, an incestuous love affair developed between Candy and

Mel Powers. Mel was far from handsome. His face was pitted by acne scars. He was crude, surly, arrogant. But there was a certain sensuality about this tall, well-built, dark-haired knockabout. And there was youth—the youth Candy herself yearned to retain and the youth that had been absent in Jacques Mossler ever since their marriage.

Whether Jacques was aware of his wife's purported affair with her nephew is unclear. But it is a matter of record that, by the summer of 1963, Mossler had become fed up with Powers. He not only ordered Mel out of the Houston mansion; he fired him from his job with a Mossler finance company. By this time Jacques and Candy—though maintaining the appearance that their marriage was still a going concern—were mainly traveling their separate ways.

Several months after ordering Powers out of his home, Jacques went off to Europe alone. When he returned, he did not join Candy in Houston. Instead, he took up residence in an apartment atop one of his business places in Miami. In his absence, Candy and Mel continued seeing each other. Mel rented an apartment in Houston. Witnesses would later say he had introduced Candy to them as his fiancée and that they had seen the aunt and nephew necking in plain view.

In May of 1964, however, Candy and several of the children went to Florida to rejoin Jacques. They stayed together in an apartment he had rented on Key Biscayne, across the Rickenbacker Causeway from Miami. Powers, at least at first, stayed behind in Texas.

On the evening of June 29, 1964, Jacques Mossler went to bed alone. In the apartment with him earlier had been Candy, her daughter Rita, and three of the adopted children, Martha, Eddie and Danny. Though it was long past the children's bedtime, Candy took them out about 1:30 A.M. on June 30 for a drive. She planned, she said later, only to drop some letters in a mailbox. But while she was out, she said, she developed a splitting migraine headache. This was not unusual. She had complained of such headaches for some time and had previously visited the emergency room of Miami's Jackson Memorial Hospital for injections to ease the pain. Thus, hospital staffers were not surprised when she appeared again early on the morning of June 30 for another injection. When a nurse offered to give her the injection, Candy said she preferred to wait for a doctor, even though it might be hours until he could attend to her. The children remained with her at the hospital.

Meanwhile, back at the Governor's Lodge—the apartment house in which the Mosslers had rented their apartment—Jacques was presumably asleep. His pet boxer dog, Rocky, lay silently on a porch adjacent to the bedroom.

In her nearby apartment was Mrs. Peggy Fletcher, a divorcée. She had gone out to buy some cigarettes about the time Candy had left. About five minutes after returning, Mrs. Fletcher heard a dog barking fiercely. Then she heard what sounded like a struggle. She recalls hearing a loud thud, then a man's voice shouting: "Don't do this to me!" There was another thud, followed by the sound of heavy footsteps—clearly a man's, she says—racing down the apartment-house corridor. She opened her door and stepped into the corridor. She saw nobody. But she could still hear the barking dog and was certain the barking was coming from the Mossler apartment.

Upstairs, another tenant named Herbert House earlier had been awakened by the barking. He walked to a balcony above the Mossler porch, heard a sliding door open and called down to ask whether the Mosslers were going to take Rocky inside. From below came the grunted reply: "Yeah." The voice sounded like that of a young man, House thought. He went back to bed. But, a few minutes later, he heard three screams. However, he dropped off to sleep.

On the floor below the Mossler apartment, the screaming awakened Mrs. Irene Durr, the building's night manager, who was off duty. She heard footsteps coming down the stairs. She opened her door in time to catch a fleeting glimpse of a figure leaving the building through a back door. Mrs. Durr watched the figure walk to a white Chevrolet in an adjacent parking lot, then pull out of a parking space. Although she could not even say whether the figure was a man or woman—much less identify the person—she recalled later that "the walk didn't seem like a woman."

Entering the front door of the building about this time was another tenant, Marvin Tavel, general manager of Miami radio station WOAH. Tavel had seen the retreating figure outside. He was sure the person had been a man—a large man wearing his hair long in back. Mrs. Durr told Tavel about the screams she had heard, and the two of them walked into the parking lot. A white Chevrolet was leaving the lot. They could not see the driver, but they noted that the car had Florida license tags and that the driver kept his lights turned off until he was some distance away.

Tavel and Mrs. Durr went to the second floor to investigate. There they met Mrs. Fletcher. The dog was still barking inside the Mossler apartment, but there were no other sounds. Mrs. Fletcher spoke through the door to the dog, telling it to be quiet. The dog, which knew her voice, obeyed. The three frightened, sleepy people decided there was nothing further to do. They went to their own apartments.

Several hours later, about 4:30 A.M., Mrs. Durr heard voices in the vicinity of the Mossler apartment. Candy had returned from the hospital with the children.

Inside lay the body of Jacques Mossler. His skull was cracked and his body was full of knife wounds—thirty-nine of them. In life, Jacques Mossler was hardly a handsome man. In death, he was grotesque. An inch-and-a-half-long scar was cut into his cheek and left ear. His arms, chest and back were covered with stab wounds. Seven wounds had penetrated his heart and dozens had penetrated his lungs and main blood vessels. Bruises scarred various parts of his body.

Thus, what confronted the returning members of his family was not only a corpse but a horribly mutilated corpse. Exactly what happened when Candy and the children entered the apartment is not certain. But, within minutes, both a doctor and a deputy sheriff were en route to the apartment. And the case that was to develop into what some called the "murder trial of the century" was under way.

When the doctor and the deputy arrived, they found Candy

waiting at the apartment door. She was not crying, and appeared relatively calm. She told the deputy, first on the scene, only that there had been some trouble and that "he's over there." In a corner of the living room, under a blanket, was the body of Jacques Mossler. The apartment did not appear to be in particular disarray.

The professionals quickly took over. The doctor arrived, examined the body and pronounced Mossler dead. Other sheriff's officers arrived and began dusting for fingerprints. Members of the sheriff's homicide squad took Candy aside and questioned her.

She told them how she had taken the children out for a drive, then gone to the hospital and returned to find her husband's body. Asked if her husband had any known enemies, she replied in effect that he had a list of them as long as a whore's dream. Her husband was a ruthless businessman, she said, and might have been murdered by any one of many business enemies. For openers, she named a Miami auto dealer with a grudge against Mossler. In addition, she said, Jacques had developed homosexual tendencies and might have been killed by one of his "boy friends." On top of that, she suggested robbery as a possible motive. Although the apartment did not appear to have been ransacked, Candy pointed out several purported clues supporting a robbery theory–such as open zippers on bags inside a closet–and claimed that several hundred dollars in cash was missing.

In subsequent days, the investigators came to feel that Candy and other members of the Mossler family were not cooperating fully with them. At one point Candy claimed some of her jewelry was missing. She promised to provide officers with a list of the missing items, but failed to do so. One officer later said he called Candy nine times in one day and her daughter Rita five times—but got no help from either of them.

Mossler's body, after undergoing an autopsy, was sent to Arlington National Cemetery for burial. Candy seemed normally upset at the funeral. Because of Mossler's prominence and the circumstances of his death, the case was headline news. But, at the outset, there seemed to be no implication that his wife was suspect.

There is no need to detail here the evidence that eventually led officers to charge Mel Powers and Candy with the murder. That will be explored in depth in a narrative of the court proceedings. Suffice it to say that the investigators felt they had a major break when they learned that Mel Powers had been in Miami about the time of the slaying, had been seen with Candy and had been driving a white Chevrolet similar to the one spotted leaving the parking lot adjacent to the murder scene.

On July 3, 1964, Florida authorities obtained a warrant charging Powers—but not Candy—with the murder. Powers was no longer in Florida. He was back in Texas, operating a mobile-home sales business at Webster (between Houston and Galveston). On the afternoon of July 3, Texas officers arrested Powers in Webster. Since they had not yet received a warrant from Florida, the Texas officers maintained the fiction that they were not arresting Powers on the murder charge, but rather on some long-standing Texas traffic charges. This transparent rationale did not, however, prevent the officers from taking Powers secretly to an out-of-the-way jail where he could be questioned about the Mossler slaying.

It was at this point that Percy Foreman entered the case. He did so in a typically flamboyant manner. Foreman had been retained by Candy to represent her nephew. She would eventually turn over to him almost 50,000 dollars' worth of her jewelry, as security against a projected fee of 200,000 dollars. Once retained, Foreman made a frontal assault on the Harris County Jail in Houston—accompanied by a swarm of newsmen he had invited along—and demanded in outraged tones that he be permitted to confer with his new client. Foreman knew Powers had been arrested, but he did not know where he had been taken. He insisted that, if Powers were being detained for Florida authorities, he should be in the Harris County Jail. But jailers insisted just as vehemently that Powers was not being held there. Just where was Powers? Foreman demanded to know. Nobody could tell him. He thereupon began a tour of all the jails, police stations, highway patrol and Texas Ranger bases in the area, repeating at each place his demand that he be given access to his client. At each place, he got the same answer: "Powers isn't here."

An attorney who had been so eloquent on so many occasions

regarding a defendant's right to consult promptly with his attorney was not going to take this sort of treatment lightly. Foreman immediately began threatening specific policemen and jailers with huge damage suits, accusing them of violating his client's civil rights. In addition, he announced to newsmen that the authorities were forfeiting any possibility of convicting Powers, even if he were guilty, since they were holding him incommunicado in violation of the law and numerous judicial rulings.

This got some action. Early on the morning of July 4, Powers was finally booked at the Harris County Jail on the traffic charges. Foreman immediately sprang him on a writ, but Powers was taken back into custody as soon as the murder warrant arrived from Florida. This time, Foreman was admitted to the jail to confer with him. What Powers told his lawyer is unknown. But what Foreman told Powers is no secret. He said, among other things, that Powers was not to discuss the murder case with newsmen or anyone else. Foreman would do all his talking for him. And, if Powers violated this instruction, he would have to get himself another lawyer. A long legal road lay ahead. But not once during that entire journey would Powers violate Foreman's order. While Candy and various others connected with the case granted numerous interviews—helping blow the case into a legal circus—Mel Powers remained conspicuously silent. It was no wonder reporters eventually took to calling him "The Sphinx."

By the time of Foreman's initial conference with Powers, Candy had come to Houston. Almost immediately, she checked into St. Luke's Hospital to rest from her ordeal. It was there that she turned over her jewels to Foreman. These jewels, like almost everything else connected with the case, would later become controversial items.

Candy's trials were just beginning. She soon left Houston for Rochester, Minnesota, where she underwent treatment at the Mayo Clinic for her migraine headaches and other ailments. But, if she thought she could escape the rigors of the murder investigation there, she was mistaken. Although she had made it difficult for Florida investigators to question her, she had not made it impossible. Moreover, disturbing word kept reaching her from

Florida and Texas—word that the investigators were probing ever more deeply into her relationship with Mel.

For more than a year, Candy was in a state of suspended animation. She feared trouble, but had no way of knowing when, if and how it would come. When it did come, it was like a thunderbolt.

The date was July 20, 1965. The occasion: the return of an indictment by a Miami grand jury. Its heading told the story: *The State of Florida* vs. *Melvin Lane Powers and Candace Mossler, Defendants. . . . First-Degree Murder.* The grand jurors charged that Candy and Mel, "unlawfully and from a premeditated design to effect the death of one Jacques Mossler, did kill and murder the said Jacques Mossler by stabbing and cutting him with a sharp instrument. . . ."

So now it was out in the open. The whispers, the snickers, the rumors that had dogged this case from the outset now grew to smug "I told you so" comments and loud demands that the "sinners" be punished.

Percy Foreman was in a peculiar position. He had been retained by Candy. But his client was Mel. And the interests of the two might well be in conflict. He could not, in good conscience, represent them both. Nor could he drop Mel and take Candy's case. Instead, with his concurrence, Candy retained her own defense team. Foreman worked closely with her attorneys—in fact, was regarded as the chief defense lawyer. But throughout the case there would be an undercurrent of discord among the defense attorneys—an undercurrent that would one day flare into open combat.

Mel Powers had been extradited from Texas even before the return of the indictment and was in jail in Miami. Candy was in Minnesota, but it would have been a relatively easy matter for Florida officials to obtain her extradition. Rather than submit to the indignity of being taken across state lines in handcuffs, she agreed to fly voluntarily to Miami and surrender at the airport.

She was swiftly taken before a justice of the peace, arraigned and ordered held without bail. Officers then tried to question her, but got few answers. "What you should be doing is finding the man who really committed this murder," Candy complained. "That's what the Dade County taxpayers are paying you for."

Though both Candy and Mel were being held without bond—as are most defendants in first-degree murder cases—Foreman and other lawyers were seeking their release. At the lawyers' insistence, an examining trial was ordered by Circuit Judge Harvie Duval. Prosecutors sometimes prefer to forego such proceedings in order to keep all their evidence secret until the main event—the trial. But Miami authorities were so anxious to retain custody of Candy and Mel that they went through with the examining trial. They lost. Judge Duval ruled Candy and Mel were entitled to bail, and freed them on 50,000-dollar bonds.

After numerous other pretrial skirmishes, the "trial of the century" ultimately got under way on January 17, 1966. The courtroom was jammed with spectators, and a waiting line stretched interminably down a sixth-floor corridor of the Dade County Courthouse. Many of the nation's leading newspaper and magazine writers were on hand. Every gesture, every word, every eyelash flicker was duly noted, recorded and hoarded.

Presiding over the trial was Circuit Judge George E. Schulz, a firm but patient man. He had been a judge for ten years, had earned a reputation as a fair, scholarly jurist and reportedly was under consideration for promotion to the State Supreme Court.

Heading the prosecution was State's Attorney Richard E. Gerstein, a veteran racket-buster with a solid record (he had never lost a case that he had personally prosecuted). A war hero with a Distinguished Flying Cross and a Purple Heart, he bore the scars of Nazi flak in plain sight on his cheek and forehead. He was an imposing figure at the prosecution table, standing every inch as tall as Percy Foreman. Seated on either side of him were his executive assistant, Arthur Huttoe, and his chief homicide prosecutor, Gerald Kogan.

The center of attention on the defense side was, of course, Percy Foreman. His fame had preceded him to Miami, and virtually everyone in the courtroom seemed awed by him. Even Dick Gerstein, as enviable as was his record as a prosecutor, would soon concede that he hardly belonged in the same courtroom with

Foreman. Seated beside Foreman at the table designated for Powers' defenders were two prominent Miami lawyers, Henry Carr and Harvey St. Jean. They had been star performers at many another trial. But here they seemed little more than spear-carriers for Foreman.

At an adjacent table sat Candy's attorneys. Her chief lawyer was Clyde Woody, a veteran defense attorney from Houston. Woody, younger and much shorter than Foreman, has a reputation as a firebrand. There is no love lost between him and Foreman. (Foreman's Girl Friday, a trim brunette named Martha Martinez Allen, left Woody's employ to accept her current job.) However, Foreman and Woody had worked together in the past, and Woody had occasionally taken over a case Foreman had chosen not to handle personally. Seated beside Woody was a beautiful blonde member of his firm—Mrs. Marian Rosen, a Miami native who was returning to her hometown as a vivacious, capable trial lawyer. Beside her was a Miami attorney, Walter Gwinn.

Although Candy's and Mel's interests were not necessarily mutual—and each team of defense lawyers was morally bound to protect just one of them—the realities were such that each team needed the other. If one defendant tried to toss the other to the wolves, they might both be lost. Only a united front could succeed. And the only logical leader for this united front was Percy Foreman. As a result, the entire defense strategy was tailored to place Foreman in the forefront. The order in which witnesses were called, the presentation of evidence and the priority in delivering jury arguments all were designed to give Foreman the edge not only on the prosecution, but also on his fellow defense attorneys.

This was one case in which Foreman could not hope to draw all the attention away from the defendants. Candy and Mel were too well known, too fascinating and too offbeat to fade into the background. Their every move was watched intently. They could not walk through a courthouse corridor without being subjected to merciless questioning. But Foreman did his best. At his insistence, Powers maintained his Sphinxlike demeanor throughout the proceedings. Candy was another story. She gave interviews, matched quips with reporters and behaved as though she were a member of royalty presiding over a festival. Foreman did not like it. But he was not, officially at least, her attorney. And Clyde Woody—perhaps secretly delighted that Candy's behavior bothered Foreman—did little to curb her antics.

The first order of business in the trial, of course, was selection of a jury. It took no fewer than ten days to choose a dozen jurors and three alternates. All of them were qualified on their willingness to see Candy and Mel, if convicted, go to the electric chair. Under questioning by Foreman, all insisted that they would not assume Candy or Mel guilty of murder just because there was evidence that the defendants had committed such other acts as incest, adultery and fornication.

The jury-selection process seemed interminable. It quickly became clear that the defense lawyers, particularly Foreman, did not want any women on the jury. The evidence would be such that a woman juror, particularly a straitlaced one, might be likely to become prejudiced against the defendants. Foreman wanted a middle-class panel, composed entirely of males, with a sprinkling or minority-group members and an absence of wealthy business or professional men. He wanted men who were both broad-minded and open-minded—who would not equate sins of the flesh with capital crimes. The jury eventually selected met Foreman's specifications almost perfectly.

It was made up completely of men. It included a truck driver, a lumber-company yard manager, a fish collector for the Miami Seaquarium, a bus driver, an aircraft mechanic, an office manager, a rooming-house operator, a bellhop, a piano player, a mailman, a construction worker and an airline clerk. Three of the jurors were Negroes and two were Jewish, giving the panel the minority-group representation Foreman wanted.

At last, it was time for the trial proper to begin. It was February 1. Court did not convene until 9:30 A.M. But, by 8:00, a noisy crowd of spectators had gathered. Even after every seat in the courtroom's spectator section had been filled, there were more than one hundred standees waiting in line outside to grab each seat as it became vacant. As every major participant arrived, he was given the sort of treatment usually accorded a celebrity showing up for a first-night performance.

Percy Foreman was first on the scene. He lumbered easily through the crowd. At the courtroom doorway, a reporter stepped in his path and asked for an interview with Mel Powers when time permitted. "My boy, all my clients have a right to be stupid," Foreman told him. "Otherwise, they wouldn't get in trouble in the first place. But sometimes they abuse the privilege." Interpretation: no interview.

Mel arrived next, dressed neatly in an Italian-cut suit. He posed for photographers, but had nothing to say to reporters. Other members of the cast drifted in gradually. Candy was the last. She made a grand entrance—waving and throwing kisses to friends in the spectator section. She wore a beige dress, high heels and a forced smile.

State's Attorney Gerstein had assigned his assistant, Arthur Huttoe, to make the prosecution's opening statement. Huttoe spoke in an unemotional tone, his voice marked only slightly by a Southern drawl.

"Gentlemen of the jury," he began, "the State of Florida expects the evidence to show the conspiracy between Melvin Lane Powers and Candace Mossler to murder Jacques Mossler was formulated several years prior to Mr. Mossler's murder. The motive for this murder was personal hatred of the deceased by Melvin Lane Powers and a sordid, illicit love affair between the deceased's wife, Candace Mossler, and her sister's son, Melvin Lane Powers. The object of the defendants' conspiracy was consummated by the murder of Jacques Mossler at approximately 1:45 A.M. Tuesday, June 30, 1964, at Apartment 2C of the Governor's Lodge, located at Key Biscayne, Florida.

"Mr. Mossler died as a result of being stabbed in excess of thirty-nine times with a sharp instrument; he was also struck in the head with a blunt instrument. Actually, this case begins several years prior to the murder when Candace Mossler attempted to hire for many thousands of dollars a person, whom she knew had a criminal record, to kill Jacques Mossler. We will prove that the defendants made additional attempts to hire people to murder Mr. Jacques Mossler.

"On June 20, 1963, one year and ten days prior to Mr. Mossler's death, investigators from the district attorney's office in Houston, Texas, at Mr. Mossler's request, told Melvin Lane Powers that he would have to move from Mr. Mossler's home. Powers, at that time, told Jacques Mossler that he would be back, that he couldn't keep him away and that he would come back anytime he wanted to. Powers also told Mr. Mossler that 'I'll be back and you will regret this the longest day of your life.' Shortly thereafter, Mr. Mossler went to Europe and, upon returning from Europe, Mr. Mossler moved to Miami in October and never returned to Houston. . . .

"On October 1, 1963, Powers rented an apartment [in Houston] and introduced Candy as his fiancée. She, Candace, would constantly visit the apartment, and witnesses observed Candace and Powers necking and smooching. Powers expressed to people how much he loved Candace and that she was having marital complications and was in the process of obtaining a divorce and that he, Powers, was going to marry her. . . . Powers even told people that he loved her so much that he would kill for her."

Huttoe reviewed several purported attempts by Candy and Mel to hire underworld characters to murder Mossler. He then laid out the state's supposed evidence placing Powers in Miami at the time of the murder, the events involving Candy and the children on the night of the slaying, the finding of the body and related material. He claimed that Mel, while in jail, had admitted committing the murder to a cellmate and that Candy, while jailed briefly, had conceded to a fellow prisoner that she was in love with Mel.

"Gentlemen, I have outlined generally a part of what the state expects to be the evidence in this case," Huttoe said. "When you hear all of the testimony from the witnesses and the physical evidence that the state will introduce during the trial, there will be no reasonable doubt or real doubt in your mind of the guilt of the defendant Melvin Lane Powers and of the defendant Candace Mossler of the murder of Jacques Mossler."

Huttoe sat down. The defense strategy called for Percy Foreman to make an opening statement. Clyde Woody, who was also entitled to speak at this time, elected to save his statement until the conclusion of the prosecution's case. He would let Foreman carry the ball.

Foreman pulled himself, with seeming weariness, from his chair. He had maintained a disdainful expression throughout Huttoe's statement. Now his expression changed. It was a gentle, compassionate countenance he turned on the jurors. He walked to center stage, took a glass of water from a court attendant, pushed a microphone aside and hooked his thumbs in the sides of his vest. His gaze moved from juror to juror. When complete silence had fallen over the courtroom, he began. And it quickly became apparent that Foreman was relying on his tried and true defense strategy. If he had his way, it would not be Candy and Mel who would be placed on trial here. It would be the dead man—Jacques Mossler.

"Distinguished gentlemen of the prosecution; Your Honor, the Court; gentlemen of the jury and alternates," Foreman began, "we believe the evidence in this case suggests that, if each of the thirty-nine wounds inflicted on Jacques Mossler on the early morning of June 30, 1964, had been done by a different person—that is, by thirty-nine different people—there would still be at least three times that many people in Florida and the Mossler empire with real or imaginary justification to want the death of Jacques Mossler."

Foreman paused for a moment, as if to ask: "How's that for openers?"

He then proceeded to offer some reasons that persons other than Candy and Mel might have wanted Mossler dead. Mossler was a ruthless businessman, a sexual deviate and a Jekyll and Hyde, Foreman claimed.

"Jacques Mossler was a dual personality," Foreman said. "He was Jacques Mossler and he was also a Dr. Wilson—or a Dr. So-and-so. He would approach high-school students and college boys . . . in bars frequented by the 'gay' people. He had an insatiable sex appetite. The evidence will show that, except for the shoe fetish, he had 'em all—transvestite, homosexuality, voyeurism, masochism, sadism, all the perversions mentioned in *Psychopathia Sexualis,* Krafft-Ebing's great masterpiece. He hired on occasion underworld thugs to rid him of blackmailers. . . . He had his favorites in every bank [he owned]. He was a swinger—not contented with homosexual partners—but he liked to pick up strangers who were responsive to his sexual deviations.

"There reposes in the files of the state's attorney a list of at least a dozen persons who have threatened to kill Jacques Mossler. The machinations of this man ruined uncounted independent automobile dealers. Because he was the mastermind of a great financial empire, there were thousands of people who blamed him for repossessed cars. Many of these people became highly infuriated. Jacques Mossler was as ruthless in business as any pirate who ever sailed the sea of commerce. . . ."

In addition, Foreman said, Mossler had numerous enemies within his organization. "The princelings, the dukes and the barons in the Mossler empire could have stood to profit by Mossler's demise," he said.

"The evidence will show a high official knew he was about to be released. And that individual forced control of a Mossler bank into his own hands. A financial consultant produced ten prospective buyers. This man refused to let a single one of the ten see the books so they could make an offer. This Mossler business that was sold would have brought two to four million dollars more under competitive bidding."

Not even Mossler's daughters escaped the lash of Foreman's tongue. He did not, of course, dare blame them for their father's death. But he did suggest that they had a stake in Candy's conviction. Pointing out that their shares of their father's estate would increase if Candy were found guilty, Foreman boomed: "They have made available funds—private funds, mind you—for the prosecution."

In a blatant appeal to the sympathies of the three Negro jurors, Foreman made one final point. "All the white witnesses for the prosecution flew to Miami by jet, first class," he said. "The Negroes took the bus."

What this had to do with the murder of Jacques Mossler and the guilt or innocence of Candy and Mel was obscure. But it was hardly more obscure than some of the other red herrings Foreman had dragged through the court. He had not confronted the state's charges against the defendants. He had merely made a series of charges of his own—charges contrived almost to make it appear that the murder of Jacques Mossler had been a mercy killing (the mercy being directed at society generally).

"I could talk on for six more hours," Foreman said. "But I think I'll stop now." He swept his hand through his hair, walked to his chair and sank into it. A surge of whispers could be heard from the gallery. It sounded like a collective "Whew!"—an expression of astonishment over Foreman's aggressive, hard-hitting approach at the very outset of the trial. Judge Schulz called a lunch recess.

When Candy returned to the courtroom after lunch, she was stopped momentarily by a newsman. "Mrs. Mossler, there have been some terrible charges against you here this morning—murder, incest. . . . Do you have any comment?"

Candy did not flutter an eyelash. "Well, sir," she responded. "Nobody's perfect."

At 2 P.M. the trial's first witness was called. He was Dr. John V. Handwerker, Jr., the physician summoned to the Mossler apartment immediately after the slaying. He told of being called to the murder scene, examining the body and pronouncing Mossler dead. State's Attorney Gerstein asked: "Was Candace Mossler in tears at the time?"

"No," the physician replied.

"Were any other persons in tears?"

"No."

"Did Candace Mossler appear to be in shock?"

"No."

Handwerker was followed to the stand by the Dade County medical examiner, Dr. Joseph H. Davis. He presented the grisly details—telling how a blunt weapon had been crashed over Mossler's head, literally rattling his brain, and how he had been stabbed at least thirty-nine times, "probably by a thin-bladed knife four to six inches in length."

(One of the weaknesses of the state's case was that the prosecutors were never able to produce the murder weapons. Nor were they able to say for certain what the weapons had been.)

The last witness of the day was a Dade County sheriff's officer, Lieutenant Jerry Evans. He described how Candy had told him on the morning of the murder that the apartment had been ransacked, but then had failed to provide a list of the items she claimed had been stolen. Percy Foreman cross-examined Evans closely about the range of the murder investigation. He particularly wanted to know what cities, besides Miami, had been visited by the lieutenant in the course of the investigation. Evans named several, including New Orleans.

"Where did you stay in New Orleans?" Foreman demanded.

"At the home of Mr. and Mrs. Lewis Clements," Evans replied. (Mrs. Clements, as Foreman instantly made clear, was Jacques Mossler's daughter Bonnie.)

Q. How long, altogether, did you spend at the Clements home?

A. I was there twice, for a total of four or five days.

Q. This was for background information?

A. Yes.

Q. Do you know how much money Mrs. Clements had furnished to Dade County for financing this investigation?

A. None.

Q. Did you pick up any cash?

A. No.

Q. Were you not, in fact, ordered to stop associating with the heirs of the fortune—that is, if Mrs. Mossler is not an heir?

Evans conceded that he had been instructed to stop seeing members of the Mossler family, but denied any sinister connotation.

Q. Wasn't this order given to avoid a scandal in the sheriff's department?

A. No.

Called to the stand the next day was Mrs. Peggy Fletcher, the neighbor of Mossler who had heard sounds of a struggle on the night of the slaying. "The first awareness I had that something was going on was when I heard a dog barking frantically—a very unusual noise, actually," she testified. "There were sounds of a scuffle and then a very distant thud and more scuffling. . . . This whole thing is very distasteful. I'd just like to forget the whole thing."

Percy Foreman, however, would not let her forget. He wanted every detail—just what she heard, exactly what time she heard it, what she was wearing at the time (a negligee). Ultimately, Mrs. Fletcher complained to Foreman: "You've got me terribly confused."

That seemed to be precisely Foreman's intention. Thus, when Mrs. Fletcher told of hearing what she took to be a man's footsteps, there was the assumption that she might be confused about that as well.

Marvin Tavel, the radio-station manager who resided at the Governor's Lodge, took the stand. He told of arriving home shortly before 2 A.M. on the date of the murder and seeing a tall man walking through the parking lot. He said the man's most notable characteristic was his long hair. "You could not tell where the hairline ended and the shirt began," Tavel testified.

Assistant State's Attorney Huttoe walked forward, holding in his hand a picture of Mel Powers. His obvious intention was to show that Mel had worn his hair long in the past. Foreman spotted the photograph and pulled himself aloft. "Your Honor, I ask that the jury be excused," he said.

When the jurors had filed from the room, Foreman demanded that Judge Schulz declare a mistrial because of what he called "the inexcusable tactics of Mr. Huttoe." What he was complaining about was that the picture had been taken while Mel was in custody. "The jurors could very well have seen that picture and seen that it was taken in a police station," Foreman said. Why that would have been so incriminating was unclear. It stood to reason that Mel, standing trial for his life, had been in a police station at one time or another. But Foreman insisted that the picture was prejudicial.

"The motion is hereby denied," the judge ruled.

"Note our exception," Foreman snapped to the court stenographer.

Other residents of the Governor's Lodge took the stand. Among them was Mrs. Irene Durr, the night manager. In addition to describing the noise in the Mossler apartment while Candy and the children were out, she testified about their return. About 4:30 A.M., Mrs. Durr said, she heard voices in the Mossler apartment. "I heard Eddie," she said. "I recognized his voice. 'Well, Mom,' he said, 'you don't want us to tell. . . . You don't want us to tell?' About twenty minutes later I heard the children at the Coke machine downstairs. I went out and said, 'Martha, what in the world—' "

Clyde Woody was on his feet. "Objection," he said.

"Sustained."

Mrs. Durr told of having seen a car pull out of the parking lot shortly after hearing signs of a struggle in the Mossler apartment. Huttoe showed her a picture of a Chevrolet Impala owned by the Mosslers. She testified that the car she had seen "looked like that."

On cross-examination, Foreman attacked this identification.

Q. Now, Mrs. Durr, you don't know if there are 10,000 or 100,000 cars of that model in Dade County, do you?

A. No, sir.

Q. And you don't know if he, she or it seen leaving had on a Japanese kimono, do you? Or pedal pushers?

Dick Gerstein objected. "Defense is badgering the witness."

"Sustained."

Before long, Mrs. Durr was excused. Another trial day had ended.

The opening witness the following day was potentially the most damaging thus far to the defense. His name was Roscoe Brown. He was a Negro, and he had worked for the Mosslers for eighteen years. Brown testified that Candy had asked him, after the murder, to twist his testimony. Not only that; the prosecution had what purported to be verbatim transcripts of two telephone conversations in which Candy made such requests of Brown. These transcripts were entered into the record. The defense charged that they had been obtained through illegal wiretaps. But the prosecution showed this was not the case, that, with Brown's permission, the conversations were overheard and transcribed on an extension telephone.

The evidence showed that, while Candy was at the Mayo Clinic about a month after the murder (when only Mel was charged with the slaying), she had written Brown and asked him to telephone her. When he did, with sheriff's officers listening in, the following exchange took place.

Candy: It would be awful nice if you don't let them [sheriff's officers] put words in your mouth. It would be awful nice if you don't let them say you remember something you don't remember. And it would be awful nice if you don't let them coax you to say you did what you didn't do.

Brown: Well, yes. I tell you, I wouldn't say anything wrong. Now, what I mean, what I would say, I just tell the truth. . . .

Candy then said Brown's call had interrupted her during a business conversation and that she would call him back in an hour. When she called, she said she planned to create a new company in Houston called Mossler Enterprises and would like him to move back to Houston from Miami to work for the firm. He agreed. This exchange followed.

Candy: I know they questioned you a lot, and I understand that you tried to help them as much as you could. Is that right?

Brown: Right.

Candy: Anyway, I would just like to say to you that, whatever you say . . . can hurt a person. Now, Mr. M. [Mossler], you can't help him and you can't hurt him. . . . He sleeps easy where he is. But the children and I and my Norman and yourself and Mel Powers, well, we die a thousand deaths with them trying to use my husband's death to discredit his children and family. So I would just ask you to be truthful about these things, please.

Brown: Yes, I will.

Candy: Don't let them put words in your mouth. I don't care, Roscoe, if they put words in your mouth before. If you said something just because you were afraid, everybody is afraid; nobody has so much nerve not to be afraid. Every hero that died in the war was afraid.

Brown: Right.

Candy: So if they coaxed you into saying something—yes, something you really didn't remember or know about before—a man's life is at stake. And we would do the same thing for you, to watch what we said to make sure it was right and true and not something that they coaxed us into saying that could cost you your life.

All the talk was couched in generalities to this point. But now Candy became more precise. The reason Brown's testimony was vital to the prosecution was that he said he had scoured the kitchen sink at the Mossler apartment with soap the day before the murder. Later, investigators had lifted a palmprint from the sink. They identified it as Mel Powers' palmprint. Powers denied being in the Mossler apartment on the day before the murder or during the early-morning hours of the day Mossler was slain. It was the defense contention that the palmprint could have been placed on the sink any time—but Brown's story of washing the sink seemed to negate that claim.

Candy: So, for instance, if they coaxed you into saying that you washed that kitchen sink that day when you hung that mirror for me—you know you didn't wash that kitchen sink. You weren't in there; you just wiped over my mirror. If they coaxed you into saying something, you were nervous and afraid. You don't have to affirm it again.

Brown: Yes.

During his testimony at the murder trial, however, Brown insisted that he actually had washed the sink "with a bar of Ivory Soap" on the afternoon before the murder. Under prosecution questioning, he testified: "She [Candy] told me to say I didn't clean that sink."

Candy shook her head and muttered: "No, no."

But Brown elaborated on her instructions to him. He substantiated that the transcript of the telephone conversations was accurate. "She told me, 'When all this is over, you will have a good job and you will have a preference for the best job,' " he said.

In addition, Brown said, Candy had suggested that he give investigators information suggesting a homosexual relationship between Jacques Mossler and one of his employees, Vincent Caltagirone, with whom Mossler had once shared an apartment. Brown quoted Candy as telling him: "You heard Mr. Mossler and Vincent Caltagirone arguing. And you heard Mr. Mossler say he didn't have any more more time for him and he was going with another girl."

Arthur Huttoe asked: "Did you ever hear such a conversation . . .?"

Brown replied: "No, sir, I didn't."

Now it became Percy Foreman's turn to cross-examine this damaging witness. As was his habit, he immediately put the witness on the defensive.

Q. Didn't sheriff's deputies threaten to put you away for twenty years if you didn't testify the way they wanted you to?

A. Captain [Pat] Gallagher told me if I didn't tell the truth they could give me up to twenty years.

Q. Isn't it true they accused *you* of killing Jacques Mossler and told you they found your prints all over the apartment?

A. I don't remember.

Q. Do you know where you were for sure between 1:30 and 1:45 A.M. on June 30, 1964?

A. Yes, sir, I'm pretty sure—

"Objection!" shouted all three prosecutors simultaneously.

"Sustained."

Several times in his testimony Brown had referred to Candy as "my boss." Foreman set out to show, instead, that his boss actually was Walter Fountain, president of one of the Mossler banks.

Q. Let's see just who your boss is, Roscoe. Is not Walter Fountain your boss? Wouldn't you want to please him, Roscoe—the big man, the boss, Walter Fountain?

Before Brown could answer, Foreman thundered at him: "Do you know that Walter Fountain is doing all he can to convict Candace Mossler?"

"Objection!" shouted the prosecutors.

"Sustained," the judge said. "The jury will disregard that question."

The prosecution shortly took steps to knock down the defense contention that Mossler had been a homosexual. It called as a witness Howard Walker, manager of Mossler's Allen-Parker Company.

State's Attorney Gerstein asked: "Was Jacques Mossler ever effeminate?"

"Never!" Walker testified.

"Was Mr. Mossler a homosexual?"

"To my knowledge, definitely not."

Foreman's co-counsel, Harvey St. Jean, handled the cross-examination of Walker. And he bore down on the witness's knowledge of the relationship between Mossler and Vincent Caltagirone.

After the murder, Walker testified, Candy telephoned him from the Mayo Clinic and told him: "If Mr. Caltagirone and seven or eight other men would come forward, they would have the murderer." Walker said Mossler, long before the murder, told him to prepare an apartment above the Allen-Parker offices in Miami for occupancy by Caltagirone. It was explained, he said, that Caltagirone was coming to work for the company and would be given the use of the apartment.

"Did Caltagirone pay any rent?" St. Jean asked.

"None."

Q. To your knowledge, did Vincent Caltagirone have any banking experience?

A. No.

Q. Did Caltagirone subsequently occupy a downstairs apartment in the Allen-Parker building?

A. Yes, he moved downstairs three months prior to Mr. Mossler's murder.

Q. Did Mr. Mossler occupy that apartment with Mr. Caltagirone?

A. Not that apartment. They occupied the same upstairs apartment.

Q. How long did these two folks occupy the same upstairs one-bedroom apartment?

A. To my knowledge, I'd say about one year.

"No further questions."

At the time of the trial, Caltagirone was working as an assistant cashier for a Texas bank. Once his name was mentioned in the testimony, he quit his job. "I don't want to put the bank in an embarrassing position," he said. But he insisted that his relationship with Mossler had been entirely innocent. The only reason he shared the apartment with Mossler, he said, was that he had taken a pay cut in accepting the job with the Allen-Parker Company and had demanded a rent-free apartment to make up the difference.

The trial was recessed for the weekend. When it resumed, the prosecution bent to the task of establishing that portion of its case which involved purported attempts by Candy and Mel to hire someone to murder Mossler. Called next to the stand was a former carnival hand named Edward Bart Diehl. In April 1962 Diehl and his wife had been hired by Mossler to oversee a ranch he owned near Galveston. Among those who worked with him was Mel Powers. Candy frequently came to the ranch without her husband and spent considerable time with Mel, Diehl testified.

Prosecutor Huttoe asked: "Did you have an occasion at any time to have a conversation with Melvin Lane Powers in regard to Mr. Jacques Mossler?"

"Yes, sir."

Q. Tell the jury approximately when this was, to the best of your recollection.

A. It was about approximately a couple of weeks after I first started working for Mr. Mossler. . . . We was building a corral there at the Mossler ranch.

Q. Will you relate to the jury what you said to him and what he said to you, please.

A. He asked me at that time what I thought about him and Mrs. Mossler and what I thought about him and Mrs. Mossler coming down together, and all. . . . He asked me not to ever tell Mr. Mossler whenever he came down and he also asked me if I knew anybody that I could get to either kill Mr. Mossler or would I do it myself.

Q. Why did he ask you this? Did he tell you why?

A. He said that Mr. Mossler knew about him and Mrs. Mossler and that, unless Mr. Mossler was killed, Mrs. Mossler would never get anything.

Q. Go ahead and relate all the conversation you had at this time.

A. Well, Melvin and I and another fellow were building the fence there and we were stretching the wire and Mel asked me if I knew anyone that I could get to help him do away with Mr. Mossler. And I told him, "No, no"—that I didn't know anybody at that particular time. And he says, "Well, we know about your record. We thought you might know somebody."

Q. Have you ever been convicted of a crime?

A. Yes, I have.

Q. How many times?

A. Twice.

Q. What was the conversation about your record?

A. He had told me him and Mrs. Mossler knew about my past record and that they had me checked out there when I first got employed at the ranch.

Q. Did you have any other additional conversation with him that day, do you recall?

A. Yes. We had talked with her [Candy] and he asked me if I knew anybody that would do away with Mr. Mossler, would I do it myself. And I said "No." And he said, "Well, there's five thousand dollars" if I knew anyone that would do it. . . . He says, "Well, think it over."

Q. Did you have any conversation with Melvin Lane Powers with regard to Melvin Lane Powers' relationship with Candace Mossler?

A. Well. . . . Yes, sir.

Q. Would you tell the jury about the conversation?

A. . . . He said he had a very good thing going for him there and that he could get money any time he wanted, wear good clothes and drive a good car. . . .

The testimony at this point got particularly spicy—with Diehl quoting Mel on Candy's boudoir habits—and vigorous objections were entered by the attorneys for both defendants. But Judge Schulz ruled that the testimony was admissible. Huttoe then asked whether Candy had ever been present when there was a discussion about murdering her husband. Diehl said she had been present once during a discussion he had with Mel in the Mossler ranch house.

"I went down there to the house and we sat there and had a drink and we were talking," Diehl said. "That's when Mel asked me a third time if I would do away with Mr. Mossler and asked me if I knew anybody that would do it. He said if I did away with Mr. Mossler I could get five thousand dollars and they said they would even raise it to ten, give me five during the time and five thousand afterwards of the insurance money."

Q. What did Mrs. Mossler say?

A. She just sat there and said "Yes" and kind of shook her head, and that was about it.

Q. Did you see any display of affection between Mrs. Mossler and Melvin Lane Powers?

A. They'd walk a few times arm in arm. . . . [Once] they were walking toward the lake and he had his arm around her, fairly close to her breast. That's the only time.

When the prosecution completed its direct examination of Diehl, Percy Foreman launched an exhaustive cross-examination. He tried to picture Diehl as a hired perjurer—a man who was along for the ride, soaking the State of Florida for all he was worth. Diehl responded that all he received from the state was four hundred dollars in travel expenses. He conceded, however, that he had been working while in Miami as a painter. And what was he painting? A hall that served as headquarters for the Fraternal Order of Police? And where had he been when he had first learned of the Mossler murder and volunteered his assistance to the investigating officers? Why, in jail—at Soledad, California.

Foreman was particularly interested in a journey Diehl had made to Galveston with a Dade County deputy in late 1965. The purpose of the trip, Diehl testified, was to find Nathaniel Allen, the Mossler employee who had been working on the ranch fence with him and Mel at the time he claimed the subject of Mossler's murder was first mentioned. Diehl said he helped the deputy find

Allen and was present during an interview between the officer and Allen.

Foreman: Did you or not tell Nathaniel Allen at that time, "I ain't doing nothin' but lying on the beach and they're furnishing me women and whiskey and I'm not going to do anything until this Mossler trial is over. I've got it made."?

Diehl: No. I did not.

Q. Did you or not tell—

A. The only thing I told Nathaniel Allen, I said, "If you come down here and tell them whatever you know, if you did hear him say—" He said, "No, I didn't hear anything." And I said, "All right." And I left.

Q. Did you tell him, "You can have it just as good as I've got it if you will just remember the way I have told it."?

A. I had told him down here, I said, "If you know anything, you come on down here." I said, "You either get yourself a job or wait down here in the hotel until it comes up."

Q. Did you not try to get him to testify that he heard these things to which you have testified?

A. No, I have not.

Q. Then you did make that trip in an effort to try to help the prosecution convict Melvin Lane Powers, did you not?

A. No, I did not.

Dick Gerstein objected to the last question and answer. His objection was sustained.

Clyde Woody took the witness. Although the prosecution had already established that Diehl had a criminal record, Woody wanted more information. Diehl, it will be recalled, had previously testified he had been convicted twice of crimes. Woody asked him again to tell how many times he'd been convicted.

"Twice, for felonies," Diehl replied.

Woody said nothing. He merely shuffled a set of papers in his hands. Diehl shifted nervously in the witness chair, then volunteered: "Counting misdemeanors, maybe ten or twelve times."

Woody dismissed him with a wave of his hand.

Prosecutor Huttoe next called a forty-year-old Houston service-station attendant, Freddie Duhart. A solidly built Negro who wore sunglasses on the stand, Duhart described himself as a wounded veteran of World War II. He testified that, several times in the week preceding the Mossler murder, Mel Powers had patronized the service station where he worked. On one occasion, he said, he drove Powers home.

"Driving back . . . we was discussing crime in general," Duhart said.

"Have you ever been convicted of a crime?" Huttoe asked.

"Yes."

Q. How many times?

A. Twice

Q. Tell the jury what the conversation was that you were discussing with Melvin Lane Powers with regard to crime.

A. Well, he asked me did I know of any perfect crime being committed. I said, "Yes, I have knowed people that steal chickens and get by with it. I mean, it's not the guys that you read about in the papers because they're caught. But there's a lot of guys have did things and never been caught."

Q. What else was said?

A. Well, we had just a general conversation about crime—that's all. The perfect crime, perfect murders or something like that.

Q. Were there any examples by yourself or Melvin Lane Powers?

A. Not at that time, no.

Q. Did you have a conversation with him at a later time?

A. Yes. . . . Well, I think I was asked about a murder—I mean, not a murder—about someone to make a hit, to knock somebody off.

Q. Who mentioned this to you?

A. Powers.

Q. Did you have any other conversation? Tell the jury the additional conversation you had with Powers at this time, if any.

A. Well, I told him I knew of people who had disappeared off the street and never have been seen. I told him that you could make a hit in Texas or anywhere and you could take the body to Mexico and . . . they would disappear.

Q. Tell the jury the other conversation you had with him at this time.

A. Well, I was offered thirty-five hundred dollars to make a hit.

Q. Who offered you the thirty-five hundred dollars?

A. Powers.

Q. The defendant in the courtroom here?

A. Yes.

Q. What did you say?

A. I told him that there wasn't no way.

Q. What did he say?

A. He say he wants a hit made.

Q. What do you mean by a hit?

A. A guy knocked off.

Q. Did you have any other conversation with Melvin Lane Powers about the hit or the person being knocked off?

A. Yes. . . . He offered me ten thousand dollars.

Q. Approximately when was it?

A. It was in June, the first week in June . . . of 1964.

Q. What was said at that time?

A. The second time I was offered ten thousand dollars to go and find a Mexican because if he made a hit—well, if he made a hit, it would be virtually impossible to extradite that man from Mexico.

Q. Who asked you to do this?

A. Powers. I was to take ten thousand dollars and pay him [the Mexican] whatever I wanted to out of it and keep the rest of it."

Q. What did you tell him?

A. No way.

On cross-examination, Foreman tried without noticeable success to shake Duhart from his story. As usual, he resorted to a diversionary tactic.

"Do you have a plate in your head?" Foreman asked.

"No," Duhart replied.

"Haven't you claimed you have a plate in your head pressing on your brain?"

"No." Duhart explained that he had received a skull wound,

which had left a noticeable scar, during World War II. But he insisted that he did not have a plate in his head.

Now Candy Mossler's past acquaintanceship with underworld figures began coming back to plague her. The next prosecution witness was Billy Frank Mulvey, thirty-five, who was brought to the trial from from a Texas prison, where he was was serving a five-year sentence. Mulvey testified that he had come to know Candy through Howard Stickney, the convicted double-murderer whose execution Candy had tried unsuccessfully to prevent. Mulvey said he had become friendly with Stickney while serving a previous prison stretch. He said Stickney had asked him to deliver some letters to Candy when he was released. He testified that in November of 1962, about six months after Stickney's execution, he telephoned Candy and arranged to meet her at a Houston nightclub to deliver the letters. At their first meeting, Mulvey said, Candy asked him to meet her again and he did so about a month later. The second meeting, Mulvey said, took place at the same place as the first—Houston's 24-Hour Club.

Prosecutor Gerald Kogan asked: "Would you tell us the conversation that took place between you and Mrs. Mossler at that time—what you said, what she said?"

Mulvey answered: "She told me she read that Howard [Stickney] talked well of me in one of the letters and that if I wanted to make some money. . . . I told her I did. And she said that she thought I could be trusted and that she had someone she wanted disposed of right away. I told her that would cost money and some of it would have to be in advance, and there would be a lot of detail to go into. . . . She asked me how much, and I told her it depends on the circumstances of who she wanted disposed of or hit or knocked off or whatever you people want to call it down here. I don't know. We call it 'making a hit.' "

Q. All right, go ahead. What else was discussed?

A. Well, I told her it would take twenty-five grand and ten grand in front; in other words, in advance. She said she would not put up any advance money. Well, I told her it was for her own protection in case . . . there was a rumble or an arrest made.

The police couldn't trace the hit man to her. . . . She said that she would have to think about it and for me to call her later.

Q. Did she tell you who it was she wanted knocked off or disposed of?

A. Her husband.

Candy rose from her seat at the defense table and cried: "I've never seen or heard of this man!" Clyde Woody and Marian Rosen grabbed her and told her to be quiet. Judge Schulz scowled at her. "We will have no more of that," he said. "Proceed, Mr. Kogan."

Q. Did you again see her?

A. Yes, sir. . . . Maybe a month later. I called her. She told me she had thought it over. She wanted to see me that night. So I met her—it was on a road, a private road, and she gave me an envelope. . . . I asked her how much was there. She said seven grand. I told her that wasn't enough, and she said that was all she could go up. I told her, well, I would see what I could do. In the meantime, she said that the old man was out of town and would be back in a few days. And I told her, well, that would give me time to work and, when he came back, to notify me or I would call her; that I had to have two days of his schedule, type automobile he was driving and the license number, because in this business you can't make a mistake. And I took the money and that was the last I seen of her.

Q. What did you do with the money?

A. I spent it.

Q. Did there come a time during the year 1964 when you saw the defendant Melvin Lane Powers?

A. Well, I had started this sentence I am doing now, this five years, in July, the tenth. And they brought him in the . . . Harris County Jail, Houston, Texas.

Q. When they brought the defendant Powers into your cell, did you have any conversation with him?

A. Well, at that time I didn't. . . . But the next day I got talking to him. I explained to him that I knew Candace Mossler . . . and he said he heard of my name. I told him he was in a lot of trouble, you see. I don't know. He seemed—

The judge interrupted him. "Do not tell us what he seemed," Schulz said. "If there was a conversation, you may relate the conversation between you and the defendant Melvin Lane Powers."

Mulvey: Melvin Lane Powers told me that he killed Jacques Mossler, if that is what you want to know. I thought you wanted the details of the conversation.

Kogan: Tell us what he said about killing Jacques Mossler.

Mulvey: He was checking certain points of law and he asked me about the hot-check law. I don't know why. But, at any rate, he told me they could trace him through a hot check. . . . Then he told me they could trace him through an automobile. . . . And as he went on—he didn't tell me nothing how he killed him other than he stabbed him. How many times or nothing I don't know about all that.

"You may inquire," Kogan told Percy Foreman. Foreman could scarcely wait to begin working on the witness—the man who had gone perhaps further than any other in putting the finger on Mel Powers as Mossler's killer. Walking briskly toward the witness stand, Foreman shoved a stack of papers at Mulvey. "Examine these thirty-four instruments and see if they apply to you," he ordered.

Mulvey stared in astonishment at his criminal record. "Great God Almighty!" he muttered. "Is this all *my* record? You sure dug deep."

A wave of laughter swept the spectator section, prompting a bailiff to call for order. Mulvey, still staring at the papers in his hand, looked up with a triumphant expression. He handed one of the thirty-four sheets back to Foreman. "Here's one where I wasn't convicted," he said.

Foreman barely suppressed a grin. "We'll keep it separate," he said.

Q. How old are you, Mr. Mulvey?

A. Thirty-five.

Q. Will you tell us, since you were seventeen years old, how many thefts you have been convicted of or crimes you have been convicted of in state and federal court?

A. Well, I have been convicted of five felonies, including the one I am doing time on now . . . but the misdemeanors I don't know. There is a lot of them.

Q. Isn't it true that you have been convicted of nine felonies in the state courts, six felonies in the federal courts and four thefts in the county courts?

"Objection," Dick Gerstein called.

"Sustained. The jury will disregard the question."

Q. Mr. Mulvey, knowing yourself as you do, if you were on this jury would you believe a word you have said?

All three prosecutors leaped to their feet. "This entire line of questioning is objectionable," Gerstein said.

"Sustained," the judge said. "I don't know how you do it elsewhere, Mr. Foreman, but you're not going to do it that way over here. The court will not tolerate it! It is most certainly improper. And you know it!"

"I apologize to the court," Foreman said.

He then asked Mulvey: "Who is your closest associate, closest friend, there among the prisoners at the Ellis Farm [a Texas prison farm]?"

Mulvey: Nelson Halford, H-A-L-F-O-R-D.

Q. With reference to Nelson Halford, did you or not tell Nelson Halford that Candace Mossler gave you the money to give to Melvin Powers to pay Melvin Powers for killing Jacques Mossler?

A. No.

Q. Did you or not tell Nelson Halford that you intended to use the money that you got out of testifying over here to get yourself out of the Texas Penitentiary?

A. No, I didn't. Money won't buy me out, Mr. Foreman. . . .

Q. Did you or not tell Nelson Halford that within thirty days after you came back from Miami that you would not be in the Texas prison system any longer?

A. No, I didn't tell him nothing about that. In fact, I didn't even know I was coming to Miami. . . .

Foreman then turned to Mulvey's purported dealings with Candy Mossler. He took him back several times over his version of his original meeting with Candy. He was particularly interested in Mulvey's story of how the second meeting had come about.

Q. How long after this alleged first meeting did you telephone Mrs. Mossler?

A. Oh, two or three weeks. I don't know exactly. It might have been a few days. I don't recall that much about it. . . .

Q. How did you happen to pick the time you did pick as a time to call her back? Why was it not the next day?

A. I don't know. You don't rush them things. I had an idea what was coming up. I didn't know, but—

Q. Without any more said than had been, you have told this jury you deduced the reason she wanted you to call was to get you to—I think you used the word "hit," knock off or kill. Is that right?

A. That's right.

Q. You deduced that. Just some sixth sense told you that. Is that correct?

A. I don't understand.

Q. You just perceived that out of the cold night air. There was nothing said to suggest it to you. You just knew that that is what that woman must want. Is that not true?

A. Why would that woman want to contact the likes of me, Mr. Foreman?

Foreman then brought Mulvey around to the next purported meeting with Candy, which Mulvey said took place on a private road in back of the 24-Hour Club.

Q. Why was this meeting held outside and on a road, instead of in the 24-Hour Club, as the two previous meetings?

A. You don't make contracts in front of a whole bunch of people, Mr. Foreman. [A "contract," in underworld jargon, is an agreement to murder someone.]

Q. How did you know there would be a contract made, if you have told us all the conversation that took place?

A. Because I didn't assume we were going to play tiddledy-winks back there.

Q. The first thing that was said then . . . upon her arrival there on this road in back of the 24-Hour Club was she said, "How is it going to be done?" Were those the first words she spoke to you that evening?

A. Right.

Q. And you answered, "I won't tell you" or "That's not your concern" or "None of your business" or what words did you use?

A. The exact words?

Q. Yes.

A. Well, I think I said, "It would be best if you don't know anything from here."

Q. What were her next words?

A. What assurance, guarantee would she have. And I told her none. I said, "I don't guarantee hits."

Q. What was the next thing said by her or you?

A. She handed me the envelope and then I told her, "I'll call you in a few days."

Q. When did you find for the first time that there was only seven thousand dollars in that envelope?

A. I knew it before I left the car. . . . I counted it.

Q. You decided to settle for the seven thousand dollars?

A. I did.

Q. How long did you keep the seven thousand dollars before it was spent, as you say?

A. Well, I was still spending on it up early—the first—around the first or the fifth or something of November.

Q. That is when you went back to the pen?

A. That's right.

Q. Will you tell us where you spent any appreciable amount of it?

A. Well, I'll tell you what I did, Mr. Foreman. It was getting close to Christmastime and I had a feeling I was on my way back to the penitentiary. I just went out and bought a whole gang of clothes for my old lady and them kids.

Q. Meaning several thousand dollars' worth?

A. Yes.

Q. About four or five?

A. Bought myself a few clothes.

Q. To wear with continental stripes?

A. Not to wear with stripes.

Q. Is it your statement that at no place, no time since you came to the Ellis [prison] Unit, have you talked at all or said one word to Virgil Nelson Halford?

A. Concerning this case or any other, no. I have spoke to him and maybe tell him to pass a spot of coffee down or pass a newspaper or something like that. . . .

Q. Now, I want to ask you, did you tell Virgil Nelson Halford that Mrs. Candace Mossler was going to give you, Billy Frank Mulvey, the money to pay him for killing Jacques Mossler?

A. No. No. I didn't. . . .

Q. Did you or not tell Virgil Nelson Halford in this unit where you and he are assigned that you did not know anything at all about the Mossler case, but that you wanted them to think you did?

A. Mr. Foreman, I didn't tell Virgil Nelson Halford anything like that.

Q. Did you or not tell Virgil Nelson Halford that a parole was what you were hoping to get?

A. No, sir, I didn't, because I've been convicted too many times to look for a parole or anything. I do all my time. I never had a parole. They won't give me one.

Q. Did you tell Virgil Nelson Halford that you were going to get in touch with Attorney Clyde Woody or with Percy Foreman and see how much money they would give you not to testify against Candace Mossler and Melvin Lane Powers?

A. No, I didn't. Have I tried to contact you, Mr. Foreman?

Q. I fix a time on that as immediately after any conversation you had with [Prosecutor] Gerald Kogan and [Sheriff's] Sergeant Maddox—that is, about seeing Percy Foreman and Clyde Woody about selling your silence. You did not say that?

A. No.

Q. Did you tell Virgil Nelson Halford that you thought this would be a real good deal moneywise if you could get in contact with Percy Foreman and Clyde Woody and not be put in any cross between the prosecution and the defense?

A. Mr. Foreman, Virgil Nelson Halford is a sexual psychopath and a mental case. You don't talk to those kind of people.

Foreman had been waiting for just such an attempt by Mulvey

to discredit Halford. He read into the record a statement given to him by Mulvey at the Dade County Jail only a few days earlier.

"I turn to page twenty-eight and ask you if these questions were asked and these answers given," Foreman said.

" '*Question:* Who were your closest friends [at the Ellis Unit]?'

" '*Answer:* Nelson Halford.'

" '*Question:* And any others?'

" '*Answer:* No. Not real close friends.' "

Foreman fixed Mulvey with a disdainful glare. "Were those questions asked?" he demanded. The best Mulvey could do was ask a feeble question about the form of the transcript—what the "Q" meant. It meant, of course, "Question"—a point that should have been clear to a man who had spent so much time in prison and who casually threw around underworld slang terms. Foreman waved that he was through with the witness.

Having produced such a string of hardened criminals as witnesses, the prosecution next put on the stand a pretty twenty-one-year-old girl. She looked prim, but it turned out she had once been a cellmate of Candy's. Her chief contribution to the case supported the defense, not the prosecution. She testified that Candy had told her in jail that Jacques Mossler had been a homosexual.

Next, the prosecution called Vincent Caltagirone, the bank employee who had quit his job after being described during the trial as a possible homosexual. Caltagirone testified that Candy had telephoned him just after Mossler's funeral. "She told me Percy Foreman was coming to Miami to investigate the case and that Foreman would be particularly interested in talking to the gay people and seeing the gay places Mr. Mossler had gone to," the witness said. "I told her there weren't any such things, that I didn't know about anything like that. She said, 'There must have been. He must have kept this from you.' "

Prosecutor Huttoe asked: "Was Jacques Mossler a homosexual?"

Caltagirone replied: "Definitely not."

When Percy Foreman got his turn at Caltagirone, he asked a typically unexpected question: "What is a homosexual?"

He struck paydirt. "I don't know," Caltagirone replied. How he could possibly know that Mossler had not been a homosexual—when he did not know what a homosexual was—remained unexplained. Compounding the confusion was Caltagirone's next statement. "If I were a homosexual, I would admit it," he said. "If I had killed Jacques Mossler, I would admit it."

Foreman and Clyde Woody then questioned him about his whereabouts on the night of the murder. He testified he was asleep in his apartment in the Allen-Parker building.

Woody: There was no one to corroborate your being asleep but yourself?

A. That's right.

Q. Did you have an argument with Mr. Mossler that night?

A. No. There were no strong words.

The next witness was Earl C. Martin, a Negro handyman who had worked for Mel Powers in his mobile-home business. Martin bolstered the prosecution's claims of a love affair between Candy and Mel. He told of seeing them "kissing and hugging." He also told of overhearing a spicy telephone conversation between them—at the invitation of Mel, who encouraged him to listen on an extension phone. But his most damaging testimony concerned a claim that he, too, had been offered money to kill Jacques Mossler.

Prosecutor Huttoe: Did you have any conversation with him [Powers] with regard to Mr. Mossler?

A. Yes, I did.

Q. Would you tell us what that conversation was?

A. Well, he asked me did I want to make some quick money. I told him yes, I could always use quick money. He said, "Like kill Mr. Mossler?" I told him no, not for that kind of money; he had to get another boy. Then I asked him what would Mrs. Mossler say about it. And he said that she knows about it; it was all right.

Q. Did he make any statements about Mr. Mossler at that time?

A. Yes, sir. He said if he had his way and wouldn't nobody know about it, he would jug [stab] him to death.

Martin testified Powers asked him several more times to kill Mossler, but that he refused each time. He said he later quit working for Powers because he was not being paid on time.

Percy Foreman and Clyde Woody tried to break Martin's story, but he clung tenaciously to it. They succeeded only in placing in the record the fact that Martin had a long police record involving robbery and assault arrests. However, it was also established that none of these had resulted in convictions.

Now, Huttoe called to the stand Arthur A. Grimsley, an Arkansas convict who had once employed Mel Powers in a door-to-door magazine-subscription business. He testified that on June 15, 1962, Mel had come to see him in Truman, Arkansas. He said Mel told him he was living with a female relative who was married to "an old mooch." Mel offered him money to kidnap the "old mooch," he said. He said that later, however, the plot turned from kidnaping to murder.

Huttoe: What conversation did you have with the defendant Powers on this occasion?

A. Well . . . the conversation most all the time was about if I would come to Houston [to kidnap the "old mooch"]. He [Powers] said he would put this fellow anyplace I would want him and, if I didn't want to do it, someone else could. As we went on into it, he said, "We don't want him back. We want him killed." I told him it would cost a lot of money. He said, "Well, you could have two . . . Cadillacs paid for."

Q. What did you say?

A. I told him I was interested.

Q. What, if anything, did he say in regard to the woman or the relative that he had mentioned?

A. Well, that he was in love with her and she was in love with him and that she frequently came to his bedroom.

Q. Did you see Mel Powers after this occasion on the fifteenth or sixteenth of June, where you more or less agreed you would do this?

A. The last time I saw Mel Powers was in . . . Arkansas.

Q. What happened to you shortly after this?

A. Shortly after this I was arrested in New Orleans and then I started—I got in trouble. . . .

Grimsley, in fact, had been in trouble most of his life—a point that Percy Foreman made forcefully in his cross-examination. He produced evidence that Grimsley had been arrested at least fifty times and had at least ten convictions on his record. Knowing full well that Grimsley had told at least one untruth on the stand, Foreman laid an elaborate trap for him.

Foreman took pains to pin Grimsley down to specific dates concerning his various meetings with Powers. Grimsley said he was "quite positive" that his last meeting with Powers before the question of kidnaping arose was in August of 1961. He was equally positive, he said, that he did not see him again until June 15, 1962, when the kidnaping was first mentioned.

Foreman: On what day did you see him?

A. I saw him on the fifteenth [of June] and possibly the sixteenth.

Q. You do not know whether you saw him on the sixteenth or not?

A. Sir, it's a long time. I certainly wouldn't say I saw Mel Powers there if he wasn't there.

Q. You are testifying, Mr. Grimsley. My question has to do with the sixteenth, as distinguished from the fifteenth, and I am asking you what your testimony is as to whether you saw him on the sixteenth, after you had seen him on the fifteenth. Did you or not?

A. I can definitely swear that I saw him . . . on the sixteenth.

Actually, as Foreman knew, it made no difference whether Grimsley testified about the fifteenth or the sixteenth. He merely wanted Grimsley to tighten the noose around his own false testimony. For the fact was that Grimsley could not have seen Mel Powers in Arkansas on either of those dates. Powers had a perfect alibi for the period from June 14 to 17. He had been in a Houston hospital the entire four days—undergoing four minor operations by four different surgeons. Not only the surgeons, but Houston police officers were prepared to substantiate this alibi.

Foreman did not immediately call Grimsley to task. He knew that the prosecution had in its files the record of Powers' hospital stay. Now he was playing for bigger game than Arthur Grimsley. If the state did not come forward and try to correct Grimsley's error, Foreman could make it appear that the prosecutors had contrived to prevent the truth from coming to light.

Court recessed overnight. In the morning, the prosecutors made no effort to set the record straight. Foreman pounced. He rose majestically, waved a fistful of papers at the prosecution and indignantly accused the state's attorneys of suppressing vital evidence. He said the prosecutors, at that very moment, had in their possession proof of Grimsley's perjury. Yet, they had tried to hide it. He accused them of conspiring to admit perjured testimony. He hinted at corrupt acts by public servants. He demanded a mistrial. And he insisted that the prosecution immediately admit the error of its ways or else produce evidence to substantiate Grimsley's claim.

At first, there was only an embarrassed silence from the prosecution table. Judge Schulz looked straight at State's Attorney Gerstein, inviting him wordlessly to speak his piece. Finally, Gerstein rose. Anxiety spread across his face. He conceded immediately that Grimsley had been mistaken. Just that morning, he said, Grimsley had sent word from his jail cell that he had realized he was mistaken about the dates and wanted to correct his testimony. There had been no perjury and no suppression of evidence, Gerstein insisted. But he did not explain why Grimsley had not been called back to court immediately.

Now, belatedly, Grimsley returned to the stand. Arthur Huttoe asked him: "Is there something you would like to tell me?"

A. Yes.

Q. Is there something in your testimony you would like to change?

A. Yes, sir. There is.

Grimsley's excuse, while reasonable, sounded feeble. He said Mel Powers' visit to Arkansas had followed by a day the date that Grimsley's father-in-law had been released from a state hospital in Arkansas. He said he had originally called the hospital, been told that the date of his father-in-law's release had been June 14 and assumed that the date of Powers' visit was June 15. Later, he said, he had realized that his father-in-law had left the hospital twice. He had checked and found that the previous date had been in March of 1962, he said. So he now claimed that his meeting with Mel had been in March.

Lie was now piling upon lie. Foreman quickly established that it was not Grimsley, but a Dade County sheriff's officer who had discovered the error in his prior testimony. And it was only after being coached by the officer—who had conferred with him improperly—that Grimsley had corrected the testimony. Sheriff's Lieutenant Alois Spath was called to the stand. He said it was he who had established for the prosecution that Powers had been in the hospital during the period Grimsley claimed he had been in Arkansas. Spath then telephoned the jail, talked to Grimsley and straightened him out on the dates. This conversation was in clear violation of court rules that bar officers from conferring with witnesses once they have testified. The rules are designed to prevent witness tampering.

The defense immediately moved to strike from the record all testimony given by Grimsley during his second appearance on the stand. Judge Schulz granted the motion. Thus, the prosecution was stuck with Grimsley's original testimony—that he had seen Powers in Arkansas on June 15 and 16. And the prosecution itself, of course, had now repudiated this testimony. It was placed in the position of leaving in the record the false testimony of a certified liar. Without question, Foreman's cross-examination of Grimsley had been one of the high points in the defense attack on state witnesses.

The prosecution presented a few more witnesses. They testified chiefly on the relations between Candy and Mel—not on the murder. Several told of seeing Candy and Mel embracing and kissing, but that was all. The prosecutors seemed worn out. At 11 A.M. on February 21, Arthur Huttoe drooped into a chair and remarked casually: "The state rests."

The defense attorneys filed routine motions for a directed verdict of acquittal on grounds of insufficient evidence. The motions were denied.

Percy Foreman and Clyde Woody had worked out an elaborate defense strategy designed to give Foreman an edge on the prosecution. Lawyers generally seek to have the last word before a jury. This permits them to try to rebut everything the opposition has said and make additional points that the opposition gets no chance to rebut. The Florida rules permitted Foreman to make the final jury summation if he produced no defense witnesses. Therefore, it was decided that he would rest Mel's case without putting a single witness on the stand. Woody, meanwhile, would run interference for Foreman. He would call, on Candy's behalf, any witnesses Foreman wanted to question.

The first defense witness was Mrs. Lois Mulvey, wife of Billy Frank Mulvey, the convict who claimed Candy had paid him 7,000 dollars to murder Mossler. Where Mulvey had claimed he had spent perhaps 5,000 dollars of this money on clothing, his wife testified he had bought only about sixty dollars' worth during the period in question. She said her husband had been a drug addict for as long as she had known him—thirteen years.

Woody: Are you familiar with Billy Frank Mulvey's reputation for truth and veracity?

A. Yes.

Q. Is it good or bad?

A. Bad.

Q. Would you believe Billy Frank Mulvey under oath?

A. I don't know. . . . He's lied to me a lot.

The defense (with Woody summoning the witnesses) then proceeded to present one witness after another who disputed the testimony of prosecution witnesses. The state had presented evidence that human hair had been found clutched in the hand of the murdered Jacques Mossler. The hair was not Mossler's, and the prosecution claimed it had come from the head of Mel Powers. But the defense produced identification experts from Washington, D.C., who testified it was not Powers' hair.

Next, the defense made a major effort to discredit even more the testimony of Billy Mulvey. It will be recalled that Mulvey had testified he had never discussed the Mossler murder with his closest prison associate, Virgil Nelson Halford. But Halford, under questioning by Woody, told a different story. "We [he and Mulvey] were talking about the case and he just told me that he thought he was going to have to come to Florida on the case," Halford said. "I asked him what he knew about the case."

Q. What did he tell you?

A. He told me he didn't know anything about the case.

Q. Is this the extent of the conversation?

A. No, sir, we talked quite a bit about it. . . . He told me again that he was going to have to come down to Miami to testify and I asked him again what he was going to testify about. And he told me he was going to testify to whatever the people wanted him to testify to—that he didn't know anything about the case. I asked him why he was going to come down here, you know, and testify like that. And he told me he had made a deal to get a habitual indictment off him in Harris County if he would help get a conviction on Melvin Lane Powers. [Anyone convicted of three felonies in Texas is subject to prosecution as a habitual criminal. Conviction on a charge of being a habitual criminal carries a life sentence.]

Halford testified he had at least five conversations with Mulvey about the Mossler case. Concerning one such conversation, he said: "He [Mulvey] told me that while he was in the Harris County Jail [in Houston] some officials had came and saw him and wanted to make a recording of an argument between him and Melvin Lane Powers that Billy was supposed to have been go-between between Mrs. Mossler and Melvin Lane Powers, that she was supposed to have hired Melvin Lane Powers to kill Mr. Mossler and that Billy was handling the money from Mrs. Mossler to Melvin Lane. And he said that the officials wanted—I don't know—to rig some kind of recording to where it was supposed to have taken place at his house, to where Melvin had come to his house asking for his money and they got in an argument. And then he said later, after that, that they brought him a knife and shown him and asked him if he would say that Melvin had given him the knife to throw away—to get rid of."

Halford testified Mulvey became irate when he was not released from prison after agreeing to cooperate with Florida officers.

Q. Did he indicate . . . whether he was coming or not coming [to Miami] or who he was going to testify for, if anyone?

A. At that time he told me that he was going to come down here; he had to come down here. But, if he came down here and the defense would make it worth his while, he would sell out to them.

Q. Did Billy Frank Mulvey ever tell you whether he did, in fact, become acquainted with Melvin Lane Powers or not?

A. He told me he didn't know Melvin Lane Powers.

Still more witnesses were summoned by Woody. Some had been unearthed originally by Foreman, but, holding to his strategy, he refrained from calling them. One witness was a laboratory technician who testified about a bloody handprint found on Mossler's buttocks. After the other attorneys had questioned him, Foreman took the witness back over his testimony. Then, peeling off his jacket, Foreman strode to the witness chair and asked the technician to exchange places with him. His purpose was to have the witness point out on Foreman's buttocks precisely where the handprint had been found on Mossler's body. Foreman bent over, his backside toward the crowded end of the courtroom.

Judge Schulz asked: "You're not going to testify, are you?" It was as if Foreman had set the judge up as his comedy partner.

"Not in this position, Your Honor," he replied.

The defense went on to try to bolster its contention that homosexuality had figured in Mossler's murder. Nathaniel Allen, who had worked for the Mosslers on their ranch, testified that Mossler once brought three young men to the ranch. He said Mossler asked him to saddle some horses so the young men could go riding. He did so. But the young men went inside the ranch house with Mossler and did not come out for two and a half hours, he said. Finally, he went to the door and knocked. He said Mossler answered the door, nude from the waist down. But he had no idea what had been going on inside for the previous two and a half hours, he said.

Later, the defense presented evidence about a man who had been beaten up on the night of the Mossler murder. The contention was that this man might have been a homosexual and that his beating might have been connected with the murder. But the man was out of the country and could not be produced as a witness.

The man's absence, in itself, brought hints that he had something to hide. But neither Woody nor Foreman did any more with this incident than use it as a red herring. It was just one in a virtually endless list of possible leads indicating that someone other than Candy and Mel had murdered Mossler. The defense, of course, was not obliged to prove anything. Thus, it grabbed anything it could find to cloud the prosecution case.

Finally, at 11:24 A.M. on February 25, the defense rested. The prosecution put on a brief, weak rebuttal—so weak that the defense did not even counter with rebuttal of its own.

Now, it was time for summations. Since Percy Foreman had put no witnesses on the stand, he not only had the privilege of delivering the last summation; he was also entitled to have his co-counsel speak first. They would be followed by Prosecutor Huttoe, then by Candy's three lawyers, then by Prosecutors Kogan and Gerstein. After all that, it would be Foreman's turn.

Foreman's co-counsel, Harvey St. Jean, went to bat first. He contended that all the prosecution evidence against Mel Powers still left room for much reasonable doubt about Mel's guilt. He named several other persons about whom a similarly strong case could have been made for Mossler's murder. Speaking of Candy and Mel, he said: "I do not believe there was a love affair between these two persons. But, if you choose to believe it, so what? We are not trying a hugging and kissing case. We are trying a murder case."

The other Foreman co-counsel, Henry Carr, lashed out at the character of the prosecution witnesses. "I think [Billy Frank] Mulvey is entitled to some sort of monument for being the biggest liar that ever sat on a witness stand in Dade County," he said.

For the prosecution, Huttoe conceded that Mulvey was a dope addict, a hardened criminal and a "no-good." But these characteristics, he contended, made it all the more likely that he would be brought into a murder plot. "You don't hire nice people to commit crimes," he said. "When you want someone killed, you don't go to your local banker, your local minister or to the man next door. You go to the worst person you can find."

Actually, Huttoe pictured Candy Mossler as one of the worst persons he could find. "She is the most guilty of all!" he shouted, pointing an accusatory finger at her. "Powers would do anything for her. Even if she did not strike the fatal blows, she is more guilty than he."

Marian Rosen, Walter Gwinn and Clyde Woody picked up where the previous defense lawyers had stopped—ridiculing the prosecution case and suggesting other possible murderers than Candy and Mel. "Candace Mossler was not put on trial here because of evidence against her," Woody insisted. "This was done because she is a very wealthy woman. This is the only reason she is in this case."

Prosecutor Gerald Kogan accused the defense of failing to prove many of its theories. Typical, he said, was the claim that Mossler had been a homosexual. "This was never more than a red herring," he said. "No evidence to support it was ever offered."

Next, Dick Gerstein made a soft-spoken appeal for conviction of both Candy and Mel on first-degree murder charges. The chief surprise in his argument was that he did not demand the death penalty.

He said he would leave it to the jury to decide whether the death penalty or life imprisonment should be imposed in case of a conviction. "If you can find any reason in this cruel and savage murder to recommend mercy for those who did it, I will not quarrel with you on that point," he said. "On the other hand, if you can find no reason for mercy, I know you will perform your sworn duty."

Gerstein spent most of his summation attacking the defense tactics. "It is an old technique—as old as criminal law itself—to put the victim on trial in a murder case," he said. "The defense has had highly skilled lawyers with unlimited funds to divert your attention from the guilt of Candace Mossler and her nephew. Who will stand up and speak for the murdered man?" He then proceeded to do so. He claimed that greed and lust had led Candy and Mel to murder Mossler, and that they were stooping to disgusting depths in accusing the victim of homosexuality. Mossler's only crime, he said, was getting in the way of the love affair.

With that, Gerstein sat down, weariness written all over him. At last, it was Percy Foreman's turn. And his summation would be no brief, offhand discourse. He would talk for five hours, holding the jurors spellbound.

He began in his most courtly manner, paying tribute to the judge, the jurors, his fellow defense attorneys and, yes, even the prosecutors. The tribute to the chief prosecutor, however, could only be called condescending at best.

"I congratulate Richard Gerstein," Foreman said, giving the impression that it was part of his duty to pass on the relative skill of his adversaries. "It took guts and courage for him to appear personally in this case when he could have given the job to a subordinate. Few prosecutors would have chosen to appear in a case where the evidence is not overwhelming—let alone almost absent. The fact that Gerstein wasn't any better was no fault of his. It was the fault of his case."

Having raised the spectre of homosexuality in the first place, Foreman now virtually washed his hands of it. He criticized Gerstein for dwelling on the subject. "I won't waste a single word on it," he said.

However, incest was another matter. If Candy and Mel had been guilty of incest, he demanded, why hadn't they been charged with it? He pulled open a Florida law book, pointed out the incest statute and noted with some amusement that the penalty was up to twenty years in a state prison or one year in a county jail. "You must have a pretty terrible county jail here if one year there is as bad as twenty years in the penitentiary," he said.

He charged that there was a pretty terrible sheriff's department in Dade County as well. He accused members of the department of engaging in "a monetary conspiracy" with Jacques Mossler's daughters by his previous marriage. "I say to you money moves in mysterious ways, its wonder to perform!" Foreman shouted. "I say that [sheriff's officers] Alois Spath, Jerry Evans and Pat Gallagher are manufacturers of perjury—money-mad and money-hungry."

Piling detail upon detail in his castigation of the investigating officers, he declared: "The verdict, gentlemen of the jury, may have a salutary effect on justice in Dade County. When this case is over, I shall be gone. You will still live here. The next victim may not be someone from as far away as Houston. It may be someone near to you for whom the bells toll. They toll for you."

Although Dick Gerstein had not demanded the death penalty, Foreman said, Prosecutor Huttoe's summation had been a cry for blood. "Let's put 'em in the electric chair," Foreman said, in a parody of Huttoe.

Foreman had a vivid description of virtually every participant in the case. Gerstein was "that tall giant of a prosecutor." Huttoe was "that silver-tongued orator" who really ought to be doing radio commercials for Billy Graham. Candy was "that sweet little woman." Mel was "that innocent boy." Every few minutes, he would inject an appropriate quotation—this time Shakespeare, that time the Bible, another time Buddha, Confucius, Wordsworth or H. G. Wells.

In a broad burlesque of the prosecutors, Foreman stalked around the courtroom, waving his arms wildly. "They want you to forget the evidence," he cried. "Let's guess these people into the electric chair. That's what they want you to do, fellows. Burn 'em, fry 'em, fellers, help me kill 'em. The newspapers are waiting for a verdict."

Returning to the purported love affair between Candy and Mel, Foreman again ridiculed the prosecution. "I'm glad we have a moral-minded district attorney," he said. "Also, an assistant district attorney who underwrites that moral-mindedness. I'm sure they will stop fornication and eliminate adultery and assignation. They're going to stamp it out. I know they are. It's a shame the world has had to wait so long for that crusade."

The prosecution evidence, Foreman said, was "a wheelbarrow of manure dumped from the witness stand." Pointing to the jurors, he said: "And they ask you to swallow it." Now he quoted still another wise man. "Plato was the smartest man in the world," Foreman said. "He was best known for the expression, 'There is one thing I know; I know I know nothing.'" He paused for effect. "I know a good jury," he said.

Foreman reminded the jurors once more that Candy and Mel were on trial for murder, not adultery or incest. Then he recited from the Bible the parable of the adulteress brought before Jesus.

"When the mob wanted to stone her, Jesus said, 'Let him who is among you without sin cast the first stone,'" Foreman said. "And Jesus was left alone with the adulteress. 'Neither do I condemn you,' he said. 'Go, sin no more.'"

Foreman, reluctant to try improving on the Scriptures, sat down without another word. There were audible groans from the spectator section. After five hours, some bystanders wanted to hear still more from Foreman. But they had heard their last. The case was now in the hands of the judge and jury.

Judge Schulz, in his formal charge to the jury, presented a reasoned explanation of the options available. He told the jurors that, although the indictment charged first-degree murder, they could convict Candy and Mel of lesser offenses such as second-degree and third-degree murder or manslaughter. And, of course, they could find both defendants innocent. He also explained the criteria necessary to find Candy guilty, even if the jurors found that she had not been present at the time of the murder. Schulz told them: "If you find from the evidence that the defendant Melvin Lane Powers committed the offense charged, and you further find that the defendant Candace Mossler—with a premeditated design to effect the death of the deceased—aided, abetted, counseled, hired or otherwise procured the services of Melvin Lane Powers to kill the deceased, Jacques Mossler, then it would be your duty to find her guilty as charged in the indictment because she would be equally liable under the law as the person who actually caused the death of the deceased."

The jury stayed out for almost three days. It appeared the case, after all this, might end in a hung jury. In fact, the foreman, James Harris, informed the judge at one point that the jurors were deadlocked. But Schulz felt it was too early to declare a mistrial. He sent the jurors back to try again. Not only Miami, but the entire nation waited impatiently for word of a verdict. The press, television and radio coverage was exhaustive. At long last, at 10:30 A.M. on Sunday, March 6, the jurors sent word that they had a verdict.

The participants were summoned to the courtroom. Swarms of reporters and photographers were on the scene. But Percy Foreman was not there. His car had broken down on a freeway, and he would not arrive until after the verdict had been announced. Mel Powers sat as impassively as ever at his counsel table. Candy, wearing dark glasses, wiped away a tear or two.

The jurors filed in. They stood before their chairs as a clerk called their names. A bailiff then took two slips of paper, bearing the verdicts for Candy and Mel, from foreman Harris. He handed them to the judge. An expression of surprise seemed to flit across Schulz's face. The judge, in turn, passed the slips of paper to a clerk, who read the verdicts aloud.

"We, the jury, find the defendant Melvin Lane Powers, not guilty as charged in the indictment, so say we all," he read. Mel slumped in his chair, smiled vaguely and whispered just one word: "Beautiful."

"We, the jury, find the defendant, Candace Mossler, not guilty as charged in the indictment, so say we all," the clerk read. Candy burst into tears even before he was finished. She cried and cried and cried. Spectators swarmed around her. Everyone wanted to congratulate her, it seemed. She and Mel thanked the jurors. "Oh, sir," Candy said. "Thank you, sir. Oh, sir, it's been such a dreadful nightmare. Oh, sir, my children thank you. My babies . . ."

And then Percy Foreman showed up. Everyone now wanted to congratulate and thank him. It went on and on and on. Later in the day, Foreman played host at a sumptuous victory party.

He posed for pictures, with Candy kissing his cheek. He served food and drinks—even to members of the sheriff's department. And he bantered good-naturedly with everyone in shouting distance.

Someone asked the best method of committing a crime. "Don't do it, son," Foreman advised. "I can get you Billy Frank Mulvey or Virgil Nelson Halford."

Someone else asked how much it would cost to hire Foreman for another case. "That depends," Foreman said. "Do you supply the witnesses—or do I?"

For all his good nature on this occasion, however, Foreman later made it plain that he did not consider Candy Mossler one of his favorite people. He took a dim view, for example, of Candy's insistence on going nightclubbing with Mel Powers shortly after their acquittal. (They would eventually announce their engagement to be married but would later become embroiled in still another legal entanglement. In March 1969 Candy would seek Mel's arrest in Houston on charges that he beat her after ordering her to "stay home where I belonged.") Several weeks after the 1966 Florida murder trial ended, a man asked Foreman for his autograph. Foreman complied. The man then asked him to write down Candy's telephone number. Foreman wrote: "BP (blood pressure) 0-0-2-HI." In other places and in other ways, he expressed his displeasure with Candy. The feeling evidently was mutual.

Eventually, Foreman and Candy would again meet in court. And, for this meeting, they would line up on opposite sides of the legal fence. Candy would thus prove the truth of Foreman's oft-repeated adage: "Most of my clients hate my guts."

9

I am not a vindictive man.
PERCY FOREMAN

THOUGH PERCY FOREMAN may not be vindictive, many of his enemies are. And he has an impressive array of enemies—ranging from cops to criminals, from clients and ex-clients to judges, and from prosecutors to fellow defense lawyers. Thus, it is hardly surprising that he seems constantly embroiled in one raging battle or another.

Percy Foreman is a man who stirs up human passions. There are few who can merely take him or leave him. Most either worship him or detest him. It is not uncommon for a grudge-bearing citizen to barge into his office, gun in hand, and threaten to blow Foreman's brains out. To date, he has survived all such attempted assaults—not by resorting to force, but by exercising his vaunted powers of persuasion. On one such occasion, as he stared down the pistol barrel of a woman defendant who was threatening to kill him, Foreman calmly remarked: "You don't want to shoot me, honey. I'm the only one who can get you off." The woman reluctantly conceded Foreman was right. She put the gun away.

Curiously enough, a number of Foreman's former clients—some of whom owe their very lives to his professional skills—are among his most adamant detractors. Foreman has found over the years that it is one thing to win a client's case and quite another to win his undying gratitude. Such gratitude, he has discovered, can be a sometime thing. Often, it fades within hours of the jury's pronouncement of the words "not guilty."

There are numerous reasons for animosity between Foreman and those he represents. First, as should be clear by now, he demands enormous fees. While faced with the loss of their lives or their freedom, the clients are willing to pay Foreman almost anything. But, once off the legal hook, they sometimes have second thoughts about the cash value of Foreman's services. Second, Foreman refuses to treat his clients with kid gloves. While defending them with all the skill at his command, he makes no secret of his contempt for some of them. Third, Foreman's courtroom tactics often offend his clients. For example, an accused killer may object to being branded insane by his own lawyer. But, if that is the only practical defense, Foreman will show no hesitation in pleading insanity. If his client does not like it, that's just too bad.

At this writing, two of Foreman's most vociferous enemies are none other than Candy Mossler and Mel Powers. Now that they stand acquitted of murder, Candy and Mel no longer sing Foreman's praises. On the contrary, they have all sorts of complaints about him. These complaints were first voiced in a lawsuit they filed against Foreman in the spring of 1967, a year after their acquittal on the murder charges.

The suit, filed in Houston, demanded that Foreman return the jewelry he had taken from Candy as collateral against his projected 200,000-dollar fee for handling the murder case. In addition, it demanded the return of a land deed he had taken from Mel as further collateral.

Candy claimed that the jewels, which she valued at almost 50,000 dollars at the time she gave them to Foreman, were now worth at least 84,000 dollars. Mel claimed that the land deed he gave Foreman—covering 4.6 acres of valuable property in Houston's southwest section—was to be held only as collateral and was not to be sold. He claimed the property was worth 75,000 dollars. However, Mel said, Foreman had violated their agreement by selling the property. What's more, he said, Foreman had received a mere 13,000 dollars for it. Mel figured this transaction had thus cost him 62,000 dollars. Moreover, he claimed he had paid Foreman 133,000 dollars in cash. Adding the 62,000 dollars and 133,000 dollars and getting a total of 195,000 dollars, he reckoned that he owed Foreman only about 5,000 dollars of the 200,000-dollar fee. And surely Candy's jewels should not be held by Foreman as security against that paltry amount, Candy and Mel contended.

Foreman, of course, was not about to take the lawsuit lying down. He immediately retorted that 200,000 dollars was a mere drop in the bucket. He wanted more than that for his services. And he filed a suit of his own against Candy and Mel, asking the court to decide how much he should be paid.

Foreman readily conceded he had taken collateral from Candy and Mel toward his fee. He said he always does that. "If you don't, you can't control the client," he said. "If they haven't paid for advice, they won't take it."

Foreman expressed confidence that a trial would result in his fee being raised substantially. "Depending on what newspaper you read, Mrs. Mossler inherited nine million dollars or thirty-three million dollars," he said. "She would not have inherited one penny of this had she not been acquitted. I was charged with the ultimate responsibility of seeing that both clients were successfully defended against the murder charges. Lawyers often work on a fifty-percent contingency-fee basis (an arrangement under which the attorney keeps half the money he collects on behalf of the client). Therefore, I feel I have a fifty-percent interest on a contingency basis in whatever amount Mrs. Mossler profited by the acquittal. I'll settle for any reasonable amount between 4.5 million dollars and 16.5 million dollars."

If Candy thought Foreman had reached the zenith of audacity in his demand for half her wealth, she was mistaken. For he was just getting started. He declared next that he would look forward to a trial for other reasons than merely deciding the amount of his fee. "As an outcome of this trial and evaluation of my services, the public might have a better opinion than it now has as to who killed Jacques Mossler," Foreman boomed.

Now the fat was really in the fire. Candy and Mel had retained Clyde Woody to represent them in their case against Foreman. And Woody seemed not only willing, but anxious, to tangle with Foreman in court. "We'll be more than happy to give him all the time in court he wants," Woody said. Moreover, he charged that Foreman's "veiled inference" regarding Mossler's killer "must be the result of his communing with spirits or looking into a crystal ball."

Woody immediately filed a pretrial motion asking the court to direct Foreman to appear in Woody's office and submit to questioning in a deposition proceeding. The motion also asked that Foreman be ordered to bring Mrs. Mossler's jewels, plus Foreman's own income-tax records, to Woody's office. Foreman retained an attorney named Levert J. Able to represent him in the case. And Able filed a petition asking the court to quash Woody's motion. Able's petition contended, among other things, that Foreman was committed to fulfill a speaking engagement on the date when Woody wanted to question him.

At this point, Clyde Woody went out of his way to demonstrate that he could be just as flamboyant as Percy Foreman. Woody filed with the clerk of the court a legal brief—in the form of a poem—that jabbed the needle of sarcasm into Foreman's hide. The poem poked fun at the pair of diamond-encrusted dancing slippers Foreman had given his wife. It implied Foreman was slowing down because of advancing years. And it even suggested that he was in such poor health he might die before Candy could win her suit for return of the jewels.

Referring to the dancing slippers, Woody told reporters: "Is Percy's wife dancing around on Candace Mossler's gems? Considering Percy's propensity to give his wife diamond-studded shoes, it is possible. Mrs. Mossler's jewels might be in Mrs. Foreman's shoe heels by now, for all I know."

For further information, Woody referred the reporters to the poem filed with the court clerk. The poem, which was co-authored by Woody's law associate, Marian Rosen, read:

> Our clients' properties were not returned,
> Which from this deposition can be learned.
> Also, what issues can be resolved,
> To take court's time when it's involved.
> Because Defendant is up in years,
> The Dead Man's Statute—a possible fear.
> His illness and known poor health
> May cause departure with others' wealth.
> Old age and illness justify our request
> Hoping sincerely his bones don't early rest.
> Subpoenaing the items to bring into court
> Is proper and necessary in a case of this sort.
> Income records are necessitous, too,
> For determination of our clients' due. . . .
> Plaintiff's compliance with procedural rules
> Is doubted by no one save only mules.
> Speaking engagements with conflicting dates—
> A Foremanish tactic subject to debate.
> For the above reasons we pray motion denial
> And ask court's assistance in proceeding to trial.

Since the poem seemed to raise more questions than it answered, reporters went back to Woody and asked for clarification. His explanation rubbed additional salt into Foreman's wounds. "Knowing how ill Percy is and his being in the twilight years, we must protect our clients' interests," the younger lawyer said. "It's a well-known fact that Percy is hardly able to start and finish a case without going to a hospital. And I'm convinced the old gent's memory is not as good as it once was, and therefore we need to preserve his testimony."

Woody's gratuitous slap at Foreman's age and purported ill health overstated the facts considerably. The truth was that Foreman had, indeed, been in and out of hospitals on several occasions in recent years—chiefly for treatment of the recurring pains resulting from his injury in an automobile accident. (He won a court judgment of $74,850 in 1967 from the owner of the truck that struck his car.) But to imply that he was in chronic poor health or in "the twilight years" was to play footsy with the facts. Surely there was no indication from Foreman's courtroom performances that he was in his dotage.

Foreman's lawyer, Levert Able, said Foreman would have no comment on Woody's poetic brief because it was "frivolous." But Able knew little about his client if he thought Percy Foreman could remain silent on such an occasion. Foreman responded to Woody by quoting a piece of poetry himself. The poem he chose was "To a Louse."

"About two hundred years ago Robert Burns wrote a poem entitled 'To a Louse,' " Foreman said.

"The last verse commences with these lines:

" 'Oh would some power the giftie gie us
To see ourselves as others see us.
It would from many a blunder free us. . . .'

"That is my poetic response to the versification of my detractors. When good lawyers need poetry, they go to the poetry books. When they need law, they go to the law books. But, when the duet representing the plantiffs [Candy and Mel] need either poetry or law, they contrive it. I realize the comparison is odious —but, of the two, their poetry is better than their law. As to my wife's shoes, I think it is a man's privilege to lay his treasures at the feet of the woman he loves. As to my age, it has been said that wisdom and understanding are their own rewards."

Who won the battle of the rhymes was an open question. Some said it ended in a Mexican standoff. But the legal battle was something else. On the specific point at issue, there was no question who was the winner. It was, as usual, Percy Foreman. District Judge John L. Compton ruled in Foreman's favor on the petition to quash Woody's motion demanding that Foreman appear for questioning and produce both Candy's jewels and his own tax returns.

But this was only Round One in the battle of the fees. Round Two commenced nine days later in Judge Compton's court. Pending a trial of the case on its merits, Clyde Woody had asked for an injunction to bar Foreman from disposing of the collateral given to him by Candy and Mel. A hearing on this injunction plea was conducted on April 20, 1967.

Candy was the star witness. She told how Foreman had come to visit her in a Houston hospital shortly after Mel's arrest in the murder case. She said Foreman demanded collateral to secure his 200,000-dollar fee.

"In tears, crying on my hospital bed, I took the rings off my fingers and gave them to him," Candy testified. She said she also took a brooch from around her neck and a watch from a bedside table, and handed them to Foreman. "He wanted more," she said. So she turned over still another ring—an emerald-cut blue-white diamond. She claimed this ring had special sentimental value.

"It was about nine carats," she said. "Mr. Mossler gave me that stone. . . . About the same time I got mine, Aly Khan gave one to Rita Hayworth. They are the only two in the United States—in the whole world—that I know about."

Each time she mentioned her murdered husband and how he had given her the diamond, Candy's voice broke. "The sentimental value of the jewelry makes it priceless to me," she said. Nonetheless, she was able to place a monetary value on the gems—about 84,000 dollars.

"We have pleaded, begged, crawled on bended knees to settle with Mr. Foreman," Candy testified. "We want to pay him what we owe . . . because I always pay my bills. All the other attorneys have been paid, but Mr. Foreman won't let anybody pay him." She did not explain this last statement on the witness stand. But later, outside the courtroom, she told reporters that Foreman "won't let us settle. . . . He wants to keep our names on those [legal] papers."

Foreman also testified at the injunction hearing. He said he had no intention of disposing of Candy's jewels or Mel's property. "I have never sold anything that didn't belong to me," he said. Levert Able argued that Foreman was entitled to keep the collateral until he was paid in full. "If enjoined from disposing of the collateral, he will probably never get his fee," Able said.

Once again, Foreman carried the day. The judge ruled in his favor, denying the injunction sought by Clyde Woody.

Thus, both Round One and Round Two had gone to Foreman. Whether the succeeding rounds will also go his way may not be clear for many months or even years. For, at this writing, a date has not even been set for a trial of the fee case on its merits. And, no matter what the outcome of the trial, an appeal is likely. It may thus seem that a long period of enmity is in store between Foreman on one side and Candy, Mel and Woody on the other.

But such is not necessarily the case. Foreman has been known on many occasions to forgive and forget. He appears to speak the truth when he says he is not a vindictive man. If any proof be demanded, one need only examine Foreman's relationships with two men known as "The Gold Dust Twins" of Texas law enforcement.

"The Gold Dust Twins" were Harris County (Houston) Sheriff C. V. (Buster) Kern and Texas Ranger Johnny Klevenhagen. Kern and Klevenhagen were prototypes of the movie-style Texas lawman—lanky, lean, leathery and tough. Together, they had cracked countless sensational murder cases. They had fought numerous gun battles. And they were known as the scourge of the Texas underworld.

For years Percy Foreman carried on a vitriolic feud with Kern and Klevenhagen. In case after case, he charged them and their cohorts with police brutality and other assorted offenses. He accused them of beating confessions out of prisoners and of jailing innocent men. The high point in the feud was reached in a tense murder trial in 1952.

Three years earlier, a Houston gambler named Vincent Vallone had been rubbed out in gangland fashion—blasted with a shotgun by an assassin firing from a passing car. (Foreman had known Vallone for more than twenty years. As will be recalled from Chapter 3, Vallone had been manager of the Hi-Hat Club—the gambling joint Foreman had raided as a prosecutor in the early 1930s.)

The Vallone murder created a sensation, receiving all-out coverage in the news media. Kern and Klevenhagen took personal charge of the investigation. After an intensive manhunt, they arrested a thirty-one-year-old Houston grocer named Diego Carlino. They spirited Carlino to an out-of-the-way jail, questioned him at length and ultimately emerged with the announcement that he had confessed the murder. It had been a gangland rubout, "The Gold Dust Twins" claimed. They said Carlino had been given an underworld "contract" to carry out the murder. And, to prove it, they showed newsmen copies of Carlino's typed confession.

Foreman was retained to defend Carlino. Since the case had received enormous publicity in the Houston press, Foreman contended that Carlino could not receive a fair trial in Houston. He obtained a change of venue shifting the trial across the state to the city of San Angelo.

Foreman conducted a typically ripsnorting defense, tearing apart prosecution witnesses and claiming that the state was trying to railroad his client into the electric chair. Kern and Klevenhagen, who had staked their reputations on Carlino's guilt, were subjected to merciless cross-examinations by Foreman. Both were seething as the case approached its climax.

They could barely restrain themselves during Foreman's summation to the jury. Foreman recalled that Kern and Klevenhagen had testified that Carlino had not only confessed to them, but had also led them to the spot where he had hidden the murder weapon. The weapon purportedly had been retrieved by a deputy sheriff named Kain, Foreman pointed out.

"Kern, Klevenhagen and Kain," Foreman boomed to the jurors. "K.K.K. They ku-kluxed this defendant. They tortured him to make him confess. Who among you can say you, too, would not have confessed to this killing—innocent though you be—if these pistol-packing, blackjack-wearing, handcuff-carrying, booted and spurred officers of the so-called law had predetermined you guilty and decided *you* were *going to confess?*"

As Foreman cajoled them, the jurors pointedly turned and gazed at Kern and Klevenhagen. Both lawmen were glaring furiously at Foreman. They did, indeed, look tough. One could almost see each juror trying to guess whether he could stand up under prolonged questioning by "The Gold Dust Twins."

Finally, the jury retired. Within an hour, it was back with its verdict: Not guilty!

This was more than Kern and Klevenhagen could stand. They leaped over a courtroom railing and charged at Foreman. The defense lawyer, several days earlier, had accidentally fallen down a flight of stairs and severely wrenched his left knee. Thus, he was walking with the aid of a crutch as he headed out of the courtroom. Before he could reach the door, he was intercepted by "The Gold Dust Twins."

Right there in the courtroom, with the jurors loking on in astonishment, Kern and Klevenhagen proceeded to beat the daylights out of Foreman. They forced him back against the rail of the jury box, pummeled him mercilessly and ultimately left him in a heap on the courtroom floor.

A doctor was summoned to patch Foreman up. He found an impressive array of injuries. There was an inch-long cut and a large swelling on Foreman's left cheek. Both his eyes were discolored, and there were cuts and scratches alongside them. He had a badly sprained and swollen finger, sustained as he raised his hand to try to ward off the blows. His previously injured left knee had been hurt anew. And he had an aching back (the doctor said he might have a ruptured disc), apparently the result of being forced back against the jury box.

From all over Texas came cries of outrage against Kern and Klevenhagen. There were demands that both be ousted from their jobs. A Texas Bar Association official, W. N. Bonner, called for disciplinary action against them. "Officers ought to obey the law—not beat up attorneys who are doing their duty," Bonner said. "An officer can't be thin-skinned. He's got to expect some things during a trial—the same as a district attorney must expect a defense attorney to get in his hair occasionally. A defense lawyer must have freedom to defend an accused person fearlessly, without the fear that he will be beaten up." A state legislator, Douglas Crouch, wired Klevenhagen's boss, State Public Safety Director Homer Garrison, demanding that the Ranger be fired. "I have known for several years that policemen have few qualms about beating up prisoners, but I didn't believe anything so high-handed as this would occur," Crouch said.

Through it all, among the few who refused to join in the onslaught against Kern and Klevenhagen was Percy Foreman himself. "I harbor no malice toward these poor, misguided minions of the law," Foreman said. "As a professing Christian, I have already forgiven them. I hope they find it in their hearts to get on their knees and ask forgiveness of the Almighty. Surely, the Lord will forgive them. 'For they know not what they do.'"

Foreman declined to press charges against the officers, explaining, characteristically, that "I am not a vindictive man." Eventually, the storm blew over. Kern and Klevenhagen returned to their normal pursuits and Foreman resumed giving them fits. But he was true to his word. He held no grudge.

About three years after the courtroom beating was administered, Kern and Klevenhagen came to Foreman to ask a favor. They had arrested a young woman in a particularly heinous murder case. The crime had been so ghastly that the defendant seemed likely to become the first woman in Texas history to go to the electric chair. Though Kern and Klevenhagen were convinced the woman had participated in the crime, they doubted that she had committed it alone. But they were unable to find an accomplice or even establish that an accomplice existed. Because of their doubts, they grew determined to try to prevent the woman's execution. They appealed to Foreman to take her case. She was a poor woman who could not afford Foreman's usual fees. Nonetheless, at the urging of his two old antagonists, Foreman agreed to handle her defense. (The case, and its outcome, will be discussed in detail in Chapter 11.)

Several years after this episode, Klevenhagen died. But Buster Kern is still sheriff of Harris County. He and Foreman still tangle frequently on a professional basis. However, Foreman has demonstrated time and again that he holds no personal rancor toward the sheriff.

On any list of Foreman antagonists, a special place must be reserved for a Houston supermarket owner named Norris Hooks.

For Hooks stirred up one of the most sensational disputes in Foreman's career. It was he who got Foreman arrested on an adultery charge.

The Foreman-Hooks imbroglio occurred in 1954 after Hooks' wife, Lora, had hired Foreman to file a divorce suit. At the time, Foreman himself was unmarried. He had already been divorced from his first wife, but had not yet married for the second time. Though he resided in Houston, he spent considerable time—particularly on weekends—at a beach house he owned in Galveston. It was not uncommon for him to take clients to the beach house for business discussions.

At 2:30 A.M. on Sunday, May 2, 1954, a "raiding party" led by Galveston Constable Sam Popovich—accompanied by a flock of news reporters and photographers—moved across the beach in the darkness and descended upon Foreman's house. Popovich had a warrant, issued on the basis of a complaint by Hooks, calling for the arrest of both Foreman and Mrs. Hooks on adultery charges.

When the "raiding party" reached the house, Popovich found that Foreman and Mrs. Hooks were, indeed, inside. The constable duly served the warrant and took them into custody amid much hubbub and popping of flashbulbs. A short time later, the two prisoners posted bonds of 2,000 dollars each and were released.

Foreman immediately denied that he and Mrs. Hooks had done anything improper. He pointed out that the circumstances hardly supported Hooks' contention of an assignation. For he and Mrs. Hooks had not been alone at the beach house. With them had been Foreman's eight-year-old son and ten-year-old nephew. Would a man and woman bent on adultery bring along two young boys for company? It scarcely seemed likely.

Foreman explained that he, Mrs. Hooks and the two boys had driven to the beach house from Houston on Saturday afternoon. He said he and Mrs. Hooks had spent the afternoon discussing in detail eighty pieces of property involved in her divorce action. Mrs. Hooks' adult son was supposed to pick her up late in the afternoon and drive her home, Foreman explained. But the son, a Houston railroad employee, was assigned to work an extra shift and could not come, he said. As a result, it was decided that Mrs.

Hooks would spend the night at the beach house. The arrangement was entirely innocent, Foreman insisted. He said that Mrs. Hooks had occupied a suite separated by a large living room from the suite occupied by himself, his son and his nephew.

A joint examining trial for Foreman and Mrs. Hooks was conducted on May 15 by Justice of the Peace Ralph Gustafson, who had issued the warrant for their arrest. Hooks explained that, after learning his wife was at the beach house with Foreman, he had consulted an attorney. He said the lawyer told him his wife "had no business being there overnight with Foreman." As a result, he said, he filed the adultery charges.

But Hooks could provide no evidence that adultery had actually been committed. All he had was his suspicion.

"Why did you file charges if you had no evidence other than what you had heard?" the judge asked him.

"I don't believe they were playing pinochle at that house on the bay," Hooks replied.

But that was hardly enough to satisfy either the judge or the prosecution. The prosecuting attorney asked for dismissal of the charges on grounds of insufficient evidence. Judge Gustafson readily complied.

That, however, did not end the Foreman-Hooks dispute. The donnybrook was just getting started.

Foreman filed a 500,000-dollar lawsuit against Hooks, claiming that the adultery charges had hurt his law practice. Not to be outdone, Hooks slapped a 200,000-dollar suit on Foreman, claiming that the attorney had prevented him from arranging a possible reconciliation with his wife. Each of the men bombarded the other with recriminations.

"Hooks just wanted to make adultery charges against us because his wife made the same kind of accusations against him in her divorce petition," Foreman said. "His accusations have seriously hurt my practice, causing me to lose at least three big cases. And they've hurt me socially, too. His action is typical of men who are being sued for divorce. Where their wives used to turn to them for help and advice, they now turn to their attorneys. So the husbands get jealous."

Hooks replied: "Foreman completely dominates my wife. He has prevented any possible reconciliation between us. He has entertained her in the Shamrock Hotel, his home in Houston, the beach house and sundry other places. Besides that, he and my wife have just about killed my business. They're out to see that I wind up digging ditches."

The battle waxed and waned, then eventually faded from the front pages. The lawsuits ended in a standoff. Hooks did not wind up digging ditches. He went on operating his successful supermarket. Percy Foreman, despite his claim that the adultery charges had hurt his law practice, also prospered. And, in time, he went on to fight still other battles against other antagonists.

In 1962, Foreman became embroiled in an acrimonious dispute with a judge. At the time, Foreman was burdened with a typically heavy load of cases. He found himself scheduled to try two murder cases on the same day in two different cities. One of his clients, Marvin Bauer, was scheduled for trial before Judge John M. Barron in Bryan, Texas. Another, Odis Hammond, was due in court at the same time before Judge Miron Love in Houston. Even Percy Foreman could not handle two murder trials simultaneously. Foreman asked Judge Barron to postpone the Bauer trial, but his request was denied. Judge Love not only refused to postpone the Hammond trial; he threatened to hold Foreman in contempt if the defense lawyer failed to appear on schedule.

Confronted with this seemingly insoluble dilemma, Foreman resigned as Bauer's attorney on the day before the trial was to begin. Judge Barron was furious, but had no choice other than to postpone the case until Bauer could retain a new attorney. The judge publicly rebuked Foreman for quitting the case. He argued that the Bauer case took precedence over the Hammond case because its trial date had been set first. "If a thing like this can go on and an attorney can get by with it, then something is wrong with the judicial structure of this state," Barron said.

Foreman fired back an angry retort. "Judge Barron is drunk on power or doesn't have any judgment or sense of propriety," he said. "He's trying to make himself a reputation at the expense of me and my client." Foreman recalled that he had previously tangled with Barron in a trial when the judge was a district attorney. He accused Barron of refusing to postpone the Bauer case because "he has a grudge against me for something I said about him when he was district attorney." Without explaining what this "something" was, Foreman said: "I had to put him in a bad light to win that [previous] case. I thought he was big enough to forget it, but he's not. He's all motor and no brake."

A reporter asked Barron if he planned to hold Foreman in contempt. The judge shook his head. "I don't consider anyone like that worthy of being held in contempt," he said.

Only five months after the Barron episode, Foreman was subjected to a steady stream of abuse from one of his own clients. The client, eighteen-year-old Gary Stephen Sizemore, objected to the strategy Foreman employed in defending him against a murder charge. Sizemore was accused of shooting a grocer to death during a robbery. The prosecution demanded the death sentence. Foreman pleaded Sizemore not guilty by virtue of insanity and presented psychiatric testimony that the defendant suffered from a split personality. This drove Sizemore into a frenzy. "He was cursing me throughout the trial for even suggesting insanity," Foreman said. Nonetheless, Foreman saved Sizemore from the electric chair. The jury, while finding him guilty, sentenced him to life imprisonment—a term that made him eligible for parole in eight years.

There is scarcely any way of predicting who will become Foreman's next antagonist. One of his most unlikely encounters—since he is noted for his courtly treatment of women—involved him in a vitriolic hassle with a young female legal secretary. The woman, Mrs. Lena Stolicky, a twenty-six-year-old divorcee, filed a court complaint accusing Foreman of using abusive language to her. The complaint stemmed from an incident at Foreman's favorite hangout, the Old Capitol Club in Houston's Rice Hotel.

Mrs. Stolicky said she had gone to the club to apologize to Foreman for breaking several job-interview appointments with him. When she got there, she said, Foreman cursed her for breaking the appointments. She said his language shocked her so much that she went to Houston's Corporation Court and filed charges against him.

The case came to trial before Judge Walter Chalmers on February 11, 1964. Foreman testified that Mrs. Stolicky had "harassed" him with thirty-eight telephone calls since the previous spring. When she appeared at the Old Capitol Club, he said, he told her he had no job for her and then asked a club employee to throw her out. Mrs. Stolicky testified about Foreman's purported cursing. She told the judge the words she claimed Foreman had used.

"Everyone knows he is a cad and a louse!" she exclaimed. The prosecutor, Gerry Adams, tried to reprove her for the outburst.

But Foreman cut the prosecutor off. "I don't mind," he said magnanimously.

When the testimony ended, Judge Chalmers took all of ten seconds for deliberation. He then found Foreman innocent. It was not one of the most important victories in Foreman's career. But it was probably the quickest verdict.

As Foreman lumbered out of the courtroom—in search of new worlds to conquer and new battles to fight—he showed no animosity over being called "a cad and a louse." After all, he is not a vindictive man.

10

The government's pitching and I'm catching.
PERCY FOREMAN, *describing his strategy for defending Texas political boss George B. Parr against federal mail-fraud charges.*

OF ALL THE DEFENSES Percy Foreman has conducted, perhaps his greatest test of staying power came in a series of trials known as the Duval County cases. Over a period of seven years, in courtrooms throughout Texas, Foreman battled local, state and federal prosecutors on behalf of one of the most corrupt political machines in American history.

The central figure in these cases was a ruthless, middle-aged political boss named George Berham Parr. For more than forty years, Parr and his father before him had ruled like feudal despots over a wide area of South Texas near the Mexican border. Their subjects included thousands of Mexican-Americans whose livelihoods—and, some said, their very lives—depended on staying in the good graces of the Parr machine. Because his headquarters was in Duval County, and because of his iron-fisted control over the citizenry, Parr was known as the Duke of Duval. Among his other sobriquets was the Sagebrush Caesar.

Parr's power, however, was not confined to Duval County. At one time he controlled the political fortunes of no fewer than five oil-rich South Texas counties. In addition, he was a force in statewide politics and his influence was felt on the national scene. So tight was his grip on the masses that he was able to deliver voting majorities up to one hundred to one for the candidates of his choice.

The Parr family's dominance over the area stemmed from a 1912 blood bath at the Duval County Courthouse in San Diego, Texas. On May 18, 1912, a band of Anglo-Americans, determined to run Duval County for the benefit of Anglos, killed three Mexican-Americans at the courthouse. The slayings split the citizenry into two rival camps. George Parr's father, Archie Parr, took the side of the Mexican-Americans in the feud. The elder Parr mobilized the Mexican-Americans—who greatly outnumbered Parr's fellow Anglos—into a formidable political bloc.

At first Archie Parr, who was a state senator, ran Duval County under a system of benevolent despotism. He helped find jobs for impoverished Latins. He provided handouts to the unemployed. And he rarely missed a Mexican-American wedding or funeral. In return, the Latins did the Parr machine's bidding at the polls. But gradually the benevolence disappeared from the system and only the despotism remained. The Parr machine turned increasingly to repressive methods to keep the masses in line.

A force of gun-toting special deputy sheriffs—called "pistoleros" by the citizenry—enforced the orders of the machine. Dissent was not countenanced. Meanwhile, it became apparent that taxpayers' money was being used to line the pockets of members of the machine. In 1934, George Parr—who was gradually taking over control of the organization from his father—was convicted of federal tax-evasion charges. (Parr was not represented by Percy Foreman in this case.) After serving part of a two-year prison sentence, Parr was released on parole. Years later, he would receive a full pardon from President Harry S Truman.

While Parr was in prison, his father held the machine together.

The son took the reins from his father upon his return from the penitentiary. In 1942, Archie Parr died, leaving George to rule alone over the empire.

Six years after that, Parr was considered instrumental in bringing about the election of Lyndon B. Johnson to the United States Senate. Johnson, then a congressman, ran for a Senate seat in the 1948 Democratic primary against former Texas Governor Coke Stevenson. In the primary, which was equivalent to election, the counties controlled by Parr delivered massive majorities for Johnson. But even these initially did not seem to be enough to prevent Stevenson from apparently winning the race by 112 votes.

All boxes (precincts) in the state had reported their vote tallies and, five days after the primary, Stevenson was considered the winner. But then there occurred what came to be known as "the miracle of Box 13." On the sixth day after the primary, Box 13, in Parr-controlled Jim Wells County, "amended" its vote tally. It gave an additional 201 votes to Johnson and an additional two votes to Stevenson. This provided Johnson with an eighty-seven–vote victory and the nickname "Landslide Lyndon." Stevenson screamed "fraud" and demanded an examination of the Box 13 election records, but the Parr forces claimed the records had somehow gotten "lost."

Stevenson got a federal court injunction to prevent Johnson from taking office. However, the case eventually went to United States Supreme Court Justice Hugo Black, who nullified the injunction—not on the merits of the vote-fraud charges, but on the ground that federal courts should not become arbiters of state primary elections. Thus, Lyndon Johnson went to the Senate and George Parr reached new heights of power.

With this power came increased arrogance. Parr became ever more high-handed. He appropriated a 500,000-dollar Duval County bond issue for his own benefit—using it to buy a 45,000-acre ranch. And his tactics for maintaining control became increasingly oppressive.

Ultimately, these tactics drove a segment of the populace to revolt against the Parr regime. In the early 1950s, an Anti-Parr party was formed to challenge the Parr party. The leader of the

Anti-Parr party was a determined Anglo lawyer named Jacob S. (Jake) Floyd.

On the evening of September 8, 1952, Floyd was sitting in his home in Alice, Texas, talking to his son, Jacob, Jr. The son, called Buddy, was studying law at the University of Texas. Floyd and his son were alone in the living room. Mrs. Floyd was at church. About 8:45, the telephone rang. On the line was a Mexican-American lawyer, Nago Alaniz, who was an underling of George Parr. Alaniz told Floyd he had to see him immediately to tell him something. He asked Floyd to meet him behind a drive-in restaurant on the outskirts of Alice.

Floyd agreed. Just before Floyd hung up, Alaniz told him in a tense voice: "Jake, don't come in your car. It might be spotted. Don't go out your back door. Come in a taxi. And be sure you come out your front door."

Following the instructions, Floyd telephoned for a taxi. He told his son he was going to the drive-in. "One of Parr's men wants to tell me something," he said. At the drive-in, he found Alaniz seated in a car. He climbed in beside him.

"They're trying to kill you, Jake," Alaniz said. "Maybe they'll kill me for telling you. But, when they start killing people, I'm getting out." Floyd scoffed at the warning. But Alaniz insisted he was telling the truth. "You've got to believe me," he said. "They've brought in Mario Sapet to handle it." Mario (El Turco) Sapet was a former bartender and brothel-keeper. Less than a month earlier, he had been sworn in as a Duval County deputy sheriff by George Parr. (Parr, who had held various public offices over the years, was then serving as sheriff.)

Floyd, remaining skeptical, pressed Alaniz for more details. Ultimately, Alaniz told him: "My God, Jake, believe me! When I telephoned you, I was supposed to let you walk out your back door to your garage. At this minute a pistolero is hiding in your garage, waiting to kill you." Finally, Floyd was convinced. He went looking for a peace officer to arrest the gunman hiding in his garage. But, unknown to Floyd, the gunman had already struck.

When Floyd had left his home, his son Buddy had feared he was walking into a trap set by the Parr forces. Buddy decided to follow his father. But he did not know about Alaniz's warning to avoid using the back door. Thus, he ran out this door toward the garage, planning to use the family car to join his father at the drive-in. Buddy was about the same height and weight as his father. In the darkness, the gunman mistook the son for the father. He fired four quick shots, fatally wounding the youth.

Neighbors heard the shots. They saw a man run to a car, then speed away. The neighbors made a cursory search of the Floyd yard with flashlights. However, they failed to spot Buddy, who was still alive but bleeding profusely. It was not until his mother returned from church, almost an hour later, that Buddy was found lying in the driveway. He was rushed to a hospital for emergency surgery, but died the next day.

Although Nago Alaniz had tried to warn Jake Floyd, he was arrested on charges of participating in the original conspiracy that had resulted in Buddy's murder. Mario Sapet was also arrested as a conspirator, but not as the triggerman. Texas Rangers developed evidence that the shooting had actually been carried out by a Mexican outlaw named Alfredo Cervantes. Among other things, Cervantes' fingerprints were found on the murder weapon.

The Rangers eventually charged Cervantes with the murder. But by that time he had skipped back across the Mexican border. All attempts by Texas to extradite him have failed. Thus, he has never come to trial. Alaniz and Sapet, however, were tried. Alaniz was represented by Percy Foreman. On the theory that Alaniz had purged himself of guilt by warning Jake Floyd, a jury set him free. Sapet was not so fortunate. The prosecution produced evidence at his trial that he had imported Cervantes to carry out the murder of Jake Floyd, had given him detailed instructions and had provided him with both the murder weapon and a getaway car. The jury convicted Sapet of being an accomplice to murder. It sentenced him to ninety-nine years in prison.

Although Sapet had been one of George Parr's deputies at the time of the slaying, no evidence was produced to link Parr with the murder. Nonetheless, as one by-product of the Buddy Floyd murder case, a massive investigation of Parr's political machine was launched by state and federal officers.

Texas Attorney General John Ben Shepperd sent hordes of investigators into Parr's territory. The federal government sent teams of FBI men, Internal Revenue agents and postal inspectors. For years, Parr had controlled the makeup of grand juries serving in his area. But now a grand jury that owed no allegiance to Parr was empaneled. Since it opened each session with a prayer, the panel became known as the "praying grand jury."

Before long, the federal and state investigators began coming up with evidence of massive corruption. They uncovered the fact that Parr had used the 500,000 dollars in Duval County bond funds to buy his ranch. They found that more than a hundred school-district checks totaling 67,000 dollars, made out to fictitious persons, had been cashed at banks controlled by Parr; that more than 130 Duval County checks had been cashed at the Parr banks without being endorsed; that still other checks had been issued in the names of persons who claimed to know nothing about them; that more than 330,000 dollars in Duval County funds had been illegally juggled around in Parr banks, and that the county had paid 250,000 dollars to a construction company controlled by Parr.

Eventually, the "praying grand jury" returned 104 indictments against Parr and his associates, charging various acts of corruption. Parr retained Percy Foreman as his defense lawyer. And Foreman, in time, succeeded in getting all 104 indictments dismissed on the ground that the "praying grand jury" had been illegally empaneled.

But a new grand jury was sworn in, and it returned swarms of new indictments. All told, including the original 104 indictments, 454 indictments were brought in against Parr and 200 of his associates. The cases were tried, on changes of venue, in courtrooms throughout Texas. Foreman traveled from city to city in a marathon defense of Parr and his henchmen. And, when all of the state's cases had been disposed of, not one of Foreman's clients had served a single day in prison.

However, the main event in the Parr cases did not come in a state court, but in a federal court in Houston. For Parr and eight of his associates had been charged in a federal indictment with using the mails to defraud the Benavides Independent School District out of more than 200,000 dollars in tax funds. Thus, all the resources of the federal government were arrayed against Percy Foreman in this case.

Indicted with Parr were D. C. Chapa, a Parr lieutenant who had served as tax assessor-collector of the Benavides school district; Oscar Carrillo, a son of Chapa who had served as school-board secretary (the discrepancy in their last names resulted from the practice by some Mexican-Americans of using their mothers' maiden names); O. P. Carrillo, another Chapa son who had been the school board's attorney; B. F. (Tom) Donald, cashier in Parr's Texas State Bank of Alice; Jesus Garza, a former school-board member; Santiago Garcia, another former school-board member; Octavio Saenz, former school-board president; and Jesus Oliveira, a director of the Texas State Bank of Alice.

Among other things, the government charged that Parr, although not a member of the school board, was the school district's final authority on hiring, firing, spending and other matters; that 200,000 dollars' worth of checks were made out by the district to fictitious persons for work that was never performed; that various defendants "short-stopped" checks mailed to the district by taxpayers, then stole the checks and cashed them; that the defendants charged personal purchases to the district; and that the mails were used repeatedly in carrying out the defendants' illegal schemes. (Tax bills and payments were habitually sent through the mails. Many of these involved large payments by oil companies operating wells within the district.)

It took four trials to get a verdict in the case. The first trial ended in a hung jury. The second was declared a mistrial when it was discovered that one of the jurors lived outside the judicial district in which the case was being tried (he had been summoned to court by mistake). The third was declared a mistrial when it was found that a juror had a criminal record.

The decisive fourth trial began on May 6, 1957, at the Federal Courthouse in Houston. Presiding was United States District Judge Joe Ingraham. Heading the prosecution was the United

States Attorney for the Southern District of Texas, thirty-eight-year-old Malcolm R. Wilkey. Seated beside Wilkey at the prosecution table was his chief aide, thirty-four-year-old Edgar O. Bottler. At the defense table, Foreman was assisted by a veteran South Texas lawyer, Gilbert Sharpe.

Shortly after the trial began, the prosecution produced evidence about a fantastic "phantom school" in the Benavides school district. Wilkey and Bottler read into the record excerpts from the district's annual reports, showing the purported expenditure of thousands of dollars for the supposed construction of the school. They then produced evidence that this school had never been built, that it existed only in the falsified records of the district. The prosecutors contended that the money that was supposed to have been spent for construction of the school had found its way, instead, into the pockets of Parr and his codefendants.

All told, Wilkey and Bottler entered into the record evidence concerning the issuance of 220,000 dollars' worth of checks by the district. They maintained this money was paid out either in the names of fictitious persons or in the names of persons who never did any work for the district. Included in the alleged payments were regular 500-dollar monthly checks to Parr's brother-in-law, B. G. Moffett, for "legal services." The prosecutors produced evidence that Moffett had never done any work for the district. Also listed as regular recipients were defendant Jesus Oliveira and the young daughters of defendants Santiago Garcia and Jesus Garza. There was testimony that Oliveira never did any work for the district and that the young girls were attending out-of-town schools during the periods when they were listed as school-district employees.

Further evidence of strange goings-on in the district was provided by a former school-board member, Troy Carey. He testified that, in effect, two separate school boards functioned within the single official board. Carey said he and two other board members conducted regular meetings at Freer, Texas, a community in the district. Meanwhile, he testified, four other board members—all defendants in the trial—conducted separate meetings in Benavides. For more than a year, Carey said, the two groups never met jointly. He said the group composed of Parr's codefendants maintained complete control over the letting of contracts and the hiring of employees.

Shortly after Carey completed his testimony, a caustic word battle erupted between Foreman and Wilkey. Foreman was cross-examining a prosecution witness who had produced documents that were potentially damaging to the defense cause. Foreman asked the witness several questions concerning whether he had testified about those same documents in a state court trial of one of Parr's codefendants, D. C. Chapa, at Tyler, Texas. Foreman's stated purpose in asking the questions was to show that state and federal officials had joined in a "political alliance" to persecute Parr and had used the same witnesses and evidence to carry out this purported persecution.

Wilkey objected to the questions, accusing Foreman of knowing "all the while" that the witness had not testified in Tyler.

"I did not know this man did not testify in Tyler," Foreman insisted heatedly.

Wilkey, just as heatedly, retorted: "Mr. Foreman knew in advance the answers to these questions—and that they were improper—but asked them so he could make prejudicial statements before the jury." He objected particularly to Foreman's charge of a "political alliance." And he asked Judge Ingraham to order Foreman to refrain from asking prejudicial questions.

This request brought on an angry tirade from Foreman. In a voice that rose from a low rumble to a piercing shout, Foreman said: "I except to Mr. Wilkey's statement that I asked something I knew was improper. The only place in my thirty years of law practice that I've ever had a prosecutor ask a judge to join with the prosecution against the defense was in this court. And the only prosecutor who has ever done that to me has been Mr. Wilkey! He has eternally and repeatedly said to judges—outside the hearing of the jury—'You ought to join with us and throw a stone at him [Foreman].' I could say he's a bald-faced prevaricator if I were as bold as he is—which I am not." Foreman further accused Wilkey of assuming "a professorial attitude" and "trying something in the courtroom that is used generally only in law-school classrooms, trying to get the judge to warn me in advance to restrict my questions."

Wilkey, his face flushed, replied: "My information comes not from any textbooks, but from continued observation of Mr. Foreman in the Parr trials."

Once again, Foreman hammered at the "political alliance" theme. He told the judge: "This prosecution was based on an exchange of information between state and federal officials. Mr. Wilkey calls it 'information.' We call it 'grand-jury testimony,' which is in violation of the law. We will put Mr. Wilkey on the stand—as we did in the first trial—and I am sure he will testify that he did use information from the state [officials]."

Judge Ingraham calmly took all this in from the bench, then mildly addressed each of the lawyers in turn. To Foreman, he said: "You should refrain from asking leading questions." To Wilkey: "I don't see any harm in Mr. Foreman referring to this as a 'political prosecution.' 'Political' in its broadest sense means 'in the public good.' "

Foreman next turned to trying to show that some of the government's witnesses did not come to court with clean hands. The prosecution put on the stand Joe Valleo, a current member of the Benavides school board. Valleo had served as board president after three of Parr's codefendants had resigned from the board. He testified to various purportedly illegal acts committed by the defendants. But Foreman drew from Valleo an admission that he had agreed to become board president only if three of his relatives and close friends were named as board members.

Knowing that the prosecution later planned to call as a witness a former board member named Richard Barton, Foreman set out to discredit Barton's testimony in advance. Foreman asked Valleo: "Will you tell us whether Richard Barton resigned as a school-board member on the same day as [defendants] Octavio Saenz, Santiago Garcia and Jesus Garza?"

A. Yes, he did.

Q. Do you know of any acts by Mr. Garza, Mr. Garcia and Mr. Saenz—while they were members of the school board—that were not likewise the acts and conduct of Mr. Barton?

A. To my knowledge, no.

Q. To your knowledge, then, all acts of these three members were also the acts of Richard Barton?

A. Yes, sir.

Because of this cross-examination, Barton's later testimony seemed to be of minimal value to the prosecution. But a subsequent government witness provided testimony that was considerably more valuable to the prosecution. The witness was Mrs. Edna Fitch, a short, plump brunette who had previously worked as a teller at the Texas State Bank of Alice. Mrs. Fitch testified that George Parr, who was president of the bank, often cashed Benavides school-district checks at her teller's cage. "He would just reach into my cash drawer and take out the amount of money on the checks," she said.

Prosecutor Wilkey: Did you ever examine those checks to see if they were endorsed?

A. No, sir—except for one time.

Q. That time, were they endorsed?

A. Yes, sir.

Q. Was Mr. Parr's endorsement on them?

A. No, sir.

Q. To whom were they made out?

A. I didn't check.

Q. Were they made out to Mr. Parr?

A. I just didn't check. He reached into my drawer and took the money and I just stamped the checks.

The significance of Mrs. Fitch's testimony lay mainly in the fact that the government had already shown Parr had never done any work for the school district to justify receiving district funds. Of course, it was possible that Parr could have cashed checks for persons who had originally received them legitimately from the district. Parr, in turn, could have taken the checks to the bank. But the prosecution contended that, if this had happened, Parr's second endorsement should have appeared on the checks. And, at least in the one case when Mrs. Fitch had examined the checks, they had borne no such endorsement by Parr.

On cross-examination, Foreman immediately attacked Mrs.

Fitch's credibility. "Were you fired from your job at the Texas State Bank of Alice or did you resign?" he asked.

Mrs. Fitch rasped angrily: "Would you like the jury to hear all about that? Are you sure you want me to tell the circumstances under which that happened? Well, I'll tell you, and it isn't going to be good!"

Foreman cut her off. "I didn't ask you that, Mrs. Fitch. Just anwer my question." Then, without giving her a chance to answer, he asked: "Do you bear an animous grudge or feeling against Mr. Parr? Or Tom Donald?" (Donald, it will be recalled, was cashier of the bank and a codefendant of Parr.)

A. No. I was glad to get out of there.

Q. I didn't ask you that, Mrs. Fitch. I asked you if you bear them an animous grudge.

A. No. I just feel pity for them.

Mrs. Fitch shortly left the stand. She never got the chance to tell her story of how she came to leave her job at the bank.

She was followed to the stand by a Duval County service-station operator, Amador Caballero. He testified that various defendants had bought gasoline and automobile supplies at his station. Although these were used in the defendants' personal cars, he said, the items were charged to the school district.

Once again, on cross-examination Foreman tried to show that a prosecution witness was biased against the defendants. He brought out through his questioning that Caballero was active in the Freedom party—an anti-Parr political party. He also showed that Caballero had been a member of the grand-jury commission that had appointed the "praying grand jury." Foreman then drew from the witness a concession that he had helped appoint a number of his relatives and political allies to this grand jury.

Q. Isn't every one of the defendants in this case now an active leader or worker in the Old party—sometimes called the 'Parr party'?

A. Yes, they all are.

Q. Do you know any member of the Parr party who has not been indicted from one to 104 times?

A. No, sir.

Q. Did you help the grand jury return the 104 indictments against these men?

A. No, sir. [He said this emphatically, but with a broad smile.]

Q. Wouldn't you like to see these men convicted? Don't you think it would be in your interest in running for office down there if these men were out of the way?

A. No, sir, I don't, either, want them convicted. That's not my duty.

The next day, Foreman displayed the kind of alertness that is one of his stocks in trade. Prosecutor Wilkey was questioning R. R. Gonzales, tax collector for the Benavides school district. Gonzales testified that he had brought some district tax records to the courtroom, but had left "a whole roomful" back in South Texas. Wilkey asked him: "Are you willing to bring whatever other records remain in the school-district office which may be relevant to the case—at the request of the defense or the prosecution?"

Foreman pounced. Two words in Wilkey's question—"the defense"—had triggered an alarm bell in his mind. "We move for a mistrial for the reason that there is no burden placed on the defendants to produce any evidence," Foreman announced. He argued that Wilkey's use of the words "the defense" had improperly implied there *was* such a burden on the defendants. Judge Ingraham said at first that he was "very much concerned" that he might have to grant the mistrial. But later, after studying legal precedents on the issue, he denied Foreman's motion. This ruling, however, left Foreman with a possible ground for appeal if his clients should be convicted.

Next, the jury heard testimony that the microfilm records of two Parr-controlled banks had mysteriously disappeared when investigators began looking into the affairs of the Parr machine. The first witness to testify about the missing microfilm was Reed Nunnally, former note teller at the Texas State Bank of Alice.

Nunnally testified that he was one of four members of the bank's loan committee, which was headed by Parr. On February 20, 1954, Nunnally said, the committee had conducted its regular weekly meeting. "Nothing was said at the meeting about the microfilm being missing," he testified. But the next morning, he said, he discovered that the microfilm was not in its ordinary place in a bank drawer.

Nunnally's testimony was supported by an Internal Revenue agent, W. A. Dimler. The agent said he was conducting an income-tax investigation in Duval County at the time the microfilm disappeared. Dimler testified that he questioned Parr's codefendant B. F. (Tom) Donald, who was cashier of the bank, about the missing film. He said Donald told him that the film was destroyed as a matter of course and that any one of a number of bank employees could have destroyed it. Dimler testified that he discovered the microfilm records were also missing from another Parr-controlled bank, the San Diego State Bank.

During the testimony of the next witness, another caustic crossfire erupted between Foreman and Malcolm Wilkey. The witness was Postal Inspector William D. Main, who had been instrumental in helping build the mail-fraud case against Parr.

In trying to bolster his contention that the state and federal governments had engaged in a "political conspiracy" to persecute Parr, Foreman asked Main to name for the jury all the places in Texas where he had gone to testify in state court trials or to aid state prosecutors. Wilkey immediately jumped to his feet and objected on the grounds that the question was immaterial, irrelevant and prejudicial. Foreman, arguing that the question was admissible, told Judge Ingraham: "As we've tried to show before . . ."

But Wilkey cut him off. Anticipating that Foreman would renew his "political conspiracy" charge, Wilkey told the judge: "Now, I don't want Mr. Foreman making another speech to the jury, Your Honor. He's done it before and I want to object before he gets started this time." Foreman replied acidly: "If Mr. Wilkey thinks I'll steal his jury from him, I'd as soon discuss this at the bench." The judge, however, declined the offer to hear the arguments out of the hearing of the jury.

Foreman continued: "We're trying to show that purely political machinations were engaged in by the federal and state prosecutors, and that these machinations reached all the way to Washington." Judge Ingraham, however, was not convinced. He said he thought Foreman's questioning had "gone somewhat afield." He thus upheld Wilkey's objection to the question.

In midtrial, the Parr case was suddenly thrown into confusion by an unexpected development in Washington. The confusion resulted from a United States Supreme Court decision. The ruling was handed down in a case unrelated to the Parr trial, but its guiding principle would become applicable to all federal criminal cases. Involved in the decision was the case of Clinton E. Jencks, a union official who had been convicted of giving a false non-Communist affidavit to the government. During his trial, Jencks' lawyers had demanded that the prosecution open some of its secret files to the defense for use in cross-examining government witnesses. The prosecutors had refused to turn over the files and had been upheld by the trial judge. But the Supreme Court had reversed the conviction on the ground that the files should have been provided to the defense.

Two days after the Supreme Court handed down its ruling, Percy Foreman walked into Judge Ingraham's court with a copy of the Jencks case decision. He promptly demanded that he be given access to secret government files in the Parr case. At this point, neither Judge Ingraham nor Malcolm Wilkey had even seen the full text of the Jencks ruling. Despite the fact that the Justice Department had been a litigant in the case, all prosecutor Wilkey had seen had been news reports on the decision and partial texts of the ruling published in newspapers. But, somehow, Foreman had managed to get his hands on the full text.

The Jencks case decision and Foreman's demand for access to government files in the Parr case caused considerable consternation for both the prosecutors and Judge Ingraham. For the ruling, while making clear that certain government files should be opened to the defense, did not set down any ground rules for future implementation of the decision. It did not, for example, say precisely what sort of files should be opened and just when they should be handed over to the defense.

At first, Wilkey tried to pacify Foreman by handing him a small batch of government documents—including several witnesses' sworn statements, investigators' reports on interviews with other witnesses and interoffice memoranda. But Foreman was not to be pacified. He demanded next the transcripts of testimony before a state court grand jury, which had been turned over to Wilkey by state prosecutors. Wilkey balked at surrendering the transcripts, arguing that state court evidence was not covered by the Jencks case ruling. But Judge Ingraham upheld Foreman, and Wilkey reluctantly handed over the transcripts.

For days, a battle raged between the prosecution and defense over just which documents were covered by the ruling. Each day, Wilkey was compelled to hand Foreman additional files. In the end, he had given up no fewer than 121 previously secret documents—including records on every government witness for whom Wilkey maintained a file.

The theory behind the Jencks case decision was that it would provide an additional element of fairness to defendants. It would permit defense attorneys to search the government files for information that might be used to challenge the credibility of prosecution witnesses. In the Parr case, the decision enabled Percy Foreman to obtain from the government files evidence that cast serious doubt on the testimony of a key prosecution witness. The witness was Diego Heras, a chunky former lieutenant of George Parr who had turned against the Duke of Duval and provided investigators with much of their original information against the Parr machine.

Called to the stand by prosecutor Wilkey, Heras had testified at length about the inner workings of the machine. He had been used by the prosecution to tie together numerous loose ends concerning the purported financial manipulations of Parr and his codefendants. In the government files, Foreman discovered a statement made by Heras to FBI agents at Benavides on April 11, 1953. The statement said: "I wish to state under oath that much of the information I gave in my statement to FBI agents in Galveston April 9 was false and I knew at the time that it was false." Foreman promptly got this admission by Heras entered into the trial record.

He seemed to have made a serious dent in the government's case. The prosecutors could argue all they wanted that Heras had lied once to FBI men, but had told them the truth on all other occasions. However, the impression lingered that a man who would lie once might lie habitually.

After presenting testimony by an FBI handwriting expert that the writing on various prosecution exhibits had been done by Parr and his codefendants, Malcolm Wilkey rested the government's case. Foreman filed a lengthy motion for a directed verdict of acquittal, but Judge Ingraham ruled against him.

In launching the defense case, Foreman called Wilkey to the stand as one of his first witnesses. He questioned Wilkey closely about the contents of some of the documents turned over to the defense under the Jencks decision. He was particularly interested in the statement in which Diego Heras admitted he had previously lied to FBI agents.

Q. Did you read that statement before you called Heras as a government witness in this case?

A. Yes, I did.

Q. Then you knew Heras was a certified liar when you called him as a witness; isn't that right?

A. The government doesn't pick its witnesses. We take no position of vouching for any witnesses.

Q. Then you, yourself, have some doubts as to the veracity of the witness?

A. I make no statement as to the veracity of that or any other witness. The jury will have to be the judge of veracity.

With Wilkey still on the stand, Foreman read into the record a portion of a previously secret statement given to government investigators by W. M. Benson, a former employee of the Benavides school district. The portion Foreman read seemed relatively innocuous. But the defense attorney managed to get additional mileage out of the statement.

Wilkey's aide, Edgar Bottler, rose to ask that the statement be read in its entirety—if at all. A broad grin spread across Foreman's face. He walked toward Bottler and said in a stage whisper that could be heard throughout the courtroom: "I don't think you'd want me to read the whole statement, would you?" Foreman then turned to Judge Ingraham and declared: "I would be taking advantage of my brothers at bar if I presented this whole statement in evidence."

Neither Bottler nor Wilkey pressed the point further. Thus, Foreman's maneuver left the jury with the impression that the unread portion of Benson's statement contained material embarrassing to the prosecution.

Foreman rarely passed up an opportunity to renew his charge that the prosecution of Parr had resulted from a "political conspiracy." He raised the question again in questioning another witness, Grady Starnes, who had formerly served as a chief supervising assistant to Texas State Auditor C. H. Cavness. Starnes testified that, while he was working for Cavness, he and other state auditors had conducted a brief investigation of the tangled financial affairs of the Benavides school district and other South Texas governmental agencies dominated by Parr. He said the investigation had been abandoned after a short time.

Foreman asked whether the brief investigation had been made at the direction of former State Attorney General John Ben Shepperd, who had spearheaded the state prosecutions of Parr. Starnes explained in reply that the state auditor's office worked independently of the attorney general's office. Nonetheless, Foreman asked whether the auditor's office would have conducted a full-scale audit of the school district if requested to do so by Shepperd.

Starnes: No. I mean it depends on the circumstances involved. Mr. Cavness is an extremely cautious man and he doesn't go into any kind of special investigation without reviewing what is involved.

Foreman: In other words, he wouldn't take part in a political crusade to pull someone's political chestnuts out of the fire? Is that what you mean?

Starnes: That's exactly what I mean.

Of the nine defendants in the trial, the only one Foreman placed on the stand was O. P. Carrillo, the former school-board attorney. As a practicing lawyer, Carrillo presumably was the defendant best able to handle himself in the witness chair. Questioned about large sums of money he and other members of his family had accumulated, Carrillo testified that he had collected considerable winnings by betting on horse races in Mexico. He said some of the bets were on quarter horses owned by his family, including a particularly fleet steed named Indian Charlie.

On cross-examination, prosecutor Bottler tried to reinforce the government's contention that the defendants had participated in a mail-fraud conspiracy. He asked Carrillo whether the mails had been used to collect school taxes while he worked for the district.

A. I have no idea how they went about collecting current school taxes. I was in charge only of collecting delinquent taxes.

Q. They could have been using the pony express to collect taxes, then, as far as you know?

A. If one existed, I guess so.

Q. Did you ever see a horse ride up to the tax office—Indian Charlie or some other horse—and see someone deliver the taxes collected from Humble Oil and other firms?

A. I attended to my work and the other people attended to theirs.

Q. Are you telling this jury you didn't know the mails were being used to collect Benavides school taxes?

A. I'm telling the jury exactly what I know. I can't tell them anything I don't know and didn't see.

Foreman called several minor defense witnesses. Then, at 10:30 A.M. on July 3, 1957, he rested the defense case. Testimony in the trial had lasted three days short of two months. Foreman filed a new motion for a directed verdict of acquittal. It was denied.

The jury arguments were begun by prosecutor Bottler. He accused George Parr and his cohorts of using the Benavides school district as a "personal vehicle for their own subversion and corruption."

"This is a fraud of a most serious nature," Bottler told the jurors. "This fraud sets out the subversion and corruption of a political subdivision by these defendants. Funds which should have gone towards the education and use of school children, it is charged, instead were used by these defendants.

"There can be no question this was a continuing scheme to defraud. It went on and on—1948, 1949, 1950, 1951, 1952 and 1953."

Malcolm Wilkey followed his aide with additional vilification of the defendants. He argued that the prosecution had presented "a mass of documentary material" proving the guilt of Parr and his codefendants.

But, when Percy Foreman got his chance before the jurors, he gave Wilkey's words a slightly different twist. "I think this would be more accurately referred to as a *mess* of documentary material," Foreman said.

He ridiculed the arguments delivered by Wilkey and Bottler. "There is a farfetched fallacy in the rationalization of that scholarly gentleman, Mr. Bottler," Foreman said. "He asks you to assume or to guess about what the burden is on the government to prove. What Mr. Wilkey and Mr. Bottler tell you is: 'We want you to do for us what the law says the burden is on us to do.'

"They ask you to guess these men into the reputation of being felons and into the four walls of the penitentiary. There's not one word of testimony on some of these things they want you to assume, guess or infer."

Foreman claimed it was prejudicial for the defendants to be tried in metropolitan Houston, far from the atmosphere of their South Texas bailiwick. He said it was "a violation of man and nature" to transport them to the big city for their trial.

"They have a right to be tried by a jury of their peers—meaning their equals," Foreman said. "Unless you live in their sleepy little community, you couldn't understand the customs and mores and practices by which they live."

To judge Parr and his cohorts by Houston standards of morality would be grossly unfair, he argued. And he cited an old French rule of agriculture to support his point. The rule, as quoted by Foreman: "A plant never does well one hundred miles north or south of its natural habitat."

Referring to Parr's South Texas domain, Foreman said: "What we have here is a section of Texas with its own traditions of Latin-American law. The defendants all have an inheritance of customs foreign to our Anglo-Saxon concepts of law."

Once again, he raised the charge of political persecution. He said the government's case was not based on solid evidence, but instead went "into the realm of conjecture, suspicion and politics."

"That, thank the good Lord, is not enough to convict these defendants," Foreman argued. He said that, if the defendants were to be convicted on the word of their political enemies, that would mean any innocent person could be prosecuted at the instigation of an enemy.

As usual, Foreman had a quotation—this time from Ali ibn-abi-Tālib, son-in-law of Mohammed—to illustrate his point:

> "A man who has a thousand friends
> Has not one to spare.
> But he who has an enemy
> Meets him everywhere."

When the arguments were concluded, Judge Ingraham delivered his charge to the jury. He instructed the jurors to cast aside "sympathy, prejudice and public opinion" in reaching a verdict. "Don't ask yourself if the government will win or lose this case," he said. "The government always wins when justice is done."

The case went to the jury at 2:08 P.M. on July 12. The jurors deliberated for almost five days. Then, at 11:35 A.M. on July 17, they filed back into the courtroom. The foreman handed the written verdicts to the court clerk, Albert Anderson. A hush fell over the courtroom. Anderson began reading the verdicts.

George Parr was found guilty on all twenty counts against him. This meant he faced a possible maximum sentence of one hundred years in prison and 29,000 dollars in fines. As the verdict was read, a slight smirk spread across Parr's face.

All of his codefendants were found guilty on at least some of the counts. D. C. Chapa was convicted on twenty counts; B. F. (Tom) Donald, on eighteen; Oscar Carrillo, on twenty; O. P. Carrillo, on one; Jesus Garza, on nineteen; Santiago Garcia, on ten; Octavio Saenz, on nineteen; and Jesus Oliveira, on one.

Judge Ingraham set sentencing for July 30. He released the defendants in the meantime on their existing bonds. As Parr walked from the courtroom, he told newsmen: "I have nothing to say."

Percy Foreman, smiling despite the verdicts, announced that he planned to file a motion for a new trial. If that were denied, he said, he would appeal the case.

On July 30, as the defendants stood before the bench for sentencing, Malcolm Wilkey urged Judge Ingraham to impose stiff terms. He delivered a scathing denunciation of George Parr.

"The actions of Parr reveal the character of a man who is completely amoral," Wilkey said. "He makes no differentiation between the money of the public, others and himself. He has maintained control and dominance over the political affairs in Duval County through his position as county judge and sheriff and through his maintenance of 200 or 250 special deputies. In addition, he has used methods of violence to maintain his control."

Wilkey reeled off a list of sums of money that he said Parr had stolen from various governmental bodies. Among the amounts he listed were 500,000 dollars in 1945, another 168,000 dollars between 1945 and 1948 and 20,000 dollars in 1949.

"In April 1952 Parr paid the sheriff of Duval County 20,000 dollars to resign as sheriff—with Parr taking his place," Wilkey said. "Immediately prior to this payment, four 5,000-dollar checks were withdrawn from Duval County funds."

Percy Foreman, after initially telling the judge that neither he nor any of the defendants would have anything to say before sentence was pronounced, later changed his mind because of what he described as "the multiplicity of insinuations that have been made by the prosecutor."

Foreman accused Wilkey of improperly dredging up a variety of matters that had nothing to do with the mail-fraud case and of attaching "odiferous insinuations to them." He asked Judge Ingraham to disregard these matters in deciding upon the sentences.

When the time came for the judge to pronounce sentence, he announced that he was not quite ready. He declared a three-hour recess. "I am sure there are many people who know exactly what should be done in this case," he said. "Being the only person who can pronounce sentence, I feel a great sense of responsibility. I want some additional time to sit with my conscience before imposing sentence in this case."

During those three hours, the judge made up his mind. When the defendants returned to court, he announced his decisions.

He sentenced George Parr to serve ten years in prison and pay a 20,000-dollar fine. Parr stood silently at the defense table and showed no emotion as the sentence was pronounced.

The sentences imposed on the other defendants were: D. C. Chapa, five years in prison; B. F. (Tom) Donald, four years in prison; Octavio Saenz, three years in prison; Oscar Carrillo, four years in prison; O. P. Carrillo, two-year suspended sentence; Jesus Garza, three-year suspended sentence; Santiago Garcia, three-year suspended sentence; and Jesus Oliveira, two-year suspended sentence.

Judge Ingraham permitted the defendants to remain free on bond, pending appeal of the case. Outside the court, Percy Foreman showed no dismay over the sentences. "This was only the first round," he said. "We have nine more rounds to go."

The next round came five weeks later. Judge Ingraham conducted a hearing on Foreman's motion for a new trial. He denied the motion.

Next, Foreman appealed the case to the United States Fifth Circuit Court of Appeals in New Orleans. The appellate court upheld the convictions.

Finally, the case reached the United States Supreme Court. Almost three years had dragged by since the trial before the Supreme Court decided the case. In June 1960, by a vote of six to three, the court reversed the convictions. Both the court majority and minority held that the trial record showed ample evidence fraud had been committed in the Benavides school district. But the majority ruled that the use of the mails had been only incidental to the fraud and had not been an essential part of the alleged conspiracy. Therefore, the majority held, the mail-fraud convictions could not stand.

Thus, Percy Foreman had kept his record in the Parr cases intact. Not one defendant in any of the cases had served a day of prison time.

11

> I work by instinct. I work and I don't play,
> I work every Saturday, every Sunday.
> And I work at law.
>
> PERCY FOREMAN

SEYMOUR KURTZ and Harold Turner were two bright young Chicago lawyers. But, in 1960, they needed a lawyer of their own. The man they chose was Percy Foreman.

Kurtz, aged thirty, and Turner, twenty-seven, had been indicted by a federal grand jury as the alleged masterminds of an international car-theft ring. The government charged that the ring had arranged for the theft of late-model automobiles in Chicago and other cities. The cars were then driven to Houston and Laredo, Texas, and turned over to accomplices, the government said. Later, the authorities charged, the vehicles were sent to Guatemala and Mexico for sale. Government attorneys said the ring had handled more than 250,000 dollars' worth of stolen cars.

Indicted with Kurtz and Turner were three other Chicago men, Max Olshon, Gerald Covelli and Michael Slepcevich. The indictment, returned in Houston, charged that the defendants had engaged in a conspiracy to transport the stolen cars in interstate and foreign commerce between about September 1, 1958, and February 6, 1959.

As part of the conspiracy, the indictment charged, members of the ring arranged for the theft of the cars, changed engine and body identification numbers on them, submitted false documents to customs officials and entered into agreements to sell the vehicles abroad.

Max Olshon and Michael Slepcevich pleaded guilty to the charges. And Gerald Covelli agreed to become the chief prosecution witness against Kurtz and Turner. When the trial of the two attorneys began in January 1960, the entire case seemed to hinge on whether the jury would believe Covelli's story. Prosecuting the case were Assistant United States Attorneys Charles D. Cottingham, Jr., and Monroe Northrop. Foreman was assisted in the defense by Frank W. Oliver of Chicago. Foreman was practicing before a familiar judge—Federal District Judge Joe Ingraham, who had presided over the George Parr mail-fraud trial.

All other testimony in the case took a back seat to that of Covelli. He was questioned for the government by prosecutor Cottingham. It was quickly established that Covelli's current residence was the county jail in Houston and that he had previously been convicted of four felonies, including robbery and burglary. He testified that he had originally known Kurtz and Turner as law partners, although he had never retained them. In the fall of 1958, Covelli said, he went to their Chicago law office at Kurtz's request. He said he met with the two lawyers and that Kurtz invited him to join them in a deal—a "stolen-car operation, disposing of hot cars in Mexico City."

"He told me they had a contact in Mexico City in which to get rid of these cars," Covelli testified. "They went on to discuss that they intended to open an export-import firm in which to handle the money from the stolen cars, and this way it couldn't be detected. They asked me who I thought should be in with us. I told them Max Olshon and Slepcevich. Seymour Kurtz said he didn't like Max Olshon because he was a bragger and loudmouth person. I said, 'If Max isn't in, I'm not in.' He [Kurtz] finally okayed that he [Olshon] was in on the deal."

Covelli told of several subsequent meetings with Kurtz and Turner to plan the stolen-car operation. He said it was decided that the ring would handle only Cadillacs because "that was the premium car" and would bring the best price in Mexico. At one meeting, he said, an elaborate arrangement was made to protect Kurtz and Turner in case authorities ever questioned their connection with other ring members.

"At that meeting 'Sonny' [Turner's nickname] gave Seymour [Kurtz] five hundred dollars," Covelli testified. "Seymour gave it to me and I was instructed to give it to Slepcevich and have Michael Slepcevich call and make an appointment at his [Turner's] office. And Mike was to go up there and discuss an import-export business with Harold Turner. This way they would be able to protect themselves in case anything went wrong."

Cottingham: Was any reason given you why this five hundred dollars was to be given by you to Slepcevich for him to go up to Kurtz and Turner's office? Did anyone give you a reason?

A. Yes. They gave the reason to hand it to Harold Turner to retain as attorney to represent an import-export business that was supposed to open up in Mexico City.

Q. Was this retainer as stated to you real or phony?

A. It was phony.

Q. Who told you that?

A. It was just a mock action.

Covelli testified he later gave the five hundred dollars to Slepcevich, to be turned back to Turner. Still later, he said, all the members of the stolen-car ring met at Turner's office. "At that time Seymour Kurtz made a long-distance call to Mexico City and he talked in Spanish, Jewish and English, and he talked about units," Covelli said.

Q. What do you mean by "units"?

A. Stolen cars.

Q. Do you refer to them or had you referred to them previous to this phone call as "units"?

A. Yes, we did. . . . After the call to Mexico City, he told us we had nothing to worry about, that everything was ready. After that, we had a drink. Harold brought out a bottle of wine from his portable bar and we had a drink to toast a success in our new venture.

Covelli testified that Kurtz and Turner told the other ring members to make arrangements to steal cars and to prepare counterfeit ownership certificates for them. He said Kurtz and Turner showed him how to make the counterfeit certificates.

A short time after this meeting, he testified, Kurtz came to his home. "He told me to get ready to go, to get hold of three [stolen] Cadillacs and we should meet in Mexico City in a week," Covelli said. He said Kurtz gave him five hundred dollars in expense money for the trip. He then obtained three stolen Cadillacs, made counterfeit certificates for them and took the cars to Mexico City, he said. Covelli testified that it was Turner, not Kurtz, who initially met him there.

Q. What happened when you did see Turner in Mexico City?

A. Well, we had dinner together at the Del Prado Hotel. Previous, when we arrived there, we picked up a captain of the highway police department in Mexico City and asked him to join us for dinner. . . . We commenced pumping for information concerning taxation on cars and different ways you could reach people in the Customs [agency] to get the price of the tax down.

Q. Mr. Covelli, at this time was Mr. Turner, to use your phrase, helping you "pump" this Mexican officer?

A. Yes, sir.

He testified that Kurtz later came to Mexico City. Covelli said he met Turner and Kurtz, who were with some other men.

Q. Did they say who they were with?

A. There was a used-car dealer and his son and another attorney.

Q. State whether or not you, Kurtz and Turner entered into negotiations with these people for the sale of anything.

A. Well, we talked about automobiles.

Covelli went on to describe the sale of the stolen cars. He later testified in great detail about other stolen autos, other trips, other meetings and other sales. Throughout his testimony, the emphasis was placed on the parts allegedly played in the manipulations by Kurtz and Turner. When Covelli's direct testimony was completed, it became clear that the main thrust of the defense case would be to try to discredit him and his story.

Percy Foreman, in his cross-examination, aimed at showing that Covelli's memory was faulty, that he had been coached on his testimony by government men and that he had agreed to testify in return for favors from the government. Foreman drew from Covelli a statement that he had been moved to the Houston jail about two weeks before the trial from a jail in Texarkana. Covelli testified the transfer had been ordered after he had complained about conditions at the Texarkana jail. After the transfer, he said, he was interviewed at length by prosecutors Cottingham and Northrop in Cottingham's Houston office.

Foreman: Who filed what motion [to move him to the Houston jail]? Did Mr. Cottingham file a motion for you?

A. Yes, sir.

Q. Oh—and when did you engage Mr. Cottingham to file a motion in your behalf in this court, and under what circumstances?

A. To start with, I never engaged Mr. Cottingham. I asked him to be transferred on account of the food situation and my ill health.

Q. Did you sign such a motion yourself?

A. I can't remember if I did or not.

Q. Now, then, you remember what happened in late 1958—in September or October, the twelfth or fourteenth, eighteenth or nineteenth—as to little details of papers. Do you have difficulty recalling what you did seven weeks ago?

A. I never did it seven weeks ago. . . . It was later.

Q. Well, then, this motion appears to have been filed October 9, 1959. . . . These conversations with reference to what occurred in September and October were really in 1957, were they not, Mr. Covelli?

A. What conversations are you referring to?

Q. The conversations which you have been going into great detail—giving dates, October the twelfth and the nineteenth, and the transactions that happened about papers prepared in Chicago, with reference to certificates of manufacture and bills of sale and so forth. You very glibly and completely remember each, any and all of those papers, don't you?

A. No.

Q. You don't? Then the things you testified to as happening in September and October and November of 1957, you don't really remember?

A. Fifty-seven. I don't remember anything in fifty-seven.

Q. It all happened in 1958?

A. That's correct.

Q. Well, do you remember definitely the things you claimed happened in 1958?

A. Well, I think I do. I recall to the best of my knowledge.

Q. You mentioned dates, mentioned February twenty-third.

A. I could have been off a week or two or three. I don't remember the specific date.

Q. You don't remember whether you signed this motion filed October 9, 1959?

A. I don't remember.

Q. Well, did you ever see it?

A. No, I didn't.

Q. Well, if you didn't see it you didn't sign it, did you?

A. I don't remember.

Q. You don't remember whether you signed it without seeing it or not?

A. I don't remember if I signed it or seen it. All I know, a motion was filed.

Q. Perhaps I misunderstood you, Mr. Covelli. I asked you if you ever saw this motion and you said you did not ever see this motion. Did I misunderstand you? Do you now want to say that you don't know whether you ever saw it or not?

A. Well, when the motion was drafted—I didn't see that motion there. I saw a motion that was being drafted. . . . It was changed . . . by Mr. Cottingham.

Q. Prior to his changing it and prior to his filing the motion on your behalf, you had not told Mr. Cottingham or Mr. Northrop about any of these alleged transgressions of Mr. Turner and Mr. Kurtz, had you, Mr. Covelli?

A. Way before that.

Q. You did? How long before?

A. Maybe three months.

Q. Mr. Covelli, in addition to the statement that you told us about . . . in Mr. Cottingham's office, please tell us whether or not on one or more occasions you have been interviewed with reference to the circumstances surrounding this case on trial in the presence of Mr. Max Olshon by any representatives of any branch of the federal government.

A. Well, when Max Olshon gave his first statement, I wasn't there. But, at a later date four or five months later, Max Olshon and I were interviewed.

Q. Were you from time to time, as Olshon would be asked a question and as he would answer it, were you called upon to see if that was . . . your recollection as well as Olshon's?

A. Max Olshon and I differed. . . .

Q. Then is it your statement that all of the facts that Olshon recalled that you were called upon either to affirm or deny, that you differed on all facts or just some?

A. I can't speak for Mr. Olshon. I can only speak for myself. The statement I gave is what I recall. . . .

Q. In other words, each of you were jointly interviewed together . . . and you recall some of them the same as Olshon and perhaps different as to some?

A. That's correct.

Covelli testified that he and Olshon were questioned jointly over a ten-day period by Cottingham and an FBI agent, James O'Connor.

Q. And you all conformed your dates and times as a result of this ten days of conferences with Agent O'Connor and Assistant District Attorney Cottingham?

A. We tried to, but we couldn't get together on dates.

Q. You did get together on a large part of it, didn't you?

A. I believe you'll find the large part of it was on the first statement. . . . Olshon and I just couldn't get together on dates.

Q. Had Olshon, so far as you know, signed a statement prior to the time this inquisition started about or shortly after the ninth of October?

Cottingham broke in with an objection. "Your Honor, I am going to object to this word 'inquisition,'" he said. "I think the proper word is 'inquiry' and Mr. Foreman knows it."

Foreman answered: "I didn't mean it in the medieval sense. I meant it in the Websterian sense, an inquisition meaning an inquiry."

Judge Ingraham ruled: "The court will not be influenced or prejudiced by the use of this word. You may continue."

Q. All right, now that we understand and we refer solely to the "interrogation" as a gentle, kindly appellation for the ordeal you and Mr. Olshon went through, would you tell us whether or not Mr. Olshon had made a statement prior to the time this questioning of you and him started after the ninth of October?

A. I believe he did.

Q. And did he make another one after this, sign another statement after this ten days of inquiry?

A. I think he did.

Under Foreman's questioning, Covelli testified that his wife, Jean, had divorced him after his arrest in the stolen-car case. He said the divorce had been granted about six months before the trial.

Q. Do you know who represented your wife in the divorce?

A. No, I don't.

Q. It was not Mr. Cottingham?

A. No, sir.

Q. All right. Was it a federal assistant district attorney in Chicago?

A. No, sir.

Q. How do you know it wasn't? You said you didn't know who represented her.

A. I can't recall the name. I did get a notice.

Q. While we are on that subject, was it part of your consideration of your getting a divorce, a part of it, to make your wife a more credible witness for the prosecution? Was that part of your considered plan in you and Jean, your wife, divorcing?

A. No, sir.

Q. Nothing was said about that?

A. No, sir.

All in all, Foreman never succeeded in completely breaking Covelli's story. But he did succeed in creating doubts about the testimony. Covelli's past criminal record, the prosecution's action in moving him to a jail of his own choice, his lapses of memory and the government's efforts to make his story jibe with that of another witness all were used by Foreman to create an aura of uncertainty about his credibility.

When the jury retired, it needed only one ballot to decide on a verdict. The verdict: Not guilty.

Seymour Kurtz and Harold Turner returned to Chicago. And Percy Foreman moved on to the defense of others in trouble with the law.

It does not always take a dramatic acquittal for Foreman to "win" a case. Frequently, he is considered victorious if he succeeds in obtaining for his client any sentence less severe than the death penalty. A case in point was that of Annie Laurie Williams.

Mrs. Williams was a pretty, red-haired twenty-eight-year-old dime-store clerk. She resided in a trailer park at Pasadena, Texas, a suburb of Houston, with her two sons, Calvin, nine, and Conrad, eight. Her husband, Hoyt J. Williams, was serving a prison term on charges of selling a stolen car.

On February 17, 1955, a friend of the family reported to Pasadena police that Mrs. Williams and her sons were missing from their trailer home. During the next five days, the police turned up no clues to their whereabouts. Then, about 1 P.M. on February 22, Mrs. Williams appeared unexpectedly at a combination home-and auto-wrecking service near Algoa in Galveston County. The place was owned by Mr. and Mrs. Morris Johnson. Mrs. Williams had known them since the previous September, when Johnson had overhauled her car.

Mrs. Johnson, who did not know about the missing-persons report, invited Mrs. Williams inside. They made small talk for a few minutes. Then Mrs. Williams said that the car she was driving that day, a 1948 Studebaker, had been borrowed from the woman who owned the trailer park where she and the boys were staying. She said the woman had loaned her the car for a week on the condition that she throw away some spoiled meat in the trunk. The meat had spoiled when a deep freeze had gone out of order, Mrs. Williams said. She said she had to get rid of it because it was venison shot out of season and she would get into trouble if caught with it.

Eventually, Mrs. Williams asked permission to dump the meat behind the Johnsons' wrecking yard. Mrs. Johnson suggested, instead, that it would be best to bury it back there.

"Okay, give me a shovel and I'll bury it," Mrs. Williams said.

But Mrs. Johnson said that her husband would do the burying. Johnson and the two women then took the Studebaker to a thickly weeded spot about a hundred yards behind the wrecking yard. There, they opened the car trunk and removed four packages. Three were bundles made of paper, cloth and plastic sheeting. The fourth was a cardboard beer carton. They put the packages into a shallow ditch. Johnson shoveled some loose dirt on top.

The trio then returned to the house and chatted nonchalantly. Mrs. Williams was hungry, so Mrs. Johnson gave her some wieners and sauerkraut. About 4 P.M. Mrs. Williams returned to the shallow ditch, inspected it and came back to the house complaining that there was not enough dirt covering it. The Johnsons noted that she appeared extremely nervous for a few minutes.

Mrs. Williams then persuaded the Johnsons' nineteen-year-old grandson, Clayton Johnson, Jr., to go out to the ditch and pile several more loads of dirt on it. About 6 P.M. Mrs. Williams left the Johnson home, gave Clayton a lift to a movie theater in the nearby town of Alvin and drove away.

After taking in a movie, Clayton was strolling down an Alvin street when he ran into a young friend named Gene Whitmore. Clayton casually mentioned that Mrs. Williams had come to the Johnson home to get rid of the spoiled meat. Whitmore happened to be carrying a copy of a Houston newspaper. On the front page was a story describing the reported disappearance of Mrs. Williams and her sons. Whitmore showed the story to Clayton. This was the first any member of the Johnson family knew of the missing-persons report. Both youths' suspicions were aroused.

"I'll bet those packages you buried contained the boys' bodies," Whitmore told Clayton.

The two of them then rushed to the Johnson home, got a shovel and dug up the packages. Whitmore's hunch had been correct. Inside the packages were the dismembered bodies of Calvin and Conrad Williams.

Sheriff's officers were notified, and a vast hunt was launched for Mrs. Williams. The Johnsons recalled the license number of the Studebaker Mrs. Williams had been driving. An alarm was issued for the car. The hunt was directed by Harris County Sheriff C. V. (Buster) Kern.

A check of motor-vehicle records disclosed that the Studebaker had been bought only a day earlier from a Houston auto dealer. The purchaser had been a woman who had given her name as "Dena T. Linden" and had given as her address a Houston apartment.

About 4 A.M. on February 23 Sheriff Kern arrived outside the apartment. Other members of a raiding party were waiting for him. An officer knocked on the door. From inside a female voice asked: "Who's there?"

Sheriff Kern and another officer hurled themselves against the door. The lock snapped and the door swung open. Inside was Annie Laurie Williams. The officers grabbed her. She offered no resistance.

At first, Mrs. Williams claimed she did not know why the officers wanted her. Later, however, she admitted dismembering her sons' bodies, though denying, at least temporarily, that she had murdered them.

Mrs. Williams gave officers a written statement. She said that when she returned to her trailer home from work on February 16 she found Calvin and Conrad in bed, apparently asleep. She later discovered that they were not asleep, but dead, she said. She claimed she examined a bottle of narcotic tablets in the trailer, found some were missing and surmised that the boys had died from overdoses.

"So I wrapped them in blankets, put them in my car and drove to the apartment [where she was later arrested], which I'd rented just a few days before," she said in her written statement. "I put them in the bathtub there and left them there for two or three days. I was afraid to call the police because I thought I'd get in trouble for having the dope—with my husband in prison—so I decided to get rid of the bodies. I tried first to use a butcher knife, but it was too dull. So I did it with a double-edged razor blade, and put them in the refrigerator. Then, yesterday, I wrapped them up and carried them down to the Studebaker. I had to make four trips. I drove around awhile, then went to the Johnsons' and had the bodies buried."

Investigating officers believed only part of this statement was true. They did not accept Mrs. Williams' version of how the boys had died. For autopsies disclosed that the boys had not died of overdoses of narcotics, but rather of skull fractures apparently suffered when their heads had been beaten with a blunt weapon.

The officers kept hammering at Mrs. Williams for the true story. Eventually, she confessed that she had killed the boys. She claimed her sons had been subjected to constant teasing from playmates about the fact that their father was in prison, and that she had killed them to spare them further harassment. She was charged with murder and ordered held without bail.

Although the murders apparently had been committed in Harris County, jurisdiction for prosecuting the case lay in neighboring Galveston County because the bodies had been found there. The Galveston County district attorney, Marsene Johnson, announced that he would try to send Mrs. Williams to the electric chair. "This is one of the most horrible crimes I have ever seen," Johnson said. "There's no question about it. I'll ask for the death penalty."

Because of the ghastly nature of the murders, there seemed to be a strong likelihood that Mrs. Williams would become the first woman in Texas history to go to the electric chair. But, several weeks after her arrest, a startling development occurred.

Mrs. Williams repudiated her confession and pinned the blame for the murders on someone else. What's more, she stuck to this new version of the killings when doctors, at her request, placed her under the effects of sodium pentathol—the so-called truth serum. In her revised account, Mrs. Williams claimed the murders had been committed by a curly-haired ex-convict named John Long. This was her new version:

She and her husband had known Long before her husband went to prison. Following her husband's imprisonment, Long began paying a great deal of attention to her. Long was a drug addict and got her to start using narcotics. Later, he persuaded her that she ought to become a prostitute in order to support the two of them. But he complained that the boys would be in their way and would have to be killed.

On the day the boys were slain, Mrs. Williams claimed, she and Long fed them large doses of sleeping pills. But the pills failed to kill them. When the pills did not "take," she said, Long sent her out on an errand. She claimed she returned to find that the boys were dead and that Long had dismembered their bodies with a straight razor which he habitually carried. Mrs. Williams said Long stuck with her until shortly before her arrest, but then fled. She said she met him after getting the Johnsons to bury the bodies, and went with him to the Houston apartment. He gave her a shot of narcotics and she went to sleep. When she awoke, she said, Long was gone. That was why she was alone when the officers broke in and arrested her, she claimed.

The problem with Mrs. Williams' revised version was that investigating officers were unable to prove that John Long existed, much less that he had committed the murders. They could find no trace of him. Since Mrs. Williams claimed her husband knew Long, investigators were sent to question Williams in prison. But he said he had never heard of John Long. And, speaking of his wife, Williams told the investigators: "I hope she burns." Mrs. Williams claimed Long had originally come from Detroit, Michigan. Officers were dispatched to Detroit in search of evidence. They found several ex-convicts named John Long, but could not prove that any of them had ever been in Houston.

Nonetheless, some officers—including Sheriff Kern and his sidekick, Texas Ranger Johnny Klevenhagen—were inclined to believe Mrs. Williams' new account. For one thing, her story had held up under the effects of "truth serum." For another, they did not believe that Mrs. Williams, a frail woman who weighed barely a hundred pounds, had the physical strength to dismember the bodies by herself. For still another, the evidence seemed to support her revised version that the bodies had been dismembered with a straight razor, rather than her original story that a double-edged razor blade had been used.

Under the circumstances, Kern and Klevenhagen were determined to keep Mrs. Williams from going to the electric chair. They appealed to Percy Foreman to take her case. Although the request came from his longtime antagonists and although Mrs. Williams could not afford to pay his usual fee, Foreman agreed to handle her defense. And, in representing her, he spared Kern and Klevenhagen not one iota of embarrassment.

At a preliminary hearing, Foreman subjected one of Kern's deputies to a merciless cross-examination. The deputy described how, after the discovery of the boys' bodies, he and other officers had traced Mrs. Williams to the Houston apartment. Instead of breaking into the apartment immediately, the raiding party had awaited Sheriff Kern's arrival before making the arrest. Foreman sought to establish that the wait had been designed to permit the sheriff to reap maximum publicity from the arrest. For, in addition to awaiting the sheriff's arrival, the raiding party had awaited the arrival of news photographers before crashing into the apartment and seizing the slight, unarmed woman.

"Why did you wait so long to enter the apartment? Were you afraid of this little lady?" Foreman asked.

"No," the deputy answered sheepishly. "We were waiting for Sheriff Kern."

Q. Why were you waiting for the sheriff?

A. We didn't know what apartment the woman was in.

Q. Well, did Sheriff Kern know that?

A. I don't know. But it was awfully dark in there.

Q. Oh, it was dark in there. Well, were all you big law-enforcement officers afraid of the dark?

A. Er–uh–no.

Q. Well, was Sheriff Kern going to bring you a candle?

A. No. I guess not.

Q. No further questions.

The cross-examination had been typical of Foreman. It had not materially changed the fact situation that had previously emerged. It had been designed as a diversionary tactic to shift the focus of attention from the accused murderess to the officers. And it had succeeded.

Each prosecution witness who took the stand at the preliminary hearing was subjected to a similar going-over by Foreman. The defense attorney failed to achieve his immediate goal at the hearing. The presiding judge denied his motion to release Mrs. Williams on bond. But Foreman had taken giant strides toward achieving his long-range goal—saving Mrs. Williams from the electric chair. For the preliminary hearing had given District Attorney Johnson a foretaste of the kind of savage defense Foreman would wage when Mrs. Williams came to trial.

Publicly, Johnson continued to insist that he would settle for nothing less than the death penalty. But, privately, he began to have serious doubts that he could persuade a jury to send Mrs. Williams to the electric chair. With Foreman defending, there was even the chance that Mrs. Williams might go free.

Thus, on the day that Mrs. Williams was scheduled to come to trial, Johnson abandoned his insistence on the death penalty. At a meeting with Foreman, Mrs. Williams and District Judge William E. Stone in the judge's chambers, Johnson offered to recommend a life sentence if Mrs. Williams would plead guilty. Foreman conferred with his client, and they agreed to accept Johnson's proposed deal.

It was still necessary to find two juries—one for each boy's murder—that were willing to assess life sentences. From the panel of three hundred veniremen, twelve jurors were quickly selected after they pledged to impose a life sentence, "no more or no less," for the murder of Mrs. Williams' younger son, Conrad.

Mrs. Williams then stood before the bench. The indictment charging her with the murder of Conrad was read.

"Annie Laurie Williams, you have heard the indictment," the judge said. "How do you plead?"

In a barely audible whisper, Mrs. Williams replied: "Guilty."

Q. Have you arrived at this plea of your own free will?

A. Yes, sir.

Q. You were not in any way coerced, you were not forced and it was not through fear that you entered this plea?

A. No, sir.

Q. Are you pleading guilty because you are guilty and for no other reason?

A. Yes, sir.

Q. The court will accept the plea of guilty.

Even though Mrs. Williams had pleaded guilty and the jurors had agreed to give her a life sentence, it was necessary to go through the motions of conducting a trial. In theory, this trial enabled the jurors to decide on an appropriate sentence. The lawyers perfunctorily questioned a small group of witnesses, then rested their cases. The jurors retired for deliberation and then quickly returned with the promised sentence of life imprisonment.

This entire process was carried out a second time the same day, with another jury imposing a second life sentence on Mrs. Williams for the murder of her older son, Calvin. The two life sentences did not necessarily mean that Mrs. Williams would spend the remainder of her life behind bars. For a life sentence, under certain circumstances, can be served in eight years in Texas. And Mrs. Williams was ordered to serve the two terms concurrently.

When she went behind the bars of the state prison, Mrs. Williams left several questions unanswered. Which of her versions of the murders was true? Did John Long really exist? And, if so, did he actually kill the boys? These questions remain unanswered at this writing.

But in any event—no matter which version was true—Mrs. Williams had been a party to the crimes. As such, she was subject to possible execution. Percy Foreman's prime mission had been to keep her out of the electric chair. He had succeeded. Thus, in spite of the fact that his client had been given two concurrent life sentences, he had "won" his case.

Usually, the cases in which Foreman becomes involved deal with purported violations of state or federal laws. But occasionally he takes a case that gets him enmeshed in the complexities of international law. Such was the case of Charles Hubert Taylor.

Taylor, a twenty-seven-year-old native Texan, was living in Mexico City with his Italian-born wife, Lilliana, during the fall of 1966. Although nearly blind, he was studying for a master's degree at the University of Mexico. Before marrying Taylor in May 1966, Lilliana had been divorced from Luis Fernando Lagarde, a Mexican diplomat whose father had served as Mexico's ambassador to France. Lilliana had custody of a six-year-old daughter, but Lagarde made periodic visits to the Taylor apartment to visit the child.

On October 11, 1966, neighbors heard sounds of a struggle and then gunfire from the Taylor apartment. Witnesses later saw a man drag a trunk down a stairway of the apartment house. The next day Lagarde was reported missing, and police began an intensive search for him. A small overnight bag containing blood-stained clothing belonging to Lagarde was soon found beside a lake near Cuernavaca. Several weeks later Lagarde's body was found inside a trunk in the same lake. Police said he had apparently been shot elsewhere, that the body had then been loaded into the trunk and dumped into the lake.

In the meantime Taylor, his wife and Mrs. Taylor's daughter crossed the border into Texas and went to the home of Taylor's mother in Austin. Taylor telephoned Percy Foreman, saying he understood he might be wanted by Mexican authorities. Foreman instructed the Taylors to come to Houston, then installed them in the home of a former client—an accused murderer who had been declared insane and committed to a mental hospital.

On November 11 police in Mexico City filed murder charges against Taylor and his wife. They said the motive for Lagarde's slaying "evidently was a dispute over the custody" of the six-year-old girl. Because of the prominence of Lagarde and his family, the case caused a sensation in the Mexican press.

In Houston, Taylor and his wife decided on a suicide pact. The day after the murder charges were filed Taylor plunged through a first-floor window of the house Foreman had provided. He fell only a short distance, however, and was not seriously hurt. When police arrived, they found Mrs. Taylor unconscious —a bottle of sleeping pills nearby. They also found a suicide note in her handwriting.

Addressed to "Mr. Percy Foreman," the note read in part: "This is one case you are not going to win. We killed the son of a bitch. We really did. It was Charles that had the idea of committing suicide. I'll follow."

Taylor and his wife were taken to a hospital. Mrs. Taylor died the next night. Houston detectives arrived soon afterward and took Taylor into custody, presumably to be held for extradition to Mexico. Two Mexican Secret Service officers appeared with a murder warrant. They said they were under the impression they could take Taylor back to Mexico "without any red tape." Since they had locked horns with Percy Foreman in the past, the Mexican authorities should have known better. Informed of the Mexican officers' arrival, Foreman routed Texas District Judge Miron A. Love out of bed and demanded an immediate hearing on a habeas corpus petition. Judge Love agreed to set the hearing, telephoned Houston police and ordered them not to turn Taylor over to the Mexican officers.

At 1:15 A.M., Foreman showed up at police headquarters and personally served a copy of his writ application upon the lieutenant in charge of the Homicide Squad. "Taylor is almost completely blind," Foreman told newsmen. "He couldn't have killed anybody himself or helped anybody much. He is not a fugitive from justice. I was told personally by a judge in Mexico City October 30th that Taylor was not wanted and that no charges were filed (at that time). There is no valid charge against Taylor in any state in the United States. He was arrested here without a warrant while under the influence of medicines—ill and dazed at the time. He was taken from the hospital in a furnished gown without clothes or shoes. He looks like a monk. The state of Texas has no more jurisdiction in this than it has to forgive sins or baptize a baby. Even if he's charged in Mexico, the city of Houston has no right to arrest him."

The validity of Foreman's contention was upheld later in the day not only by Judge Love, but also by the local district attorney. Without opposition, Foreman's writ was granted. But Foreman, conceding he had won a mere temporary victory, told the judge: "I am sure the FBI will come for this man, and I will produce him when he's wanted." He kept his word. Federal authorities and the Mexican government agreed on procedures aimed at extraditing Taylor, and a Houston federal judge ordered his arrest. While federal marshals hunted unsuccessfully for him, Taylor walked into their office with Foreman and surrendered.

The marshals put Taylor back in jail. Foreman immediately filed another petition for a writ of habeas corpus, contending the new incarceration was improper. This time there would be no mere five-minute hearing. Jurisdiction in the case now rested with Federal District Judge Allen B. Hannay. One of the most highly regarded federal judges in the Southwest, Hannay was also something of a "character." He was cut from the same general mold as Foreman—a country boy who had come to the big city and had, to some degree at least, conquered it. Lyndon Johnson is among Hannay's friends; so is Percy Foreman. Yet, the judge has ruled against Foreman—and against Johnson's political allies—on many occasions. And, while making clear his affection and respect for Foreman, he has also rebuked him both privately and publicly. Once, Hannay remarked in open court that Foreman seemed to be going high hat—"duding up" in fancy clothes to "look like a riverboat gambler."

The hearing in the Taylor case got under way before Judge Hannay on December 20th. Foreman asked for dismissal of the extradition case. He argued that the evidence against Taylor was not sufficient to connect him with Lagarde's murder. Assistant United States Attorneys James Gough and William B. Butler contended that the facts merited extradition. They did not argue that Taylor had actually participated in the murder, but rather that it had been committed by his late wife and that he had become an accessory after the fact. Taylor, they claimed, had helped get rid of Lagarde's body and had aided his wife's escape to Texas.

The government produced evidence indicating Taylor had dragged a trunk down some stairs outside his Mexico City apartment a few hours after the shooting. The evidence seemed to show that this trunk had contained Lagarde's bloody clothing, not the body. Foreman contended that, even if Taylor had been an accessory after the fact, the 1899 extradition treaty between the United States and Mexico did not provide for extraditing a defendant in such circumstances.

Judge Hannay ruled, twenty months after receiving the extradition request, that Foreman was right. In his decision, handed down on June 27, 1968, Hannay held that Taylor did not have to return to Mexico. He ruled that Taylor and Lilliana were legally married, although there was some evidence indicating it was a common-law marriage. Even under Texas common-law provisions, Hannay wrote, a husband could not be extradited as an accessory to a crime committed by his wife. Moreover, he held, the evidence of murder gathered by Mexican authorities was insufficient to warrant extradition.

The decision caused headaches for the U.S. State Department, stemming from anti-American reaction in Mexico. But that was not the concern of Percy Foreman. He had freed his client. Taylor, after periodic treatment at a mental hospital, returned to Austin to reside with his mother and continue his studies.

Having successfully represented a man arrested in the murder of his wife's former husband, Foreman turned to the defense of a more orthodox client—a husband-slayer. There was no question that Mrs. Virginia Deane Thomson had killed her husband, Arthur, an attorney and accountant. In fact, after shooting him, Mrs. Thomson telephoned Foreman—one of her neighbors—and said simply: "I'm sorry to bother you, Percy, but I just killed my husband and I wish you'd come on over."

Foreman arrived to find that Thomson had been shot four times with a pistol. His body, clad in trousers and an undershirt, bore two bullet wounds in the back of the head, another in the chest and a fourth in the back. The dead man had been forty-nine; his widow was forty-eight. Their three children, aged twelve to sixteen, had been awakened by the shots about 12:30 A.M.

Police arrested Mrs. Thomson and took her before a magistrate, where her rights were explained. There, she complained of a leg injury. Foreman insisted that she be taken to a hospital for an immediate examination. Physicians found several bruises on her body. And Foreman thereby began building his defense. The case attracted national attention when the trial was filmed by CBS television for use in a documentary about famous trial lawyers, including Foreman. The documentary opened with a scene from the trial, showing Foreman presenting his case to an all-male jury.

It was another case in which Foreman put the murder victim on trial. He accused the slain man of trying to hire a farm laborer to kill Mrs. Thomson; of being a sexual deviate; of becoming "an almost unbearable tyrant" to his family; of physically abusing his wife; of poisoning Mrs. Thomson's pet animals; and of beating her the night of the slaying.

Three physicians testified that Mrs. Thomson's body bore numerous bruises, plus a hairline fracture of a pelvis bone, when she was examined at the hospital after her arrest. Other witnesses described in detail her mistreatment at the hands of her husband. Mrs. Thomson herself took the stand to testify that she fired the pistol in self-defense, fearing her husband might kill her. She denied prosecution allegations that she had slain her husband to prevent him from divorcing her and thus putting a halt to her "high-style life." The night of the slaying, she said, "everything went blank." She conceded firing the shots, but added: "How many times I shot, I don't know. But (I recall) I thought he was going to kill me."

Foreman made a typically impassioned jury summation, assailing the dead victim and seeking to place God's seal of approval on the slaying. "The Almighty intended Arthur Francis Thomson to die," Foreman told the jurors. "Perhaps he died that others might live in peace. He lived by force, and he died by force and violence."

All this drama, with the exception of the testimony of the three physicians (who objected to appearing on camera), was filmed by CBS. The televising of the case, perhaps as much as the trial itself, made major news. It was an experiment in use of television in the courtroom. From the jurors' viewpoint, the cameras had not intruded. "We did our best to see that personalities of the lawyers [and use of cameras] did not influence us," said jury foreman G. F. Dickinson. "Maybe we didn't succeed, but we tried."

Whether the jurors had succeeded in this regard depended on which side you supported. An objective observer would find it difficult to see how a juror could help but be swayed, one way or another, by the personality of Percy Foreman. It is such an overpowering personality that it can scarcely be ignored.

In any event, the jury found Mrs. Thomson not guilty. As so many husband-slayers had done before her, Mrs. Thomson thanked Foreman profusely for saving her from possible imprisonment or death. "It's so wonderful that it is all over, but I am sorry my husband is dead," she said.

Not all of Foreman's cases deal with issues where the alleged crimes are so clearly defined as murder and theft. Occasionally, he tries a case where the purported offense lies in one of the gray areas of the law. A notable trial of this kind took place in the summer of 1966. Foreman led the defense of seven individuals and four companies charged with interstate shipment of obscene paperback novels.

Once again, Foreman found himself practicing before Judge Joe Ingraham in Federal District Court in Houston. He shared the defense table with four other attorneys—Newton Schwartz of Houston, Stanley Fleishman of Los Angeles, James Carroll of Cleveland and Donald H. Cole of Sandusky, Ohio. The prosecutors were Chief Assistant United States Attorney Morton Susman (later named U.S. Attorney), Assistant U.S. Attorneys Ronald Blask and Donald Stone, all of Houston, and Edward Pesce, a Justice Department lawyer from Washington.

Individuals standing trial were William L. Hamling of Palm Springs, California, former publisher of *Rogue Magazine* and owner of two California publishing companies, Corinth Publications and Reed Enterprises; Richard A. Yerxa of San Diego, California, president of the Corinth and Reed firms; three other persons connected with the two firms, Stephen A. Keegan of San Diego, Donald M. Partrick of El Cajon, California, and Mrs. Shirley R. Wright of La Mesa, California; Howard E. Stephens, owner of Stephens Printing Corporation in Sandusky, Ohio; and Walter H. Lonsdale, owner of New-Cal Publications of Gardena, California. The Corinth, Reed, Stephens and New-Cal firms were also defendants in the case.

The defendants were charged with shipping hundreds of copies of seven purportedly obscene paperback novels to Houston area newsstands from Los Angeles and Sandusky. The government charged that the books were published and distributed by the Corinth and Reed firms and printed by the Stephens and New-Cal companies.

The books were entitled *Sin Summer, Temple of Shame, Swap Sect, Passion Carousel, Virgins Inc., Orgy Club* and *Shame Hunger.* Foreman and his fellow defense attorneys did not try to dispute the fact that the books had been shipped to the Houston area by the defendants. Instead, they challenged the government contention that the novels were obscene. They contended that the books had social value because "they depict life as it is."

The pulling and hauling between the prosecution and defense began even before a jury had been chosen. During the jury-selection process, defense attorney Stanley Fleishman charged that the Justice Department had picked Houston as the site for the obscenity prosecution—although the defendants had shipped identical books to many parts of the country—because religious factors in Houston would make it easier to find a jury that would convict. Fleishman's charge prompted *The Houston Chronicle* to publish a headline that read: "Bible Belt Houston Called No Place for a Smut Trial." Percy Foreman moved to strike the entire panel of prospective jurors on the grounds that panel members might have been prejudiced by seeing the headline. Fleishman, arguing in support of the motion, pointed out that he had never used the term "Bible Belt." But Judge Ingraham denied the motion. He said he had instructed prospective jurors not to read newspaper accounts of the trial and that there was no assurance members of future jury panels might not read other headlines referring to the case.

As the jury-selection process continued another defense lawyer, Newton Schwartz, disclosed that the defense would try to show that sexual practices described in the defendants' books occurred in Houston and all parts of the country. Among the practices he named were wife-swapping, homosexual acts, prostitution, sadism and masochism. Judge Ingraham indicated he was not inclined to admit such evidence in the trial. He said he did not see how the conduct of Houston residents had any bearing on the charges against the defendants. In a bank-robbery trial, he pointed out, it would not be relevant to review other, unrelated bank robberies.

But defense attorney Fleishman argued that the authors of the seven books involved in the case had cut "a slice of life" in their novels. "Many of us have had insulated lives, and what the books depict may seem impossible," Fleishman said. "That is why we want to show what really takes place." The judge decided to hold the matter in abeyance until later in the trial.

Because of the nature of the case, it took three days to select a jury. Many of the prospective jurors were excused when they conceded they might be prejudiced against the defendants. One, for example, said he was concerned about the effect of obscene materials on children. Another said literature concerning sexual matters had once caused him trouble at home. Still another said his religious background might prejudice him.

The jury ultimately chosen was composed of ten men and two women. Since the trial was expected to be lengthy, four alternate jurors were also selected. The alternates would hear all the evidence and would be available to replace any jurors who might have to leave the case because of illness, disqualification or other reasons.

The prosecutors opened their case by presenting evidence tracing the shipments of purportedly obscene books from California and Ohio to Houston. The evidence indicated that at least 2,440 copies of the seven books in question had reached Houston area newsstands. Foreman and Fleishman countered by producing evidence that many other books dealing with sexual matters could be found at the same newsstands. They introduced fifty such books into evidence. Among the titles were *The Anatomy of Rape*, *Lolita* and *Sexual Behavior of American Nurses.*

At this point in the trial, Houston's supposed status as a "Bible Belt city" arose again. The city's mayor, Louie Welch, was asked at a press conference about Fleishman's statement that Houston had been chosen as the site for the trial because religious factors there would make it more likely for a jury to convict the defendants. Welch replied that he was proud of "the charge" that Houston was a "Bible Belt city" when it came to pornography.

The mayor's statement received broad coverage on radio and television, as well as in the newspapers. Foreman promptly moved for another mistrial, contending Welch had "poisoned the air" for the trial. He claimed that news reports on the mayor's press conference had made it impossible for the defendants to receive a fair trial in Houston. But Judge Ingraham denied the motion, pointing out once again that the jury had been instructed to disregard news reports on the case. "It is not appropriate to impeach the mayor here," the judge said.

Reporting this episode in the trial, *The Houston Chronicle* published a large page-one headline that read: "Smut Trial Poisoned, Percy Says." This prompted Foreman to make still another motion for a mistrial. He charged that the *Chronicle* was making "an obvious effort to influence the community [against the defendants], perhaps in an effort to sell papers." This purported attempt by the newspaper to influence the community, Foreman contended, made it even more impossible for the defendants to get a fair trial. Once again, Judge Ingraham denied the motion.

The prosecutors called to the stand a Los Angeles vice-squad policeman, Louis McClary. He testified that one of the defendants, Richard Yerxa, president of Corinth Publications and Reed Enterprises, had once described the companies' books as "roughest on the market."

McClary testified he had met with Yerxa and another defendant, Donald Partrick, in January of 1964. They told him that the Corinth and Reed firms planned to distribute books in the Los Angeles area, he said. He testified Partrick told him "somebody big" was behind the Reed firm, but that Partrick said he could not disclose the identity of this somebody.

On cross-examination, Foreman tried to ridicule McClary's testimony. With a straight face, Foreman asked the policeman whether he knew the two long-dead puritanical reformers Carrie Nation and Anthony Comstock.

With an equally straight face, McClary replied simply: "No, sir."

Another witness, Samuel Campagna, Jr., who had served in the Marine Corps with Yerxa, testified that Yerxa had paid him five hundred dollars after Campagna had signed some papers making him one of three incorporators of the Corinth and Reed firms. At Yerxa's request, Campagna said, he had left his job as a Chicago milkman to work briefly for the Reed firm in California. He said Yerxa had told him the Reed firm collected 20,000 dollars to 30,000 dollars a week in receipts from book sales. Under cross-examination by Foreman, Campagna conceded that he had lied when he told an FBI agent he had been offered 2,000 dollars a month to serve as secretary-treasurer of the firm.

Next, the jurors began reading the seven novels involved in the case, in order to judge whether the books appealed to the prurient interests of the average American. The reading was done in the courtroom. Each of the jurors and alternates was first given a copy of *Swap Sect,* a novel about wife-swapping. Judge Ingraham instructed the jurors to read a chapter at a time, then wait for all the others to finish before moving on to the next chapter. The judge had a copy of the book and read along with them. When all of them had finished *Swap Sect,* they went on to the next book. It took them a week to finish reading all seven.

During the reading of the books, spectators drifted in and out of the courtroom. Some arrived under the impression that the books were being read aloud. When they discovered that the reading was being done silently, they left disappointedly.

Before the reading of the novels was completed, two of the

jurors were disqualified because of a chance remark they overheard in a courthouse elevator. The jurors, Mrs. Virginia Moraitis, a housewife, and King D. Fariss, a retired government employee, were riding down in the elevator during a lunch recess. Also in the elevator were United States Attorney Woodrow Seals (who was not participating in the trial), defense attorney Newton Schwartz and Judge Ingraham's law clerk, Carroll Shaddock. Seals, mistaking Shaddock for another judge's law clerk, asked him: "What is your judge doing today?" Shaddock answered jokingly: "He's reading smut."

After the lunch recess, Schwartz asked Judge Ingraham to declare a mistrial or disqualify the two jurors on the ground that Shaddock's remark had been prejudicial. Percy Foreman, arguing in support of Schwartz's motion, contended that the jurors would think Shaddock had been reflecting the judge's opinion of the books. Judge Ingraham denied the mistrial motion, but disqualified the two jurors. They were replaced by two alternates.

Shortly after the jurors finished reading the novels, the prosecutors rested the government's case. Foreman and his fellow defense lawyers moved for a directed verdict of acquittal on the ground that the prosecution had presented insufficient evidence. Judge Ingraham denied the motion. He said the case involved "a gray area of the law" and that he did not know what action an appellate court might take. "But I am going to give you a trial," he said.

The defense subpoenaed voluminous records of the Houston Police Department Vice Squad, intending to show that certain sexual practices described in the defendants' books occurred in Houston. Prosecutor Morton Susman opposed issuance of the subpoena for the records. He accused the defense of trying to harass the police, convert the trial into a "sensational exposé" and make "a parody of a court of law."

Foreman, Schwartz and Fleishman argued, however, that they needed the records to prove that the novels described real-life situations. Fleishman said the defense wanted to demonstrate the books were not obscene by showing that they had social value. "Holding a mirror even to the dark side of life has social value," he said. Judge Ingraham approved issuance of the subpoena, but indicated he might admit few of the vice-squad records into evidence. He questioned their relevance to the case.

In the end, none of the records was admitted. Instead, at the request of the defense, the judge instructed the jury that "in the nation as a whole, including the state of Texas, people engage in a wide variety of sexual conduct, including conduct which is contrary to law, morality and religious teachings." He read to the jurors a list of twenty-two examples of such conduct, including wife-swapping, sodomy and "the use of teenaged boys for the sexual pleasure of older women."

The defense then called a series of expert witnesses in efforts to show that the books were not obscene, that they appealed to persons with normal sexual interests and that the sexual behavior they described occurred in real life. Among the experts was Dr. Wardell B. Pomeroy, a psychologist who had been one of the authors of the Kinsey reports on sexual behavior. Pomeroy had worked at the Kinsey Institute at the University of Indiana for twenty years before becoming a marriage counselor in New York.

"About ninety-five percent of the men and eighty-five percent of the women in the country could be doing time in prison for what they have done sexually," Pomeroy testified. He said research indicated that high percentages of the population were violating state laws forbidding such practices as adultery, premarital intercourse and homosexuality.

Pomeroy testified that "the normal average male is more aroused by viewing a living person than by openly sexual depictions in writing or pictures." He said the average man is "tremendously interested in sex," is sexually stimulated by many things and engages in a broad variety of sexual behavior before, during and after marriage.

Pomeroy was followed to the stand by a literature professor from the University of Oklahoma, Dwight V. Swain. In questioning Swain, Foreman employed a geographical analogy to defend the seven novels. He showed the professor a map of the United States. If the limits of candor on sex in literature extended from Houston to the Canadian border (with Canada representing the extreme of candor), Foreman asked, how far would the seven novels go?

"The seven books would lie within the state of Texas," Swain replied.

The professor testified that he was a former pulp-fiction writer. Under Foreman's questioning, he gave the jury a short lecture on the writing of popular fiction. He said that readers of such fiction are looking for a chance to worry about the fate of the main characters in a story. The writer must give his characters desires, then interpose dangers that threaten to prevent them from achieving those desires, he said.

Swain testified this pattern was followed in *Passion Carousel,* one of the seven novels involved in the trial. The book concerned a young woman trying to escape from a cult of devil-worshipers. Swain said that orgiastic rituals described in the novel accurately portrayed actual rites practiced by devil-worshipers in the past.

The professor was questioned about another of the defendants' books, *Orgy Club,* which described the adventures of a group of housewives who went to work in a bawdy house. By coincidence, their husbands showed up as their customers. Swain admitted that the chances against this happening were astronomical, but said it was not an unreasonable exaggeration for popular fiction.

Another defense witness was Mrs. Vivian Ayers Allen, a Houston writer and editor who also worked as a librarian at Rice University. Mrs. Allen testified that numerous books described by the defense as more sexually candid than those involved in the trial were widely available in Houston. She also said that the Rice University library contained a pornography collection.

Mrs. Allen was followed to the stand by the author of four of the books involved in the case, Thomas P. Ramirez of Fond du Lac, Wisconsin. Ramirez, forty, who writes under the pen name of Tony Calvano, testified he was the author of *Passion Carousel, Orgy Club, Swap Sect* and *Shame Hunger.* A former school teacher, he staunchly defended the literary quality of his books.

"They have characters, plots, motivation, action and resolution," he said. "The roughest language used is an occasional 'damn' or 'God.' It is ridiculous these books are being questioned."

Ramirez testified he was paid nine hundred dollars per book and wrote each one in ten to twelve days. While writing, he said, he pictured "a rather unsophisticated reader—one whose reading must be done in a hurry." But he added that he knew some "intellectuals and some darn nice people" who also enjoyed such books.

Defense attorney Fleishman asked: "Is there going to be a story on Houston?"

"Very likely," Ramirez replied.

He testified he had written *Passion Carousel* to demonstrate that "witchcraft has not died" and to expose the activities of what he described as a burgeoning sadomasochistic movement "in our country and the world." He said this movement is made up of "jaded, wealthy, powerful people who seek extremes in sexual depravity."

Ramirez's wife was the last defense witness. She testified that she was the author of sixty published Sunday School lessons. And she was proud of her husband's books, she said.

Percy Foreman tried to introduce into evidence fifty letters from servicemen in Vietnam. He said the servicemen requested that they be sent books such as those involved in the trial, and described Tony Calvano as their favorite author. But Judge Ingraham refused to admit the letters into evidence. After ordering the jury withdrawn from the courtroom, the judge said he had received a letter he was sure Foreman would not want introduced. It was from a woman in Alaska who wrote that she hoped the defendants would be convicted and given stiff sentences.

Judge Ingraham said the issue in the trial was not whether readers liked the books, but whether the books were obscene. He observed that the case might be easier to decide if it were turned into a "Roman trial" and moved to a local arena, the Sam Houston Coliseum, where the public could vote "yea" or "nay." But, since the law precluded such a popularity contest, the judge ruled that the various letters had no relevance to the trial.

After the defense attorneys rested their case, the prosecutors called several rebuttal witnesses to counter the expert testimony presented on behalf of the defendants. The best known of the rebuttal witnesses was novelist David Westheimer, author of *Von Ryan's Express,* among other works. Although he was then living in Los Angeles, Westheimer previously had been a longtime Houston resident and had served as television critic for *The Houston Post.*

Westheimer testified that the seven novels involved in the trial lacked literary merit and accused the authors of dishonesty for failing to use four-letter words. He charged that the writers had intentionally omitted such words "to attempt to avoid accusations of the type that have been brought [in the prosecution]." The use of four-letter words in the books "could eliminate erotic appeal by making sex acts so ugly or shocking as to bring a reader out of his fantasy," Westheimer said. He said the books "would have been more honest" if the words had been used, since some of the characters normally would have used them.

"The story [in each of the seven books] is vestigial, merely a framework upon which to hang scenes of a sexual nature, normal or perverted," Westheimer testified. "The books are very poorly written. Their characters are one-dimensional, like cardboard figures." Westheimer said the authors' descriptions of sexual sensations and women's figures were virtually identical from one book to another. "The books' endings are abrupt, as if the author had suddenly decided he had written enough," he said.

On cross-examination, Foreman asked Westheimer about his World War II experiences. As a bomber navigator, the witness had been shot down and imprisoned in Europe.

"Would you say you know more about B-24 bombers and prisoner-of-war camps than sex?" Foreman asked.

"I am not sure I can answer that without sounding like I am bragging," Westheimer replied.

Foreman then introduced into evidence paperback copies of three of Westheimer's novels. He pointed out that the pictures on the covers seemed suggestive, and he read from the cover blurbs passages that emphasized the books' sexual appeal.

After reading one blurb, Foreman asked: "Did I read that correctly?"

Westheimer answered: "If I were directing you, I would have changed the emphasis."

Later in the cross-examination, Westheimer described as improbable some of the sexual scenes in the defendants' novels. He said such improbability in literature could not be artistically justified.

"Do you recognize the Old Testament as literature?" Foreman asked.

"Yes," Westheimer replied.

Foreman then asked whether the scenes in the defendants' books were any more improbable than a series of passages from the Old Testament. He referred Westheimer to the Biblical account of Lot and his "two virgin daughters." Foreman recounted how Lot had thrown the daughters to a mob to be ravished, and how the girls had later plotted to get Lot drunk so that he would father children for them. He also asked Westheimer about the Old Testament account of King Ahasuerus, who was said to have had sexual relations with "3,000 virgins" before making Esther his queen.

Westheimer said he would consider these events improbable today, but that he could not say whether they would have been in another era.

Under further questioning by Foreman, Westheimer testified that he had never lived next door to any women such as the sexpots described in the defendants' books.

"Where did you live in Houston?" Foreman asked.

"On Aberdeen Way."

"I don't know any women like that on that street, either," Foreman said.

"I wouldn't question your expertise in these matters," Westheimer replied.

"I wouldn't, either," Foreman snapped.

Westheimer testified that some of the sexual acts described in the books were "medically impossible."

"You say they are impossible because they are impossible for you?" Foreman asked.

"Yes, sir!" Westheimer answered emphatically.

Another rebuttal witness called by the prosecution was a woman psychiatrist from Toledo, Ohio, Dr. Ann Hankins Ford. The prosecutors tried to use her testimony to attack the expertise of defense witness Dr. Wardell Pomeroy, the former Kinsey Institute researcher.

Pomeroy had testified that the defendants' books did not appeal to unhealthy sexual appetites. But Dr. Ford testified that they did appeal to such appetites.

Pomeroy had testified that the average male's sex drive reaches a peak when he is eighteen, then gradually declines. But Dr. Ford said the male's sex drive peaks during adolescence, then stays on a plateau until senility. She testified that the average woman's sex drive also is long-lived. She said it begins in adolescence, rises gradually until it peaks when a woman is forty to fifty, then remains on a plateau for virtually the remainder of her life. Dr. Ford testified that people don't enjoy sex more as they get old, but that their interest in it doesn't diminish, either.

While conceding that "the average normal adult" should be able to choose for himself what he wants to read, she criticized the defendants' books for describing sexual activities as divorced from love.

Under cross-examination by Foreman, Dr. Ford admitted that sex without love is not uncommon in real life. "But that doesn't make it healthy," she said.

Foreman asked: "If a person had to settle for either sex or love, which do you think he would take?"

Dr. Ford replied: "No one has to make that kind of choice."

She testified that she was sixty years of age and was a grandmother. Foreman asked her: "Is your sexual drive greater now than it was when you were thirty?"

Dr. Ford replied with a smile: "I'm doing all right."

A short time later, both sides rested their cases. In closing arguments, prosecutors Morton Susman and Donald Stone contended that the defendants' books were obscene, that they appealed to prurient interests and that the defendants should be found guilty. They told the jurors to disregard the expert testimony, if they chose, and to decide for themselves whether the books were obscene.

In his summation, Foreman accused the prosecutors of fostering "lynch law" by encouraging the jurors to cast aside the experts' opinions and to judge the books by their own standards of what constituted obscenity. If jurors were to decide such cases according to their own notions of obscenity, he said, "we might just as well go back to lynching." Such a system would mean that obscenity laws would change with each new jury, Foreman said. He argued that the jury was supposed to judge the books against national standards, but could not do so without the benefit of expert testimony.

Foreman contended the prosecutors were trying to make scapegoats out of the defendants. "These defendants were cut out of a great herd to be branded and barbecued," he told the jurors. "They [the prosecutors] are asking you to do the barbecuing, but they haven't given you enough firewood."

Accusing the government of an attempt to impose censorship, Foreman pointed out that there was a time in history when the Bible was banned as pornographic and when anyone found possessing it was subject to execution. "I dare you to find any more obscene character than King David," he said. "Neither *Fanny Hill, Candy, Orgy Club* nor *Passion Carousel* are nearly as obscene as the Book of Genesis."

He argued that neither the courts nor legislative bodies should try to impose standards of morality by decree. "I don't believe someone else has a right to tell me anything about what is right and proper for me except the minister of my church," Foreman said. He argued that the defendants' books should not be condemned because they were not great literature and because they were aimed at unsophisticated readers.

"Every man is entitled to what he can enjoy," he said.

The case went to the jury on August 24, 1966. On August 29, the jurors reported that they were hopelessly deadlocked. But Judge Ingraham sent them back to the jury room with instructions to keep trying to reach a verdict. The next day the jury foreman, Robert W. Heflin, reported to the judge: "We feel progress is being made at this time. If the time arises this is not the case, we will advise you."

That time arose on September 2, the tenth day of deliberations. Heflin advised the judge that the jury was "hopelessly deadlocked with no unanimous agreement possible." He said the jury had once stood nine to three for acquittal, then switched to nine to three for conviction and finally to six to six.

Judge Ingraham, convinced that further deliberations would be fruitless, declared a mistrial.

A disgruntled professional football player once grumbled that "a tie game is like kissing your sister." The remark might just as well have been made by a lawyer involved in a case ending in a hung jury. Usually, such a case settles nothing. It may be retried, if the prosecution chooses, at a later date.

But the Houston obscenity case may prove to be an exception. Shortly after declaring the mistrial, Judge Ingraham expressed grave doubts about whether the defendants should have been prosecuted in the first place. He advised the government lawyers to "take a long, hard look" at the evidence before deciding whether to seek a new trial.

The judge commented: "There were many times during the trial that I thought, 'Is it worth it?' Obscenity is a gray area of the law. Some of it is blackish and some whitish, but none of it is black or white. Education and cultivation of better tastes might be a better answer to the problem of obscenity."

While the government lawyers were pondering their next move, the United States Supreme Court handed down a decision that placed sharp new curbs on obscenity prosecutions. The court, in throwing out convictions in three other obscenity cases, hinted strongly that it would not permit the suppression of publications on grounds of obscenity except in special, extreme cases. Involved in the cases decided by the Supreme Court were two spicy paperback novels of the general type involved in the Houston case—entitled *Lust Pool* and *Shame Agent*—plus ten "girlie" magazines. The court held that none of these publications was obscene.

Ultimately, it was decided that the Houston case would not be tried again in Houston—if it were tried again at all. Jurisdiction in the case was transferred to the federal district court in San Diego, California. At this writing, the case has not been set for a new trial there. Whether it will be retried is an open question. But, even if it is, the prosecution will have to meet the severe new tests imposed by the Supreme Court decision.

Thus, time may prove that even a hung jury can work to the advantage of Percy Foreman's clients.

12

I had been in trouble all my life, in jail most of it. But in all my crimes I was proud that I had never hurt anybody. I had never molested any child or pistol-whipped any victim I held up.
JAMES EARL RAY

IN LATE 1968 the defendant who unquestionably needed Percy Foreman most was James Earl Ray—accused assassin of the Reverend Dr. Martin Luther King, Jr. Ray stood accused of committing perhaps the most baffling crime of our generation.

The assassinations of John F. Kennedy and Robert F. Kennedy, despite all the newspaper and television reports to the contrary, were essentially simple cases. That is, the police work involved was minimal. If we are to believe the Warren Commission, other experts and members of the Kennedy family itself, no conspiracy was involved in either assassination. Each was evidently committed by a man who fit the classic pattern for an assassin—a lone assailant, mentally disturbed, harboring deep-seated resentments against society.

The evidence was not quite so clear in the assassination of Martin Luther King. Not only did James Earl Ray appear to fall outside the classic pattern; there was also some evidence indicating a conspiracy, at least to aid his escape, if not to carry out the murder itself.

When Percy Foreman entered the Ray case as chief defense counsel, Ray already was suffering the effects of a spate of unfavorable publicity and a certain amount of confusion among those trying to help him. To grasp the enormity of the problem, it is necessary to consider briefly the fact situation.

Martin Luther King—by that time a Nobel prize winner—had gone to Memphis, Tennessee, in April 1968 to lend his prestige to a strike by city garbage collectors. The Memphis crisis, such as it was, paled in comparison with some others King had precipitated. The Montgomery bus boycott, the Freedom Rides, the Birmingham rioting, the violence in Danville, Virginia, the March on Washington, the Poor People's Campaign and countless others had brought to King the brutality of physical violence and the martyrdom of filthy jail cells.

Now, however, he was riding the crest of a respectability that had long been denied him. He was a hero of sorts, even to many white people in his home state of Georgia. A native son who had won the Nobel prize was not to be denied his place in the sun.

Thus, it was as an elder statesman—albeit a young one—that he had gone to Memphis. His presence was expected to help the garbage collectors, many of them Negroes, win some sort of accommodation from the city.

At midafternoon of April 4 a white man of medium height, with dark hair trimmed neatly in place, entered a small rooming house at 422½ South Main Street. He seemed out of place in the rundown structure. He wore a presentable black suit, a white shirt and a slim black tie. The rooming-house manager, Mrs. Bessie Brewer, was not used to renting rooms to men dressed that well. The man said he wanted a room—just a room to sleep in, nothing more—but was choosy about its location.

They finally settled on room 5, which rented for eight dollars and fifty cents a week. The man handed her what appeared to be a fresh twenty-dollar bill, said he would pay for a week in advance and received his change.

"What's your name?" Mrs. Brewer asked.

"John Willard," he replied. Authorities would later charge that his real name was James Earl Ray.

Room 5 allowed its occupant a view of Mulberry Street. And, across Mulberry Street, he could see room 306 of the Lorraine Motel—an addition to the old, Negro-occupied Lorraine Hotel. In room 306, Dr. King was meeting with his aides—including the Reverend Andrew Young, executive vice-president of King's Southern Christian Leadership Conference; the Reverend James Bevel, a fiery maverick who later would claim he could prove Ray's innocence; and the Reverend Jesse L. Jackson.

There had been some civil disorder in Memphis following an earlier appearance by King. Now he and his staff were planning a rally scheduled for eight o'clock that night.

It was no secret to the public that King was occupying room 306. The location had already been publicized in newspapers and on television. "John Willard" could see the room from his vantage point, but the view was not ideal. He had to bend over to do so. A rooming-house bathroom, however, provided a window with a much clearer view. Other roomers noticed that Willard made several visits to this bathroom during the afternoon. They also noticed that a 1966 white Mustang automobile was parked outside.

At the Lorraine Motel, King wound up his meeting. He told his friends he was tired of restaurant food and would dearly love some "soul food" before making his appearance at the rally. A local minister invited him home for dinner, and he agreed to go. Before leaving, however, he walked out on a balcony outside his room. Ben Branch, also involved in planning the rally, asked King what spirituals he preferred to hear sung.

"My man, be sure to sing 'Precious Lord' and sing it well," King replied.

It was 6:01 P.M.

Crack!

Inside the rooming house, roomer Charles Stephens heard the noise and knew immediately it was a shot. "It was very loud," he later recalled. "It sounded like a German .88." Stephens was certain the shot had come from the bathroom.

Dr. King lay sprawled on the balcony. "Oh," he said. "Oh."

While some of his friends rushed to his aid, others pointed toward the rooming house, shouting that the shot had appeared to come from there.

Despite the fact that Dr. King had not requested protection, Memphis authorities had taken the precaution of having about forty peace officers in the general area of his motel. Thus, although these precautions had failed to thwart the assassin, they did permit a manhunt to begin almost immediately. Wearing blue helmets and toting rifles and riot guns, the officers swept swiftly through the streets, sealing off the immediate vicinity.

Somehow, "John Willard" got through the roadblocks. And his ease in escaping—plus other mysterious events—has fostered the notion that he may have had some sort of help.

Dr. King was rushed to a hospital. But, at 6:31 P.M., an aide emerged and announced: "They have killed Dr. King."

"They," he said. "They" had killed Dr. King. But who were "they"? The answer remains a secret to this day and may forever. For, even if James Earl Ray's guilt stands affirmed in the highest courts of our land, there will still be the lingering mystery of who, if anyone, helped him.

Only by tracing his movements from the time of the assassination until his capture is it possible to assess the probability of aid at some point. There is little question at this point that Ray was, indeed, the man who called himself Willard. The question, if any, is whether he actually fired the fatal shot or was the patsy for someone else. He and his closest advisers do not deny that he was in Memphis and was somehow involved in the murder.

Assuming, then, that Ray was the man in the rooming house, what happened to him after the shooting? The known facts are these:

Charles Stephens, the roomer, heard shouts from the Lorraine Motel after the shot, and rushed into a hallway. He saw a man, presumably Ray, carrying a bulky bundle about the size of a rifle. It was wrapped in newspapers. Another roomer also saw the man and said to him: "That sounded like a shot." The man with the bundle replied: "Yes, it was." He appeared to have a smile on his face as he said it.

A few minutes later a rifle and a small suitcase were discarded outside a music shop near the murder scene. A policeman, called to the scene, opened the suitcase and found a set of binoculars, some underwear, tools and a sales receipt for forty-one dollars and five cents. The officer rushed into the rooming house, was directed to room 5 and found a strap that fitted the binoculars perfectly.

The white Mustang that had been parked near the rooming house was driven away, apparently without being noticed, shortly after the shooting. But only a few minutes elapsed before police were made aware of the possibility that it might be a getaway car. At 6:25 P.M. the radio dispatcher at Memphis Police Headquarters reported that a white Mustang was spotted heading north on Danny Thomas Boulevard "at a high rate of speed."

By that time, it would have been possible for the actual getaway car to have crossed state lines into either Arkansas or Mississippi. Such a route would have been logical for an assassin. The crossing of state lines—while liable to bring the FBI into the case—would allow for possible red-tape delays in transmitting a "pickup" order among various law-enforcement agencies. As a practical matter, the FBI entered the case shortly in any event.

Just two minutes after the dispatcher reported the white Mustang spotted on Danny Thomas Boulevard, another car of the same description was reported stopped two miles away. Eight minutes after that, there was a radio report that a police car was pursuing such a car north on Danny Thomas Boulevard. But a northbound car would have been going in the wrong direction for flight into either Arkansas or Mississippi.

Meanwhile, a car identifying itself as Police Car 160 radioed that a "complainant" had just reported a white man driving a white Mustang east on still another street. The police dispatcher then radioed: "White male east on Summer from Highland in a white Mustang, responsible for this shooting. Cars 36 and 42 pull down. Subject is exceeding the speed limit on Summer from Highland."

At that very moment another police car was chasing down a Mustang and reporting that its driver appeared innocent of any connection with the shooting. Somehow, despite the speed with which Memphis police had launched the manhunt, the slayer had escaped. It would later be reported that at least one major report broadcast over the police radio network had been phony. This would lead to speculation that a "pirate" radio transmitter of some kind had been used, as part of a conspiracy, to facilitate the killer's flight.

But, if the assassin was gone, he had left behind numerous clues. There were some who said he had left too many—too many, that is, to be genuine. It appeared almost as though some of the clues had been left deliberately to point the finger of suspicion at a man who might be a patsy. James Earl Ray and his associates later would seize on this theory and try to build it into a defense.

Within hours, FBI agents, Memphis police and state authorities were piecing together part of the background of the man who called himself John Willard. The day before the assassination Willard had entered a Memphis store and bought the binoculars later found in the suitcase. That same day he had taken a room at a motel at the intersection of Interstate 240 and U.S. 78. He had registered at the motel as Eric S. Galt. Employees recalled that he had been driving a white 1966 Mustang.

Authorities at this point did not know Ray's true name, of course. But they did know for sure that John Willard and Eric S. Galt were one man. The next step, aside from trying to find him, was to trace his recent movements. The murder weapon provided a key clue. It was a pump-action Remington .760 rifle—a 30-06 bearing the serial number 461476. It had been fitted with a telescopic sight bearing the serial number A17350.

A check of firearms records disclosed that it had been sold on March 30, five days before the shooting, by the Aeromarine Supply Co. near the municipal airport at Birmingham, Alabama. A salesman there recalled selling the rifle to a man who gave his name as "Harvey Lowmyer." Not only the salesman but a customer as well remembered the buyer. He had originally bought another Remington model, the .243, but had returned a day later to exchange it for the murder weapon. The .243 is similar in design to the murder weapon, but is used for smaller game. "Lowmyer," in exchanging the first rifle for the second, explained that he and a relative planned to go hunting for large game in Wisconsin. (There is some confusion whether he said the relative was his brother or brother-in-law.) The Birmingham shop fitted the rifle with the telescopic sight.

It is now clear that the purchaser of the rifle was James Earl Ray. It is also clear that, the day after he bought the weapon, he was in Dr. King's home city, Atlanta. Indications are that he made the 155-mile trip from Birmingham in the white Mustang. Ray had previously rented a room on Fourteenth Street in Atlanta under the name of "Eric Starvo Galt."

On March 24, Galt paid the ten dollars and fifty cents weekly rent in advance. On March 31, he paid another ten dollars and fifty cents—meaning the room would be his until at least April 7. But he never returned to the Atlanta room after the murder.

It seems evident that Ray, under the name of Galt, was stalking Dr. King. Within three miles of the Atlanta rooming house were King's residence, his home church and the headquarters of his Southern Christian Leadership Conference. Birmingham, where Ray had bought the murder weapon, had been the scene of King's most difficult struggles and some of his greatest triumphs. His brother, the Reverend A. D. King, resided in Birmingham. A. D. King's home and church had been bombed more than once, as had other Birmingham churches at which Martin Luther King had preached and homes at which he had stayed. One of Dr. King's most famous writings, the heralded "jail letter," had been composed in a Birmingham cell.

After Dr. King's assassination, officers found among Ray's belongings a map of Atlanta. Circled on the map were the locations of Dr. King's residence, church and the SCLC headquarters. Also circled was an area known as the Capital Hill Housing Project. It was near this project that the authorities found their next major clue in the case. It was the white Mustang, evidently abandoned by Ray the morning after the murder.

Investigators then followed a tortuous trail indicating Ray had fled from Memphis to Atlanta, then to Toronto, Canada, then to London, England, Lisbon, Portugal, and back again to London.

It was in London on June 8, 1968, that his flight came to an end. Ray had just checked out of the Pax Hotel and gone to Heathrow Airport, apparently intending to catch a plane to Brussels, Belgium. He was carrying two passports—both in false names. Immigration authorities detained him, then turned him over to Scotland Yard.

Under questioning by the Yard's chief superintendent, Thomas Butler, Ray insisted his name was Ramon George Sneyd. But Butler—who had been cooperating with American authorities in the manhunt—knew better. He ordered Ray taken to the Cannon Row Police Station, and told him: "I now believe your name is not Sneyd, but James Earl Ray; that you are also known as Eric Starvo Galt and by other names and that you are wanted at present in the United States for serious criminal offenses, including murder in which a firearm was used."

Ray dropped deep into a chair, covered his face with his hands and groaned: "Oh, God. . . . I feel so trapped."

A series of legal maneuvers followed, in which Ray was provided with counsel in order to fight extradition back to Memphis. At an extradition hearing on June 27, he was questioned by British defense lawyer Roger Frisby.

Q. Did you know Martin Luther King personally?

A. No, sir.

Q. Had you any kind of grudge against him?

A. No, sir.

Q. Did you kill Martin Luther King?

A. No, sir.

While still being held in England, Ray obtained the counsel of Arthur Hanes, an Alabama lawyer. Hanes had been the mayor of Birmingham during that city's racial violence in the early 1960s. He had frequently vilified Dr. King, who had led the demonstrations opposing the city's segregation policies. Later, Hanes had won a measure of national attention by defending various accused members of the Ku Klux Klan.

Thus, Hanes's entry into the case immediately spurred speculation that Ray might have been a hired gun involved in a conspiracy—hatched by the Klan or someone else—to assassinate the leader of the civil-rights movement. Neither Hanes nor Ray did anything to mute this speculation. In fact, they heightened it. Hanes and Ray made a deal to sell the rights to Ray's story to William Bradford Huie, an author with an enduring interest in race-violence cases.

Huie (a friend and sometime colleague of the author of this book) paid 25,000 dollars for the rights, which Hanes expected would be used chiefly for his own counsel fees. For this money, Huie got a series of handwritten notes from Ray's various jail cells, giving his version of the story. The problem was that, as any law-enforcement officer can attest, purchased information is often suspect information. Huie, though diligent in his efforts to verify the information provided by Ray and Hanes, was stuck basically with their version. His first writing on the subject—published by *Look* magazine in the fall of 1968—bore a huge cover headline entitled: "THE STORY OF JAMES EARL RAY & THE CONSPIRACY TO KILL MARTIN LUTHER KING."

Later, however, Huie himself concluded that there had been no conspiracy. In a subsequent book version of the Ray story, he made plain that his purchased information had been misleading at the least. Nonetheless, there will be lingering doubts about this case—just as there will be lingering doubts about other assassinations.

In any event, Arthur Hanes was ultimately fired by Ray. There had been some talk early in the case that members of Ray's family wanted to retain Percy Foreman as defense counsel. Foreman indicated mild interest at the time, saying once again that he always intended to go "where I'm needed the most." But weeks dragged by without his formal entry. There was some talk that Jesse Stoner, a long-time Klan lawyer, would take over. Foreman said he would not come in if Stoner did. As in the case of Jack Ruby, he insisted on clear control over the defense if he were to prepare Ray's defense.

It was not until November 10, 1968, that Foreman agreed to take over. The case was due to go to trial two days later, with Hanes still listed as chief counsel. But Foreman visited Ray—by then jailed in Memphis after extradition from England—in his cell. With him during the visit were Ray's brothers, John and

Gerry. When they emerged, it was disclosed that Hanes had been formally discharged and that Foreman had entered the case. Foreman is a stickler for the niceties of legal protocol when replacing another attorney—even one far his inferior in the courtroom. He takes great pains to make clear that he is not forcing his entry; it must be sought and the prior defender must make a clean break or else subordinate himself to Foreman's control.

Once Hanes had made his exit, Foreman made his own presence felt immediately. All eyes were on him when he first appeared in court on Ray's behalf. The appearance was made for the purpose of seeking a delay in the trial, so that he could study the case. His very presence precipitated a show of petulance by a Memphis prosecutor, Robert K. Dwyer. Irritated by the last-minute change of attorneys, Dwyer accused the defense of stalling tactics. He then took a gratuitous personal whack at Foreman—referring to him bitingly as "this gentleman from Texas. . . . Foreman, I believe, is his name."

Foreman, for once, did not reply in kind. "I know I can get along with Mr. Canale [Shelby County Attorney General Phil Canale, who was Dwyer's boss]," Foreman said. "And I hope, before this day is over, I can get along with Mr. Dwyer."

But, as many participants in the case were to learn, it was growing increasingly difficult for them to get along with Foreman. Even attorneys with whom he had long been associated in trying individual cases said that, with age, he was becoming ever more cranky. This he may have been, but it hardly seemed that his crankiness was hampering his efficiency very much. He lost a few more cases, perhaps, than he had in earlier years. But no serious student of criminal law believed Foreman was in his dotage.

The point in the Ray case was, of course, one that Foreman had made many times. Winning and losing in the courtroom are relative terms at best. And, in the cases of Foreman's clients, a victory is often any verdict less severe than the death penalty.

In arguing before Judge W. Preston Battle for the delay and formal permission to replace Hanes, Foreman said: "In most of the world today, the state says who can represent a defendant. But, in those countries deriving their jurisprudence from England, the common law and Anglo-Saxon principles, the defendant has a right to [say who represents him]. Frankly, Your Honor, I would be much better off physically [he was in ill health] and financially if the court adhered to the adjurations of the distinguished prosecuting attorney. However, I feel it is my responsibility to my oath as a lawyer and to my profession—if this man wants me and needs me and feels that he does, and this court will so permit—to make myself available to the defense of this case. This man is not at liberty. He is in jail. He is not a danger to the community. There might be some expense [involved in granting a delay], but justice doesn't have a price tag on it."

Judge Battle was reluctant to grant Foreman's requested postponement. "This motion comes not only at the eleventh hour but, so to speak, at the fifty-ninth minute and the fifty-ninth second before trial," he said. "It is also true that an immense amount of human energy and time and thought and money has gone into the preparation of this case for trial. It's an awful thing at this time to have to continue the case. But all other considerations yield to the defendant's right to be represented by counsel of his own choosing in a trial for his life."

An indication of Foreman's defense technique was provided by the length of the delay he requested and received. He told the judge he always made it a practice to interview every potential prosecution witness who would cooperate with him in the preparation of the defense. Since the Ray case involved a multitude of potential witnesses—many of whom presumably would agree to talk to him—Foreman sought a three-month delay. The judge gave him 111 days, then granted an additional postponement because Foreman was hospitalized with a mild case of pneumonia.

There was great speculation about the pending trial. Once again a case of Foreman's was billed as a potential "trial of the century." But Foreman, very early in the game, knew it would not be—at least if he could help it. He became convinced after examining the evidence that there had been no conspiracy, that Ray (a long-time criminal who was being hunted as a prison-breaker at the time of the killing) had murdered King alone and that any sentence less severe than death would be a victory in this case. In mid-December Foreman visited Ray's cell—an air-conditioned affair that allowed guards to watch the prisoner around the clock on closed-circuit TV—and proposed the possibility of making a deal with the state. Ray resisted at first. He knew he had the best lawyer available; that there were sufficient holes in the published versions of the assassination to leave room for reasonable doubt; that Southern juries have rarely sentenced a white man to death for murdering a Negro; and that his own machinations had made him something of a hero among professional racists with a violent bent. Ray was confident he would never go to Tennessee's electric chair.

With Foreman in his corner, he figured, he might even beat the rap. But Foreman did not see it that way. He saw virtually no chance that Ray would be acquitted. The evidence seemed clear. Only the most flagrant miscarriage of justice could possibly turn Ray loose. Thus, Foreman's prime duty became keeping Ray out of the chair. He encountered continued distrust from his client. "It took me several months before I convinced him I was working in his best interest," Foreman said.

The physical evidence in the case was what caused Foreman the greatest problem. He could, perhaps, shake the eyewitness testimony of those who placed Ray in the vicinity of the murder. But the physical evidence was so damning that Foreman despaired of taking the case to a jury. There had been ballistics tests on the rifle abandoned at the scene. The tests identified the rifle as the murder weapon. Other evidence showed Ray owned the rifle. The white Mustang used as the getaway car contained strands of hair identified as Ray's. Moreover, his fingerprints had been found on the rifle and in the rooming house from which King had been shot. "Those fingerprints—they were everywhere," Foreman said.

In his talks with Ray, Foreman emphasized the hopelessness of going through with a trial if a deal could be arranged with the prosecution. He told Ray that Memphis juries were noted for dealing out stiff sentences in first-degree murder cases. There were other aspects. The citizenry of Memphis had reacted to the King murder in much the same fashion as the citizens of Dallas had reacted to the assassination of John F. Kennedy. Ray was considered an outsider—just as Lee Harvey Oswald had been considered an outsider—who had brought unfair, unjustifiable criticism to the city as a whole. Therefore, it was reasoned, local jurors might be inclined to deal more severely with him than with the average white man who committed the average murder of an average Negro (that is, if any murder or person can be called average).

Besides consulting with Ray, Foreman also discussed a possible deal with members of the Ray family. "Foreman warned us that, if the trial were to take place, Jimmy would possibly go to the chair to be made an example of," said Ray's brother John.

By early 1969 Ray himself seemed amenable to entering a guilty plea in return for a promise of leniency. Foreman went to see Judge Battle and sounded him out on the possibility of a negotiated sentence. Battle indicated he had no objections, but suggested that Foreman first discuss the situation with the prosecutors. Conversations with Canale produced tentative agreement by the prosecution to accept a guilty plea in return for a sentence of ninety-nine years in prison. (A ninety-nine-year term actually is stiffer in most states than a life sentence. With good behavior, a life term would make Ray eligible for parole after twelve and a half years. A ninety-nine-year sentence would demand that he serve at least thirty years before becoming eligible for parole.)

The agreement by the prosecution to take the deal only on a tentative basis was prompted by Canale's desire to get the opinions of various third parties. He wanted to know, for example, what Dr. King's widow thought of the proposition. Mrs. King told him she had no objection to the ninety-nine-year sentence, since she did not believe in capital punishment. But she emphasized that her informal approval of the deal indicated no acceptance of the theory that Ray had murdered her husband alone, without help from one or more conspirators. Canale elicited a similar response from the Reverend Ralph David Abernathy, King's successor as leader of the Southern Christian Leadership Conference and other civil-rights organizations. The prosecutor also sought, and received, assurances that federal authorities had no objection to the negotiated sentence. (Although Ray was being prosecuted by the state on the murder charge, he had also been accused of lesser federal charges and federal agents had been instrumental in bringing about his capture.)

Shortly before the trial was scheduled to begin, full agreement was reached. Ray would cop a plea and receive the ninety-nine years. But, as has happened numerous times in Percy Foreman's career, his client proved difficult to control both during and after the supposedly climactic day in court.

Under Tennessee law, any negotiated sentence in the case would have to be ratified by a jury. This was a mere formality. But it required a semblance of a trial, giving the jury the opportunity to hear the basic facts of the case before placing its seal of approval on the sentence.

Word was released to the press and public that a previously unexpected hearing in the case would be conducted on March 10, 1969. Speculation was rife that Ray would enter his guilty plea and draw the ninety-nine-year term. But, on the eve of the hearing, this speculation suddenly shifted. News reports said Ray had changed his mind, would refuse to plead guilty and might even dismiss Foreman as his lawyer. Foreman refused to discuss the speculation. "I am trying to save a man's life—not help sell newspapers," he said.

On March 10 Foreman entered the courtroom just after the forty newsmen assigned to cover the case, who had been admitted only after a tight screening process that included a physical search for weapons. Foreman examined some of the prosecution's trial exhibits—among them, a model of the murder scene. The model had been covered with a white sheet. "It looks like the Last Supper," Foreman quipped to reporters.

The prosecutors entered next. This time they were more cordial to Foreman, shaking hands ceremonially. Foreman's presence seemed to overshadow even the entrance of his client, who was led into court by a deputy sheriff. Ray sat down at the defense table, staring first at the floor and then at the judge's bench. Judge Battle shortly made his entrance, the spectators rose, a bailiff called the court to order and the trial of James Earl Ray—such as it was—got under way.

Foreman, decked out in his customary dark suit and vest, opened the proceedings. "May it please the Court," he said. "In this cause, we have prepared [and] the defendant and I have signed . . . a petition for waiver of trial and request for acceptance of plea of guilty."

"This is a compromise and settlement on a plea of guilty to murder in the first degree and an agreed settlement of ninety-nine years in the penitentiary; is that true?" Judge Battle asked.

"That's the agreement, Your Honor," Foreman said.

The judge then questioned Ray to be sure he fully understood the implications of the legal maneuvers being made by Foreman on his behalf. The questioning was detailed.

Battle: Do you know that you have a right to a trial by jury on a charge of murder in the first degree against you, the punishment for murder in the first degree ranging from death by electrocution to any time over twenty years? The burden is on the State of Tennessee to prove you guilty beyond a reasonable doubt and to a moral certainty and the verdict of the jury must be unanimous, both as to guilt and punishment. In the event of a guilty verdict against you, you would have the right to file a motion for a new trial addressed to the trial judge. In the event of an adverse ruling against you on your motion for a new trial, you would have the right to successive appeals to the Tennessee Court of Criminal Appeals and the Supreme Court of Tennessee and to file a petition for review by the Supreme Court of the United States. Do you understand that you have all of these rights?

Ray: Yes, sir.

Battle: You are entering a plea of guilty to murder in the first degree as charged in the indictment and are compromising and settling your case on an agreed punishment of ninety-nine years in the state penitentiary. Is this what you want to do?

Ray: Yes, I do.

Battle: Do you understand that you are waiving, which means giving up, a formal trial by your plea of guilty although the laws of this state require the prosecution to present certain evidence to a jury in all cases on pleas of guilty to murder in the first degree? Has anything besides this sentence of ninety-nine years in the penitentiary been promised to you to get you to plead guilty? Has anything else been promised to you by anyone?

Ray: No, it has not.

Battle: Has any pressure of any kind by anyone in any way been used on you to get you to plead guilty?

Ray: Now, what did you say?

Battle: Are you pleading guilty to murder in the first degree in this case because you killed Dr. Martin Luther King under such circumstances that it would make you legally guilty of murder in the first degree under the law as explained to you by your lawyers?

Ray: Yes, legally, yes.

Battle: Is this plea of guilty to murder in the first degree with an agreed punishment of ninety-nine years in the state penitentiary freely, voluntarily and understandingly made and entered by you?

Ray: Yes, sir.

Battle: Is this plea of guilty on your part the free act of your free will made with your full knowledge and understanding of its meaning and consequences?

Ray: Yes, sir.

These questions and answers seemed sufficiently clear that there would later be little doubt of their meaning. But any who assumed the Battle-Ray colloquy would put a halt to all the mystery concerning the identity of King's assassin were due for further disappointment. Ray had not yet had his final say, either in court or out.

The next step was to empanel a jury willing to approve the deal worked out between Foreman and the prosecutors. With little formality, ten white men and two Negro men were placed in the jury box. Prosecutor Canale explained the substance of the agreement and received assurances from all twelve jurors that they were prepared to assess the negotiated sentence of ninety-nine years. He then told the jurors:

"There have been rumors going all around, perhaps some of

you have heard them, that Mr. James Earl Ray was a dupe in this thing or a fall guy or a member of a conspiracy to kill Dr. Martin Luther King, Jr. I want to state to you as your Attorney General that we have no proof other than that Dr. Martin Luther King, Jr., was killed by James Earl Ray and James Earl Ray alone—not in concert with anyone else.

"Our office has examined over 5,000 printed pages of investigation work done by local police, by national police organizations and by international law-enforcement agencies. We have examined over 300 physical bits of evidence, physical exhibits. Three men in my office . . . have traveled thousands of miles all over this country and the many cities in foreign countries on this investigation, our own independent investigation, and I just state to you frankly that we have no evidence that there was any conspiracy involved in this."

Canale's statement, in a sense, was gratuitous. Nobody had asked him to tell the jurors or the world the substance of his belief that Ray had acted alone. But it is easy to understand why he would want to make such a statement. The court of public opinion might well be James Earl Ray's court of final jurisdiction. Canale knew very well there would be rumors, *ad infinitum*, suggesting a conspiracy. He knew, as well, that his statement would not still the rumors. But he felt obliged as a public official to make known his views—even though the formal charge against Ray had never included a conspiracy count.

(Those who wonder why federal charges in the case were never pursued against Ray, except for a "holding" charge giving the FBI jurisdiction to bring him back from England, may find part of the answer in the absence of a conspiracy. Had Ray been part of a conspiracy to murder Dr. King, the federal government would have had clear jurisdiction to prosecute him under the civil-rights laws. Jurisdiction in the murder case itself would have remained, however, in Memphis.)

Percy Foreman also found himself compelled to make a statement on the subject of the presence or absence of a conspiracy. Rising and taking his place before the jurors, Foreman said:

"It is an honor to appear in this court for this case. I never expected or had any idea when I entered this case that I would be able to accomplish anything except perhaps save the defendant's life. . . . It took me a month to convince myself of the fact which the Attorney General of these United States [Ramsey Clark, Lyndon Johnson's last Attorney General] and J. Edgar Hoover of the Federal Bureau of Investigation announced last July. That is, what Mr. Canale has told you—that there was not a conspiracy. I talked with my client more than fifty hours, I would estimate, and cross-examination most of that time—checking each hour and minute, each expenditure of money down to seventy-five cents for a shave and a haircut, pursuing it. . . . If there is any one of you who feels for any reason you would rather be excused, I am sure His Honor will excuse you at this time before the jury is sworn and call someone else to take your place."

Foreman then asked each of the jurors whether he was prepared to ratify the negotiated sentence. Each juror said he was. Foreman and Canale went through the motions of accepting the jury. It was at this moment that Ray suddenly turned an otherwise perfunctory court case into a piece of theatrics.

Rising to his feet, his face a mask of determination, Ray addressed Judge Battle: "Your Honor, I would like to say something. I don't want to change anything that I have said, but I just want to enter one other thing. The only thing that I have to say is that I can't agree with Mr. Clark."

The statement caused a mild commotion in the courtroom. Ray's statement had not been heard or comprehended by all the participants in the case, much less by newsmen or spectators. Judge Battle and prosecutor Canale seemed mystified. Foreman, who understood quite well what his client had in mind, said more in explanation than exploration: "Ramsey Clark."

Battle then asked: "Mr. Who?"

Ray: Mr. J. Edgar Hoover [as well as Clark]. I agree with all these stipulations [regarding the guilty plea], and I am not trying to change anything.

Battle: You don't agree with those theories [about the absence of a conspiracy]?

Ray: Mr. Canale's, Mr. Clark's and Mr. J. Edgar Hoover's about the conspiracy. I don't want to add something on that I haven't agreed to in the past.

Foreman: I think that what he said is that he doesn't agree that Ramsey Clark is right or that J. Edgar Hoover is right. I didn't argue that as evidence in this case. I simply stated that, underwriting the statement of [Attorney] General Canale that they had made the same statement. You [jurors] are not required to agree with it all.

Battle: You [Ray] still. . . . Your answers to these questions that I asked you would still be the same? Is that correct?

Ray: Yes, sir.

Battle: There is nothing in these questions that I have asked you and your answers to them—you change none of them at all. In other words, you are pleading guilty, and taking ninety-nine years. I think the main question that I want to ask you is this: Are you pleading guilty to murder in the first degree in this case because you killed Dr. Martin Luther King under such circumstances that it would make you legally guilty of murder in the first degree under the law as explained to you by your lawyer? Your answer is still yes? All right, sir, that is all.

Judge Battle then ordered the jury sworn, and the testimony began. But Ray's outburst was to touch off a new wave of speculation about the conspiracy theory—a wave that probably would never ebb.

Swiftly, the prosecution and defense went through the motions once again, this time covering the chain of evidence that had been gathered to prove the guilt of Ray. The chain was forged tightly enough. It was not quite what one commentator—Clay Blair, Jr., author of *The Strange Case of James Earl Ray*—called it: "clearly the most well-prepared case in the annals of murder." There were too many loose threads for it to be that. But it probably was the case in which local, state, federal and international investigators had expended the most time, effort and money. Even the assassination of John F. Kennedy had not received such detailed investigation, if only because of Lee Harvey Oswald's own murder.

But the fact remained that persons of enormous stature, with differing perspectives and motivations, had all concluded James

Earl Ray alone had committed the murder. It was inevitable that certain charlatans and perhaps some well-intentioned do-gooders would contend otherwise. History would have to be the judge.

Ray's own possible motivation could be explained simply. He had nothing to lose, and much to gain, by continuing to encourage a conspiracy theory. For one thing, the cash value of his life story was bound to increase if he kept the mystery alive. He had agreed to pay Foreman as much as 150,000 dollars for defending him. This money, if it were to come at all, would have to come from sale of film rights, magazine-serial rights, book-club rights and the like. Foreman thus stood to gain monetarily from the continuing mystery. To his credit, he appeared on the surface at least to place this consideration second to his responsibility to history as an officer of the court. For another thing, any chance Ray might ever have to walk out of prison legally depended at least in part upon his ability to persuade the authorities that he was either a conspirator or a dupe. His initial defense strategy called for employing one or the other strategy, and perhaps a combination of the two. Foreman, however, recognized that such a strategy would falter under the test of judicial scrutiny. For that reason, he had urged Ray to "take a plea."

Now, despite Ray's partial disclaimer (which was irrelevant to the court case), the trial sped to a conclusion. The jurors, without leaving the courtroom, rendered their unanimous verdict by raising their right hands to signify ratification of the deal. Judge Battle directed Ray to stand.

"On your plea of guilty to murder in the first degree as charged in the indictment, it is the judgment of the court that you be confined for ninety-nine years in the state penitentiary," Battle said.

Ray sat down, showing no outward sign of emotion. He seemed resigned to the sentence. Battle then made a gratuitous statement of his own:

"The fact was recognized soon after this tragic murder took place that there was no possible conclusion to the case which would satisfy everybody. It was decided at that time that the only thing the judge could do was try the case as nearly as possible to other like cases and to scrupulously follow the law and his own conscience. This I have done. Memphis has been blamed for the death of Dr. King . . . wrongfully and irrationally. Neither the decedent nor his killer lived here; their orbits merely intersected here.

"How about conspiracy and punishment of any co-conspirators? It has been established that the prosecution at this time is not in possession of enough evidence to indict anyone as a co-conspirator in this case. Of course, this is not conclusive evidence that there was no conspiracy. It merely means that, as of this time, there is not sufficient evidence available to make out a case of probable cause. However, if this defendant was a member of a conspiracy to kill the decedent, no member of such conspiracy can ever live in peace or security or lie down to pleasant dreams because in this state there is no statute of limitations in capital cases such as this. And, while it is not always the case, my thirty-five years in the criminal courts have convinced me that Hamlet was right when he said: 'For murder, though it have no tongue, will speak with most miraculous organ.' I believe the settlement of the case a just one to both defendant and the state. I have accepted and approved the settlement. The defendant is represented by able and eminent counsel, and all rights and safeguards surrounding him have been zealously and conscientiously observed."

Minutes later, Judge Battle adjourned court. The trial of James Earl Ray was over. Or was it? He had scarcely left the courtroom before cries were heard throughout the world that justice had not triumphed. Some critics of the court action argued that the state should have settled for nothing less than the death penalty. Others, while satisfied with the ninety-nine-year term, complained about the handling of the case in such a manner as to blur the facts.

Dr. King's widow, Mrs. Coretta King, an opponent of capital punishment, was dissatisfied with the statements indicating absence of a conspiracy. "This plea of guilty cannot be allowed to close the case or to end the search for the many fingers which helped pull the trigger," she said. But she failed to make clear whether she meant there had been an actual conspiracy or whether she was referring merely to the climate of hatred that had plagued her husband's life. The murder victim's father, the Reverend Martin Luther King, Sr., commented: "No one man took my son's life." Other civil-rights leaders echoed these sentiments. The Reverend James Bevel, an aide to Dr. King, took a different tack. He claimed at one point that he had evidence proving Ray's innocence. Bevel had even tried to join the defense team, but been denied permission by Judge Battle.

The expressions of disapproval that immediately followed the trial, however, were mild compared with what followed. Percy Foreman was to become a major target of the later abuse. On the morning of March 11, Ray, disguised as a deputy sheriff to avoid possible assailants, was slipped out of the Shelby County Jail in Memphis by sheriff's officers. He was taken to the state prison at Nashville to begin serving his sentence. During the ride to the prison, Ray told a state highway-patrol captain that he had pleaded guilty only because he feared he might draw a death sentence. He said he wanted to get a new lawyer to examine the possibility of reopening his case.

The next day Judge Battle reported receiving a letter from Ray. The letter said Ray had fired Foreman and wanted a new hearing. Foreman, for his part, said Ray could not fire him because his obligation had ended with the adjournment of court on March 10. "I'm very happy to be out of it," Foreman said. "I think that James Earl Ray enjoys the spotlight and any way he can keep the center of the stage, he will do it. . . . In my view, there was no conspiracy. In my view, James Earl Ray decided, and he alone decided, to kill Martin Luther King so he could claim the glory. I think that James Earl Ray was a racist. He thought he would be a hero. He completely misconceived the thinking of the white race."

Foreman said he was not surprised that Ray wanted the case reopened, but that he had assumed his former client would wait a year or two before making such a bid. "He probably believes that if he can get a new trial, since he's already saved his life, he has no chance to get the death penalty. I wish him well. I don't think it [Ray's legal maneuver] is advisable, but that's his responsibility. I've discharged mine."

So saying, Foreman closed the books—except for the account books—on the Ray case. Ray's brothers have claimed that Foreman, for reasons of his own (mainly monetary), pressured Ray into entering the guilty plea. The road ahead seems long and tortuous for James Earl Ray. As for Percy Foreman, he has already given notice that he has other fish to fry. In his wake, as usual, he has left a storm of controversy.

13

I know nothing about his practice. He never speaks about it. But he is such a good husband, so tolerant and sweet. I couldn't have asked for a better man.

MRS. PERCY FOREMAN

PERCY FOREMAN is a man of many contradictions. He is alternately brusque and charming, grasping and benevolent, hard-nosed and compassionate, sophisticated and naïve.

One minute he may play the role of the knowledgeable world traveler. The next he may play the big ol' country boy from Polk County. The Percy Foreman seen by his wife and children is rarely glimpsed by those he meets in the courtroom.

Just how does this complex man live his life? What are his abiding beliefs, his likes and dislikes, his satisfactions and disappointments?

The side of Foreman least familiar to the public is that of the devoted family man. He is married to the former Marguerite Obert, a onetime ballerina and film actress in her native Germany. They met in 1956 during one of Foreman's business trips abroad and were married a year later. Mrs. Foreman, twenty years her husband's junior, is a striking woman with a warm smile. She is the daughter of the late Albert Obert, a distinguished German painter.

The Foremans have a pretty blonde daughter, also named Marguerite (and nicknamed "Sputnik"), who is ten at this writing. In addition, as previously mentioned, Foreman has an adopted son by a previous marriage, William, who is twenty-three at this writing. William, an Army private, was married in January 1968 at Fort Polk, Louisiana, to Marguerite Elizabeth Gracey of Houston. His father, characteristically, was tied up in a murder trial and could not attend the ceremony.

Foreman, his wife and daughter reside in a sprawling, ranch-style home in Houston's plush Memorial Drive area. (The house, it will be recalled, was turned over to Foreman by a wealthy client.) As a precaution against cranks and other intruders, the house is guarded by four tough Rottweiler watchdogs. The dogs are trained to attack anyone who climbs the fence surrounding the property. Once, in 1964, one of the dogs severely bit Foreman's daughter on the left leg. But Foreman found no fault with the Rottweiler. "You can't blame the dog for doing what he was trained to do in a certain situation," he said. "He was trained to guard and he was guarding."

Anyone who stays around Foreman for a length of time soon becomes aware of his frequent changes of mood. After spending a day with him, Van Hetherly, editor of the Houston *Chronicle's Texas Magazine*, wrote: "Foreman is gentle and hard, jocular and grim, all in the space of seconds."

A typical Foreman day starts early—about 5:30 A.M. His aching back, the result of his 1962 automobile accident, gets him out of bed by then. Because of the sore back, he is a restless sleeper. He usually awakens every half hour during the night.

Once out of bed, he heads for the kitchen and heats a pot of coffee. Next, he walks outside and picks up his copy of *The Houston Post.* He reads the paper while drinking coffee in the breakfast nook, his massive hand surrounding a small demitasse. Shortly after 6, the telephone starts ringing. As likely as not, the call is long-distance—a client, a prospective client or a fellow lawyer involved in a case in a distant city. Despite the early hour, Foreman is all business on the phone.

But his tone softens when his wife and daughter join him. He jokes with his daughter, affectionately calling her "Sputnik." The breakfast nook is decorated with paintings done by little Marguerite. "She inherited her grandfather's artistic ability," Foreman says.

He delights in teasing his wife about the fact that she has retained her German accent. "I never saw a German woman in this country three months who didn't speak better English," he says. "I accuse her of not wanting to lose her accent."

The demands of his law practice cut sharply into the time Foreman can spend with his family. Often, he is out of town for weeks—even months—at a stretch. "But my wife knew how I lived when she married me," he says. "She understands. I have no time to spare. I belong to the people who hire me."

His wife, helped by their daughter, prepares his breakfast. Normally, it consists of fresh fruit and cream, eggs "over easy," toast and more coffee. Mrs. Foreman says she doesn't mind arising at the early hour. "If he has his eggs, he's OK," she says. "Otherwise, I feel he might not get anything to eat all day."

After breakfast, the three of them troop into Foreman's bedroom—a spacious expanse crammed with stacks of reading matter ranging from Shakespeare to *Playboy* magazine. His wife and daughter help him choose the clothes he will wear for the day. His daughter presents him with a flower, picked from their garden, for his lapel.

His wardrobe donned and approved, he kisses the two Marguerites and climbs behind the wheel of his Cadillac. He drives downtown to the Rice Hotel, where he parks his car. Then, following a habit of almost forty years' standing, he drops into the hotel coffee shop for a last cup of coffee before heading for his office.

The office is in the South Coast Building, a skyscraper several blocks down Main Street from the hotel. This modern building is a far cry from the structure in which he practiced for almost thirty years. It was a rundown three-story walkup in a neighborhood of beer joints and honkytonks—but was conveniently close to Houston's courthouses. Foreman owned the building and felt he did not need a swanky office to attract clients. He had more than he could handle.

"The old building was constructed in 1911," Foreman says. "It was used by a drug company, which manufactured prickly-heat powder. Then it became a kind of shady hotel. I bought it in 1936 for 35,000 dollars."

Foreman long made his office on the second floor of the building and rented space to a loan company and other tenants. In 1960 he decided the neighborhood needed sprucing up, so he gave the building a face-lifting. The renovation featured typical Foreman touches. The front exterior of the building was adorned with an eight-foot-high bas-relief mural of the figure of Justice, complete with golden scales and sword. Beneath the mural was a representation of the Golden Rule, in the form of an actual ruler. Much of the renovation work was done by Foreman clients who could not afford to pay his legal fees.

Eventually, however, Foreman moved out of the old building and opened an office in the South Coast Building. He arrives at his eighth-floor office before 8 A.M. One of his first tasks is to skim through a large accumulation of mail. Invariably, the stack contains some crank letters. Every day for one entire year, Foreman received a package from the same woman. Frequently, the package contained nothing but some old newspapers or letters. On other occasions, it contained such assorted items as an artificial flower, a pillbox and a paperback book.

"I get nut calls, too," Foreman says. "Sometimes, when I get annoyed at another lawyer, I send him a series of nuts and tell them he's the only man in the world who can help them."

By 8 A.M. Foreman's waiting room is filling with clients, prospective clients and witnesses. His Girl Friday, Mrs. Martha Martinez Allen, briefs him on those who are waiting. One by one, the visitors are ushered into Foreman's office. Only rarely do they get his undivided attention. While talking with them, he continues reading his mail. And he is interrupted repeatedly to take telephone calls. Nonetheless, he manages to keep perfect track of each conversation. After a telephone call, he picks up the threads of his talk with a visitor as though they had never been interrupted.

His time is so limited that he is forced to be abrupt. Windbags with sob stories get short shrift.

"I know, damn it, you need the money!" he shouts to a telephone caller. "I'm trying to get it for you. Goodbye." Then, in a soft voice, he resumes his talk with a visitor.

"I don't have time to go into the narrative," he tells someone else. "What's your legal problem?"

When he is involved in a trial, which is almost always, he rarely is able to talk with all those in his waiting room before it is time to go to court. So the remainder tag along with him as he walks to the courthouse. Like a Pied Piper, he leads his flock of clients across the sidewalks—conferring on the run with first one, then another.

After the morning session of court Foreman heads for his "second office," the Old Capitol Club in the Rice Hotel. Between more telephone calls and conferences, he eats lunch—most often a rare steak, trimmings and coffee. For years he drank a Scotch and soda with lunch. But, not long ago, he gave up liquor. He settles now for a Dry Sack sherry.

His pace never seems to slow. He goes back to court for the afternoon session. Then, when court closes for the day, he returns to the Old Capitol Club. "If I went back to my office, I wouldn't get away until midnight," he says. But it is not uncommon for him to continue working until late into the night at the Old Capitol Club.

More clients and prospective clients meet him for conferences at the club. He installs them in booths, orders them drinks, then summons them in turn to join him and talk. Some wait several hours before being called to Foreman's table. Most cheerfully accept the delays as part of the price of having Percy Foreman represent them.

Shortly after Foreman arrives at the club, a typed list of his day's telephone callers is delivered from his office. While clients shuttle to and from his table, he returns the phone calls. His conversations are peppered with pungent comments. Van Hetherly, in his *Texas Magazine* article, reported hearing the following Foremanisms within the space of a few hours at the Old Capitol Club:

"Your motives are noble, but your course of action is for the birds. . . ."

"Honey, if I owned the courthouse, and a lot of people think I do, I'd send you justice in a sealed envelope. . . ."

"He's an honest man. But, like a lot of honest men, he stayed honest for lack of temptation. . . ."

"No, honey, I don't pretend to be the greatest lawyer who ever lived or even the greatest living lawyer. But, on the other hand, I don't deny it. . . ."

"I don't know how to pull punches. . . ."

"He reminds me of a Hollywood set. You go in the front door and you're in the back yard. . . ."

When the last client has left and the last telephone call has been returned, Foreman goes home. But his working day is still not over. He takes correspondence and legal papers home with him, and reads for a good part of the night in his king-sized bed. He gets about four hours of sleep. And then the process starts all over again.

Foreman works seven days a week. He makes a partial concession on Sundays, waiting until noon to go to his office.

When he is trying a case in a distant city, his life becomes even more complicated than usual. Hotel beds rarely accommodate Foreman's huge frame comfortably. His normally sparse amount of sleep is cut still further. He spends hours a day on the long-distance phone to Houston and other cities, dealing with matters that might better be handled in person.

Petty annoyances keep cropping up when Foreman is away from home. While he was trying a lengthy case in Hartford, Connecticut, an earpiece on his eyeglasses broke. Because he has a massive head, he must wear oversized glass frames. He hunted all over Hartford, but was unable to find an optician with a set of frames large enough to fit his head. As a result, he was compelled to finish the trial with the broken glasses held precariously in place by only one earpiece.

No matter where he is—in Houston, in some other American city or even abroad—Foreman is constantly called upon by newsmen, legislative committees, fellow attorneys and others to express his opinions on perplexing legal questions. Not surprisingly, Foreman has strong opinions on almost everything related to criminal law. And, also not surprisingly, some of these opinions are far from orthodox.

On the relationship between capital punishment and the murder rate, Foreman says:

"I don't think there is any relationship to the degree of punishment for murder. If a person is going to stop to think about the penalty, he is not going to commit the murder in the first place. Murder is a crime of passion. It is sudden. The theory that some prosecuting attorneys hold—that there is a relationship between the death penalty and the murder rate—is, in my opinion, unfounded.

"Actually, law enforcement is handicapped by asking for the death penalty in many cases. People who do not believe in executing or being responsible for executing a man, don't believe in some other man executing a fellow man, either."

What can be done to cut the murder rate?

"There are mechanical things that could be done in the courts that could reduce the murder rate," Foreman told a Houston *Chronicle* reporter. "In Houston, for example, we have only one justice of the peace who will grant a peace bond. A peace bond is supposed to stop assaults and assaults-to-murder by putting a person under bond to keep the peace. Therefore, the only thing we have on the statute books that is designed to help stop murder is not used. . . . Many murders might have been prevented by a peace bond being granted. Peace bonds should be granted by every magistrate when a person is threatened and has grounds to seek protection. The only reason it isn't done in courts in Houston is lack of personnel."

How has he managed to win such a large percentage of murder

cases, even though many of his clients have admitted slaying the victims?

"There are thirteen grounds upon which murder is justifiable by statute in Texas," Foreman says. "A person is innocent when one or more of these grounds is applicable. My clients are innocent either because they did not perform the acts of which they are accused or because the acts were justifiable. In most murder cases in which I have worked, there has been an element of self-defense. And the heart of presenting testimony is true salesmanship, selling the idea as to the justification or lack of justification. The district attorney is attempting to sell the lack of justification to the jury and the defense lawyers are attempting to sell the justification within the terms of the law. And any skill that I have over and above the average in that regard is probably due to my having made a study—a lifetime study—of human nature."

What about accused killers who are not lucky enough to be represented by Foreman? Are some of them unjustly convicted because of lack of talent or diligence on the part of their lawyers?

"More people are convicted on account of the lawyer than on the facts," Foreman says. "A license to practice law is a license to work. It is not a license to hornswoggle or sit back and talk like an owl, wisely, without doing anything. The person who works the hardest, whether it be the defense counsel or the prosecution attorney, is going to wind up with the best-prepared case—the one acceptable as a theory to the jury."

How high is the standard of justice dispensed in American courts?

"I don't think there is abstract justice anywhere except, I hope, in the hereafter," Foreman says. "It is only finite minds of judges, juries, prosecuting attorneys and grand jurors. And they are not omniscient. God is not the judge in these cases and, as long as we are working with human beings and haven't the divine insight to the motives, there will never be completely abstract justice. . . . The trial of a criminal case, theoretically, is to administer justice. But, actually, it is a game the way it is played by most prosecuting attorneys.

"You find a young man going into prosecuting for the purpose of getting the trial experience. As soon as he has accumulated and absorbed all of the technique and art that he thinks is necessary, then he withdraws and uses it solely for his private purpose. This, in my opinion, is a mistake. There are countries, for instance Italy, where a man who starts out as a prosecuting attorney stays there.

"France is several hundred years ahead of us in organized jurisprudence. The [criminal] case is pretty well established in France before there is any charge filed. In England, from which we obtained our Anglo-Saxon jurisprudence, that is likewise true.

"I think that the files of the police department ought to be as available to the defense as they are to the prosecution. I think that people who take it upon their conscience to write a death penalty or any term that would brand a man a felon should have the benefit of all the evidence that might have been available."

Is there a basic difference in the type of person who commits murder and the type who becomes involved in other forms of crime?

"As a rule in every penitentiary the best characters—the most trusted, reliable, dependable people, the people most apt to be readjusted to society—are the murderers," Foreman says. "A person who engages in the life of crime—such as writing hot checks, selling marijuana, stealing automobiles, burglarizing—intentionally and willfully goes into crime with a criminal bent and a crooked mind. The murderer falls into a trap. More than ninety percent of the killings are done because a man does not have control of his mind. Of course, you can pick out isolated, sensational cases to disprove this. But, by and large, it is true. And, actually, I prefer trying a murder case because of that. You deal with a higher class of person."

Is it unjust for a man who commits one crime during his life, murder, to be subject to the death penalty when an habitual criminal with three or more felony convictions (under Texas law, at least) can get no more than life imprisonment?

"Completely, and it isn't hard to make any man or woman sitting on a jury see that," Foreman says. "We attempt to make that recognition in what we call the suspended-sentence law. It is designed for the purpose of giving recognition to any useful life a person may have lived. The murderer may be a man who has paid his bills and observed all the responsibilities of citizenship, reared a family and perhaps served his country in two wars. And then, in some heat of passion, he commits a homicide which is sensational enough in the way it is carried out to make some prosecuting attorney think he's got to get a death penalty or his political opponent will use it against him in the next election. Or he wants to use it for the purpose of calling attention to himself so that he might advance his own political fortunes."

Is it time, then, for us to revise our entire system for dispensing punishment?

"We are in our infancy [in this field]," Foreman says. "It will take centuries to develop the civilized attitude. There are states which have a more advanced theory of crime and punishment that eventually we all will come to [adopt]. More intelligent thinking and planning has been done by the state of California than all the other states put together. For instance, out there, no punishment is set until the individual has been to the penitentiary. The individual is studied for at least a year or sometimes two years before a group of people who have made a study of the possibilities . . . for rehabilitation. It is called the sentencing authority. Eventually, that will be the law everywhere. But it may be a hundred years, maybe longer."

What can be done to curb juvenile delinquency?

"Juvenile crime, like murder, is a carbuncle on the social body," Foreman says. "The thing that worries me most, however, is the decadence of the moral fiber that made America great. It is very discouraging. The juvenile passes through a stage, as the administration of justice and our laws are passing through a juvenile stage. Frequently, the man who was the wildest juvenile becomes the most exemplary citizen—sometimes because of it.

"But it is an age when juveniles are energetic. They run and kick their heels like colts. The problem is to control that energy. And [the best way] to control it is by permitting them to have jobs. Permit them to train and to work. Keep them busy, ration their time, so that mother and father will know where a child is at all times."

What can the courts do to curb crime in general?

"Normally, the stock answer is swift, sure punishment," Foreman says. "But I don't adhere to the theory that there is a necessary relationship between crime and punishment. Of course, if there were no punishment at all, we would be in a jungle. There has to be some relationship between crime and punishment in that regard. But one does not necessarily affect the other. It gets down to individual advancement or personal glory at the expense of justice. The object of the district attorney ought to be to help conserve the citizen. The mere fact that a long and severe punishment can be obtained on the facts of a case does not necessarily justify its being obtained. I don't recognize that a man is a greater district attorney when he can print on his campaign cards how many death penalties he obtained. If he got very many, it is likely at least one of them was against an innocent man."

What about psychiatric testimony? Are psychiatrists being used properly by the courts?

"Psychiatrists are not being used adequately," Foreman recently told a *Houston Post* reporter. "Furthermore, in Texas, we call upon untrained people to make judgments as though they were psychiatrists. In Texas a cab driver, newsboy, janitor or deputy sheriff can testify as to his or her belief in the sanity of the suspect. If there is any other state that permits this, it is unknown to me.

"As for the psychiatrists themselves, they are often reluctant to appear in court. Not many years ago, the American Psychiatric Association urged its members to avoid appearance in the courtroom under any circumstances. The association deplored the damage done to this field by psychiatrists testifying to diametrically opposite conclusions in court and therefore in the press. This made it difficult for defense attorneys to obtain the agreement of reputable psychiatrists to examine and express a professional opinion as to the mental capacity of the defendant.

"No sincere psychiatrist is willing to conduct an examination behind bars or in a prison cell, because of the impact of the confinement itself on the suspect.

"Some states, upon a plea of insanity being made, require that the trial judge appoint three independent psychiatrists, who are not paid by the state as an adjunct of its law enforcement, to examine the defendant; that the defendant himself be committed to a psychiatric institution for this examination and for so long a period as the last of the three appointed psychiatrists believes is necessary for him to arrive at a proper conclusion; and that the defendant be given all psychological tests by psychologists selected by the panel. The findings of this panel of three are final on the issue of insanity.

"Texas has no such provision. I would say that such legislation should be adopted, and that none of the three psychiatrists be regularly employed by the state.

"Furthermore, the judge should make his appointments throughout the profession as a whole and should not be permitted to appoint the same psychiatrists time after time. It is my experience that 'county psychiatrists' soon become an adjunct of the prosecution."

Is there a need to revise the traditional McNaghten Rule for determining legal sanity—that is, the rule that applies the test of whether the defendant can distinguish right from wrong?

"The 'right or wrong' theory has one additional qualification, which is [whether the defendant knew right from wrong] 'with reference to the particular act charged' in the indictment," Foreman says. "The legal test is not did the defendant know the difference between right and wrong as a general abstract proposition. This distinction is overlooked by most lawyers, psychiatrists, judges and, therefore, juries.

"The most brilliant intellect it has been my privilege to defend [Dr. Harold Eidinoff; see Chapter 5] was more than ninety-nine percent normal so far as general intelligence is concerned. But, within a small percentage of the remaining one percent of his thinking, he was one hundred percent abnormal. He knew that killing was wrong. But he thought the killing of the particular person he killed was not only right, but that it would have been wrong not to kill that individual.

"If properly understood and properly applied, I do not feel there is any need to liberalize the McNaghten Rule. But the temptation and tendency to oversimplify and thereby fail to appreciate, comprehend and apply the McNaghten Rule probably will require amplification."

How about the theory that some crimes are committed while the defendants are under the influence of unconscious, internal forces?

"That is sometimes called 'compulsion,'" Foreman says. "In the latter part of the nineteenth century, the Supreme Court of New Hampshire ruled that an individual should not be held accountable for an act he could not resist committing, even though he might know that its commission was 'wrong.' Then, and until the late 1950s, New Hampshire was the only state that gave any legal appreciation to the newly recognized field of psychiatry. The U.S. Circuit Court of Appeals for the District of Columbia, in the case of a defendant named Durham, applied the New Hampshire rule for the first time in the federal courts.

"Subsequently, the state of Illinois has recodified its criminal law so as to recognize the New Hampshire–Durham Rule. Likewise, the state of Kentucky. Also, numerous states that are new in the process of recodifying their rules of criminal procedure are giving consideration to writing into and spelling out as a part of the law a modification of the McNaghten Rule in the light and appreciation of the New Hampshire–Durham Rule. Texas is not among those more enlightened states yet."

What about recent court decisions limiting use of confessions in criminal trials? What should be done about procedures concerning the questioning of suspects?

"I believe that suspects should be questioned concerning any crime—but I do not believe that an arresting officer should be entitled to do the questioning," Foreman says. "Experience shows that the arresting officer is usually overzealous in justifying his suspicion as to the guilt of the suspect. Most countries in the world today forbid the questioning of a suspect by the arresting officer. Their procedure calls for questioning of the suspect by a magistrate or a law-enforcement officer who is also an attorney and is conversant with the law of the respective country. I endorse such a system. . . .

"I don't think the interrogation room presided over by a person with a billy club and handcuffs is any better than a dungeon with all its torture devices. The best interrogation room is that presided over by a magistrate."

Foreman says limitations on national police power have never handicapped law enforcement in federal courts. "The state constabulary, on the other hand, has followed the line of least resistance—prejudging the guilt of the suspect and then, by either brute force or psychological brainwashing and cajolery, inducing a confession that is later claimed by the officer to be 'voluntary,'" he says.

What about the practice by some law-enforcement officers of permitting newsmen to interview a defendant while he is in custody?

"The news media should not be permitted to interview a defendant except with permission, and in the presence, of his attorney," Foreman says. "And any attorney who grants such access by the press should be reprimanded and appropriately punished by the bar association. When a prisoner is interviewed and the results of it are spread over the newspapers and through broadcasts to the public from which the jury must be eventually selected, as much harm may result to his case as through unbridled interrogation by officers."

What about proposals to curb generally the press coverage of criminal cases?

"The issue is whether an individual has a right to be tried on evidence, rather than emotions whipped into frenzy by headline writers trained to put as much emotional impact as possible into the smallest amount of space," Foreman says. He favors extensive press coverage of criminal trials themselves, but opposes pretrial release by officers and prosecutors of purported details about alleged crimes.

"As a person who has spent four decades at the bar in the trial of cases, many of which were of the sensational variety, I have had to change venue in at least three hundred cases because of unfavorable publicity caused by an unbridled, uninhibited press and the appeal by the news media to sensationalism," he says. On the other hand, Foreman concedes that press coverage can help produce a fair trial. "More than a few lives have been saved in cases that I have tried by a full and fair treatment in the news media of arrests which would have otherwise been suppressed until such time as the peace officers had worked their will and obtained the incriminating statement they set out to secure by secret arrest."

On a less weighty subject, what's his opinion of television dramas about criminal lawyers?

"I never look at them," Foreman says. "I'd charge a fee to watch one. Not because they're not good entertainment, but I don't watch any drama. I get surfeited with drama every hour of the day."

This examination of Foreman's strong opinions, the frenetic pace of his career and his devotion to his family provides only three views of a many-sided man. There are so many sides, in fact, that Foreman's acquaintances rarely agree when asked to name his most notable characteristic.

Some mention the quickness of his mind and tongue. They speak, for example, of the time Foreman got involved in a caustic word battle with a prosecutor during a murder trial.

"Did you have it in mind to prejudice the jury by introducing as evidence a photograph of the dead woman?" Foreman asked the prosecutor.

"What was in my mind was not material," the prosecutor replied.

"If it was in your mind, it must have been minuscule!" Foreman snapped.

Other acquaintances mention Foreman's impassioned jury summations. They recall cases such as the murder trial of Mrs. Ethel Simpson, a middle-aged Fort Worth housewife accused of shooting her husband to death.

The prosecution charged that Mrs. Simpson had murdered her husband in order to collect on his 13,000-dollar life-insurance policy. Foreman contended it was a case of self-defense—that the dead man had repeatedly beaten his wife and had been coming at her with a hunting knife at the time she shot him. What's more, to show the brutal character of the murder victim, Foreman produced witnesses who testified that Simpson had been a sadistic hater of animals. The witnesses said Simpson might have been responsible for poisoning about twenty dogs and for stomping a puppy to death.

In his jury argument, Foreman hammered repeatedly at the theme of the dead man's cruelty. Then he placed his hand softly on Mrs. Simpson's shoulder.

"This woman's life was hell on earth," he told the jurors. "Any man who would beat his wife and even stomp a poor puppy to death . . ." Foreman paused, as if too overcome by emotion to continue. He shook his head ruefully. Then, finally, he said: "Send this woman back where she belongs—to the people who love her, to her children."

The jury found Mrs. Simpson not guilty. When the verdict was announced, she burst into tears and shouted: "Thank God for Percy Foreman!"

(It was Foreman, incidentally, who wound up getting the 13,000 dollars from the dead man's insurance policy. Mrs. Simpson assigned the policy to Foreman as part of his fee, and he collected the money from the insurance company.)

Still other acquaintances mention Foreman's proclivity for doing things in a big way. There was, for example, the time that he accumulated 122 parking tickets and paid them all off at once—shelling out a total of 315 dollars in fines. (He simultaneously beat the rap on 112 other parking tickets on technical grounds.) As he left the traffic court, a newsman asked Foreman whether he planned to accumulate another batch of tickets. "Sufficient unto each day is the evil thereof," Foreman replied. When the reporter asked what that meant, Foreman snapped: "That's from the Bible. I always quote from the Bible."

Others mention Foreman's capacity for doing the unexpected.

They recall such occasions as the time Foreman offered to donate his services in a divorce case as a door prize at the Gala Ball of the Houston Museum of Fine Arts. The offer was declined. But, as *Houston Post* columnist Bill Roberts later commented, "There was more than one at that affair who would have liked to win that gift."

Still others mention Foreman's seemingly boundless energy, his keen memory, his ability as a cross-examiner, his flair for the dramatic, his disdain of orthodoxy and his single-minded determination. It is not any one of these attributes, but a combination of all of them and some others, that has been responsible for Foreman's success.

As should be obvious, not all of Foreman's characteristics are attractive. He has his faults. He is vain, stubborn and arrogant. He sometimes seems to lack compassion.

But even his detractors concede that his assets as a human being and his contributions to society far outweigh his liabilities.

In the final analysis, what seems most notable about Percy Foreman is that he is an original. His like has not been seen before and probably will not be seen again.

But one can always hope.

ACKNOWLEDGMENTS

BECAUSE OF the controversial nature of Percy Foreman's career, many persons agreed to provide information for this book only on the condition that their contributions be kept confidential. Rather than provide a partial list of sources, I have decided to permit all my informants to remain anonymous. Suffice it to say that I was the beneficiary of generous help from numerous attorneys, judges, law-enforcement officers, newspaper and magazine writers, court clerks, court stenographers and ordinary citizens. I would like to thank all of those who graciously shared with me their time, information and counsel.

Once again, I am indebted to Miss Elizabeth Otis, Ross Claiborne and Richard Kennedy for advice, faith and encouragement.

And, also once again, thanks are due to my wife, Jeanne, and daughters, Pamela and Patricia, for enduring the hardships and frustrations of life in a writer's household.

THIS BOOK WAS SET IN

CALEDONIA AND CASLON 540 TYPES BY

BROWN BROS. LINOTYPERS, INC.

IT WAS PRINTED AND BOUND BY

MONTAUK BOOK MFG. CO.

DESIGN IS BY BARBARA COHEN